"Carol Bradley has written a necessary book about the horses and the stuntmen that made possible the action exploits of the great Western stars, as well as the bonds of shared trust and devotion between rider and mount—and the cruelty imposed by Hollywood's invariable need for expedience and speed."

—Scott Eyman, *New York Times* best-selling author
of *John Wayne: The Life and Legend*

"The Western, Hollywood's earliest and most enduring genre, couldn't exist without horsepower. . . . If you love horses—and who doesn't?—you'll enjoy Bradley's authoritative and thoroughly entertaining account of the rise and fall and rise again of the men and animals who tamed the West, at least in the movies, and created a legend all their own."

—Glenn Frankel, Pulitzer Prize–winning journalist and author
of *The Searchers: The Making of an American Legend*

"This is a book about Hollywood's glory days and its stuntmen, about the barbaric ways we used to treat movie animals, how that slowly improved, and how one amazing thoroughbred-quarter mix named Cocaine (think Seabiscuit) learned the hard way the art of fast falling. It'll change how you watch animals who appear on the big screen."

—Larry Tye, *New York Times* best-selling author of
Satchel: The Life and Times of an American Legend

"*Twisting in Air* is by turns a well-researched and damning indictment of Hollywood's callous disregard for the welfare of horses (and their riders) from the days of the nickelodeons to the present, as well as an endearing account of the relationship of one of the industry's most famed stunt horsemen, Chuck Roberson, with his extraordinary 'falling horse' Cocaine. Chock-full of anecdotes from the glory days of the Westerns, including unvarnished glimpses of famed director John Ford ('he looked like a sack of walnuts in the saddle'), John Wayne, Cecil B. DeMille, and many more, this book will appeal to horse lovers, fans of the genre, and students of the American experience alike. Mount up!"

—Les Standiford, author of the *New York Times* best-selling *Last Train to Paradise*

"From silent film horse actors such as Fritz to latter-day superstars like Cocaine, *Twisting in Air* celebrates the bravery and athleticism of equine entertainers. More importantly, it shows how the bond between horse and human can help both achieve great things."

—Cynthia Branigan, author of *The Last Diving Horse in America*

Twisting in Air

THE SENSATIONAL RISE OF A HOLLYWOOD FALLING HORSE

Carol Bradley

UNIVERSITY OF NEBRASKA PRESS
LINCOLN

© 2024 by Carol Bradley

All rights reserved
Manufactured in the United States of America

The University of Nebraska Press is part of a land-grant institution with campuses and programs on the past, present, and future homelands of the Pawnee, Ponca, Otoe-Missouria, Omaha, Dakota, Lakota, Kaw, Cheyenne, and Arapaho Peoples, as well as those of the relocated Ho-Chunk, Sac and Fox, and Iowa Peoples.

Library of Congress Cataloging-in-Publication Data
Names: Bradley, Carol, 1957– author.
Title: Twisting in air: the sensational rise of a Hollywood falling horse / Carol Bradley.
Description: Lincoln: University of Nebraska Press, [2024] | Includes bibliographical references.
Identifiers: LCCN 2024002460
ISBN 9781496239006 (paperback)
ISBN 9781496240712 (epub)
ISBN 9781496240729 (pdf)
Subjects: LCSH: Cocaine (Horse) | Animals as actors—California—Los Angeles—History—20th century. | Horses in motion pictures. | Horses—California—Los Angeles—Biography. | BISAC: HISTORY / United States / State & Local / West (AK, CA, CO, HI, ID, MT, NV, UT, WY) | NATURE / Animals / Horses
Classification: LCC PN1995.9.A5 B73 2024 | DDC 791.43/66296655—dc23/eng/20240611
LC record available at https://lccn.loc.gov/2024002460

Designed and set in Janson by K. Andresen.

Dedicated to every horse who performed on the silver screen

CONTENTS

List of Illustrations *ix*
Acknowledgments *xi*

1. A Mortifying Gaffe *1*
2. The Lure of the West *5*
3. First Came Fritz *15*
4. Then Came Tony *23*
5. Trip Wires and More *33*
6. Ratcheting Up the Risks *41*
7. Making Headway against Abuse *51*
8. Learning the Ropes *61*
9. In Search of the Right Horse *69*
10. A Debilitating Injury *77*
11. Learning to Fall Again *85*
12. Tough Riders, Tough Horses *91*
13. Doubling for John Wayne *113*
14. *The Searchers* *123*

15. Doubling for the Stars   *147*

16. Aging and Still Falling   *163*

17. The Return of Cruelty   *173*

18. Out to Pasture   *193*

Epilogue   *203*

Notes on Sources   *207*

ILLUSTRATIONS

1. Cowgirls demonstrating their prowess at the 101 Ranch   7
2. Tom Mix and his horse Tony   24
3. Horse killed by a trip wire   38
4. American Humane Association ad   59
5. Chuck Roberson   62
6. Fred Kennedy delivering a knockout blow   65
7. Jerry Brown Falling Horse initiating a fall   101
8. John Ford with Harry "Dobie" Carey and Yak Canutt   116
9. Series of photos showing a horse galloping   137
10. John Wayne riding Cocaine   139
11. Chuck Roberson and Cocaine in *The Wonderful Country*   150
12. Drugged horse in *Cat Ballou*   176
13. Chuck Roberson and Cocaine jumping through a candy-glass window   199

ACKNOWLEDGMENTS

I'm immensely grateful for the enthusiastic support of Senior Acquisitions Editor Clark Whitehorn. This manuscript sat on my shelf for three years and might be languishing there still if Clark hadn't learned of it and urged me to send it in. He's been a delight to work with, as has copy editor Hope Houtwed and the entire University of Nebraska Press team.

I'm indebted to everyone whose knowledge helped me understand the world of Western stunt horses. Special thanks are owed to Chuck Roberson's daughter, Charlene Roberson, who offered an insider's look at her father and his favorite horse, and to Ellen Powell for shedding light on the personalities of Twinkle Toes and Iodine, the falling horses who belonged to her ex-husband Chuck Hayward.

I'm enormously appreciative of Dorrica Brewer for making available photos of Chuck Roberson and Cocaine collected by her late stepfather, John Hagner, founder of the Stuntmen's Hall of Fame. Photofest and the Oklahoma Historical Society also provided photos, and I'd still be pulling my hair out if computer whiz Karen Vanni hadn't helped me format my work.

I'm profoundly thankful to my late parents for their support. My mom, Irene Bradley, instilled a love of reading that has lasted a lifetime, and my dad, George Bradley, was my biggest fan. My brother, Jeff Bradley, and sister Brooke Bradley have lent much-appreciated support, as have a half dozen goal buddies—Robin Catalano, Judy Gruen, Valerie Harms, Joni Iraci, Kathy McCoy, and Deb Pines—who have bolstered my spirits for more than five years now. My friends Su Suits, Kathy Johnson, and Candi Short have been there for me too—knowing when it was okay to ask how my writing was going and when to steer clear of the subject. And at a point when I was ready to give up on writing, life coach Jill Kahn helped me remember why I do what I do.

I thank my husband, Steve L'Heureux, whose support makes my writing possible. This book wouldn't exist if it weren't for him.

Finally, a shout-out to anyone who has picked up this book. Reading about the treatment of animals isn't always easy, but as James Baldwin so eloquently said, "Not everything that is faced can be changed, but nothing can be changed until it is faced."

TWISTING IN AIR

1

A Mortifying Gaffe

Tall, ebony-haired Chuck Roberson had landed his dream job in Hollywood. Not as an actor—he had no desire to grab the spotlight on the big screen. Roberson's greatest desire was to perform as a cowboy stunt double in Western movies. And now, finally, he'd gotten a break. The year was 1949, and director John Ford at Republic Studios wanted to meet with Roberson to talk about a stunt role in *Rio Grande*, the tale of an army officer defending a cavalry post in Texas against warring Apaches. Box-office favorite John Wayne had the starring role, and Ford was moviedom's preeminent creator of Westerns. Penetrating his tight circle was the goal of every cowboy stuntman. If Roberson did his job well, he would more than likely be cast in Ford's next movie and the one after that.

Roberson had heard Ford could be difficult, so he wasn't surprised when the director arrived late for their appointment. Ford didn't even bother to say hello. The first words he said to Roberson were, "Stand up, I want to look at you." He then motioned for Roberson to turn around so he could check him out from the rear.

"Hmph," Ford muttered. "Not bad."

Wingate Smith, Ford's brother-in-law and assistant director who was also in the room, was a bit more encouraging. "We hear you're a good man with a horse," he told Roberson.

"I guess I can do about as well as any man," Roberson replied.

"Now you're being modest," Smith said. "Duke Wayne says you're a pretty good double. Fred Kennedy says you're a fine stuntman."

Ford offered Roberson a role, but he had already accepted a small part

A MORTIFYING GAFFE

in an Errol Flynn movie slated to begin filming at the same time as *Rio Grande*. Errol Flynn was a major star, and a part in his movie would probably pay better, but *Rio Grande* offered a chance to double Wayne again, and getting an in with Ford was an opening Roberson couldn't afford to pass up. If he didn't accept a part now, who knew when, or if, he would get a second chance? Still, he agonized over his dilemma for two days before calling Ford to say yes.

Ford had chosen the desert-y terrain outside Moab, Utah, for the filming of *Rio Grande*. Moab was barely a town at the time. It had no motels, so the cast and crew slept in army tents with wooden floors and lumpy beds that creaked loudly anytime anyone rolled over. Roberson shared his sleeping quarters with five other stuntmen, but the code of the West dictated that no one complain, so he kept his mouth shut. He felt lucky just to have a part in the movie, especially after watching Ford angrily dismiss an extra for whistling on the set. The worker was innocently whistling along to "Bringing in the Sheaves," the song Ford always had accordionist Danny Borzage play on-site. But Ford was superstitious, convinced that whistling brought bad luck.

Roberson tried to quash his nerves by reminding himself that he deserved to be there. Roberson felt comfortable around horses. He'd ridden them ever since he could walk and had done stunt work with horses in smaller movies before this. Here was his chance to show off his know-how and skill, and filming started off well. But then Ford threw a curveball and asked Roberson to perform a feat he'd never attempted to pull off.

The script called for someone to "fall" a horse—cue it to hit the ground as though it had been shot. Another stuntman, Fred Kennedy, had been scheduled to execute the trick. But Kennedy begged off; he said he was too roughed up from falling a horse the night before. He suggested to Ford that Roberson take his place instead.

Roberson had never fallen a horse in his life—Kennedy knew that. But he was offering Roberson a chance to impress the mercurial Ford. Only a fool would turn down the opportunity.

From the edge of the set Roberson stood quietly, stifling his misgivings, as Ford described the type of fall he was looking for. The assignment sounded simple enough. Decked out as an Indian, Roberson was to ride directly toward the camera while being chased from behind by actor and fellow stuntman Ben Johnson. Johnson's character would intercept Roberson's from the left and shoot him. As soon as that happened, Roberson was to fall his horse in front of the camera. The fall didn't have to be spectacular; it could take place at a relatively slow canter, a lope. The horse would appear to be moving faster once editors got hold of the footage and stepped up the speed anyway.

Still, the idea of making a horse hit the ground made Roberson nervous.

"Yes, sir," he mumbled in response to Ford's instructions, trying desperately to conceal his doubts. "Where do you want it?"

Roberson lacked a stunt horse of his own, so he'd borrowed a bay gelding belonging to a fellow performer, Jerry Brown. Roberson had some time to kill before the shoot, so he changed into an Indian costume, dabbed a few stripes of war paint on his cheeks, and spent the lunch hour and the early part of the afternoon acquainting himself with his equine partner, also named Jerry Brown. Roberson tried to picture himself taking the horse down as though it was something he did all the time. Even if he hadn't fallen a horse himself, he'd watched them take place many times over. And truthfully, it didn't look all that difficult. It occurred to him, in fact, that if a horse could fall at a canter, why not at an all-out gallop? Think how dazzled Ford would be if Roberson could crash his horse to the ground at lightning speed.

The time came to film the sequence. Roberson rode the horse a hundred yards out and turned him around. The second Ford called, "Action," Roberson spurred the horse into a fast run. From his left, he heard Ben Johnson holler, "Damn it, slow down!" But Roberson was convinced he could fall the horse at a gallop. When he reached the designated spot, he jerked hard on the reins, the way he'd seen Kennedy do.

To Roberson's dismay, the horse kept going, dashing another fifteen feet before Roberson could yank his head hard enough to the right to initiate the fall. The horse did a half twirl before keeling over and hitting the dirt, shoulder first. He fell so fast that he slid across the ground and headed straight for a row of cast members. Dust flew as actors bolted out of their seats in time to flee the mayhem. The horse knocked out an entire row of chairs before coming to a stop. No one, including the horse, was hurt, but as Roberson clambered to his feet, Johnson approached him, shaking his head.

A MORTIFYING GAFFE

"What the hell were you doing?" Johnson said. "Nobody can make a horse fall from that speed."

Roberson got to his feet, brushed off his pants, and shrugged. Granted, the fall was calamitous, but nothing he couldn't rectify. When they reshot the scene, he'd simply fall the horse at a slower pace, a canter this time. Everything would go as planned, and he would be able to redeem himself in Ford's eyes.

But Ford had seen enough. He was finished with this reckless newcomer. His face set in a grim smile, the director refused to even look Roberson's way. Instead he called for Fred Kennedy to change into the Indian outfit and perform the sequence the way it was supposed to go down. From the sidelines Roberson watched, chagrined, as Kennedy cantered his horse in slowly and fell him to the applause of the crew. Roberson was staring at the dirt when he felt someone's gentle touch on his back. He turned to see flame-haired costar Maureen O'Hara gazing at him with a look of sympathy. She had witnessed his blunder and wanted to offer a little encouragement. "I think the way you do it is much more exciting," she told him. "I think it would be wonderful if you really could do it that way."

Roberson nodded, trying not to look mortified. In the dining tent that evening, no one broached the subject of his gaffe, but he couldn't help feeling as though everyone was side-eyeing him. He excused himself early, walked back to his tent, and stretched out on his cot, thinking through his next step. No question he had blown it trying to fall Jerry Brown at such a fast speed. Knocking over all those chairs was an embarrassing fiasco, one he would be lucky to live down. But getting a horse to fall at a dead run *was* possible; Roberson was certain of it. Falling at a slower pace looked acceptable if the horse was heading directly toward the camera, but viewed from the side, it looked fake, even when the camera speed was accelerated. Combat sequences in movies would look infinitely more realistic if the falls appeared to be instantaneous, and to accomplish that, a horse needed to hit the dirt at full speed.

Westerns showed no signs of flagging as the 1950s got underway, and to make it as a stuntman Roberson needed a falling horse, one with confidence and bravado, who trusted him implicitly. And to develop that close of a relationship, he needed to find a horse of his own. The sooner the better.

2

The Lure of the West

To appreciate the circumstances Roberson found himself in 1940s Hollywood—to understand how and why filmmakers needed horses to fall on cue—it helps to realize how important Westerns had become to moviegoing audiences, the critical role horses played in those films, and the abysmal ways they were treated in the early days.

The cowboy era in America lasted just twenty years or so before railroads took over the job of shipping cattle, and wranglers were no longer needed to herd steers to stockyards hundreds of miles away. But Americans never lost their infatuation with that mythical image of the rough-and-tumble West. Even before movies came into being, audiences clamored to experience a taste of the wide-open life that beckoned beyond the Mississippi.

P. T. Barnum was the first to capitalize on the public's interest. And not with horses, but with buffalo.

In 1843, while attending anniversary festivities at the Battle of Bunker Hill site near Boston, the legendary showman glimpsed a dozen young bison pacing aimlessly inside a tent. On impulse, he bought the small herd for $700 and had the animals shipped first to New York and then to a large barn outside of Hoboken, New Jersey. Newspapers caught wind of the buffalo's existence, and unaware that the animals belonged to Barnum, rumors circulated that the exotic animals had been bagged out West, near the Rocky Mountains.

More than one reporter suggested that the owner of the buffalo stage a chase so urban dwellers could see them in action. Obligingly, Barnum scheduled a "Buffalo Hunt." The day of the much-ballyhooed event, more than twenty-four thousand curiosity-seekers crossed the Hudson River from New York to watch the show. If they were expecting to see robust, aggressive animals, they would have been sorely disappointed. Dressed as an Indian, a white man named C. D. French prodded the skinny, apprehensive buffalo into the arena, where they trotted around nervously. When French managed to lasso one of the bedraggled animals, the audience laughed so loudly at his lackluster performance that the rest of the frightened buffalo bolted out of the arena and fled to an area swamp.

Despite that third-rate presentation, Barnum was onto something. Five years later he unveiled a more sophisticated animal act, and in 1860 he formed a partnership with James C. "Grizzly" Adams to present Adams's collection of wolves, lions, bears, buffalo, and a gigantic sea lion. Audiences couldn't get enough. By the late 1890s, Wild West shows were commonplace. Wild Bill Cody and Buffalo Bill's extravaganzas were the best known, but smaller troupes like Buckskin Ben's Wild West and Dog and Pony Show, Cherokee Ed's Wild West, Hulberg's Wild West and Congress of Nations of the World, and Lone Star Mary's Wild West also crisscrossed the country displaying ragtag menageries.

The more successful of the shows drew large crowds. Cody's operation featured aging Indian chiefs and cowboy performers along with elephants, camels, and an assortment of other creatures. But audiences turned out to see even the skimpiest productions—ones that relied on a handful of old cowboys riding old and weary range horses. Over the next forty years, more than a hundred Wild West shows came and went, some of them has-been outfits repackaged with different owners or fresh new names. One of the most successful was Colonel G. W. Miller's 101 Ranch in Oklahoma. Miller and his sons started the ranch on 101,000 acres along the Salt Fork of the Arkansas River, hence the name. By 1904 the 101 had become the biggest Wild West spectacle in the country, with productions involving as many as three thousand participants, one thousand of them Indians.

The ranch outdid itself on June 7, 1905, with an "Oklahoma Gala Day" that attracted a crowd of sixty-five thousand spectators from all over the country. The 101 already boasted many skilled bronco fighters and rope tossers, but most of the hired hands were rough saddle tramps and unpolished working cowboys. For this performance, the Millers added a

1. Before Western movies there were Wild West shows. Cowgirls demonstrate their prowess as part of the 101 Ranch's famous productions in Oklahoma. Courtesy of the Oklahoma Historical Society.

few rousing specialty acts, among them spirited nineteen-year-old Lucille Mulhall, a bona fide world champion rodeo performer billed as the "original cowgirl." Schooled by stern nuns at two convents, Mulhall had busted out of her conventional life and learned to throw steers, bust broncs, stalk prairie wolves, brand cattle, and rope as many as eight running range horses at once. Also on the bill were George Elser, who called himself the "Champion Trick Rider of the World," and Texas cowboy Bill Pickett, the inventor of bulldogging: he would tackle cattle by bending upside down over a steer's face, clamping down on its lips with his teeth, and yanking it to the ground.

Fascination with the West emanated from many corners. President Theodore Roosevelt's escapades as a cowboy and a Rough Rider generated enormous buzz for the promising expanse of country west of the Mississippi. The paintings of Charles M. Russell and Frederic Remington fueled interest with their portrayals of mortals facing staggering challenges in a beautiful and unforgiving landscape. And Owen Wister's novel *The Virginian*, the tale of a cowboy at a cattle ranch in Wyoming who romances the new schoolteacher and faces ongoing conflicts with an enemy, cemented the glamourous image of the American West. For a nation still reeling from the searing trauma of the Civil War, *The Virginian* offered a cowboy hero Americans could root for. More than 1.8 million copies of the book sold over the next fifty years, and it's still regarded as the most influential Western novel ever written. *The Virginian* opened the door for other novels that idealized the West and helped perpetuate the romantic myths of the frontier. Jack London wrote of high adventure and heroic struggle in the wilderness. New York dentist Zane Grey gave up his practice to churn out scores of popular adventure novels of the West. From O. Henry—the pen name of William Sydney Porter—came the irresistible stories of the fictitious Cisco Kid.

Horses played a huge role in these Wild West shows. In the Westerns that began appearing on the big screen, their contribution was even bigger. One of the first movies, *The Great Train Robbery*, just twelve minutes long, climaxed with a thrilling chase on horseback. It further stamped the West into the nation's consciousness and created a roadmap for nearly every Western movie that followed.

Movies got their start in 1894, when inventor Thomas Edison launched the Black Maria studios in New Jersey. There he produced a wave of documentary-style Westerns, sometimes using cast members from Buffalo Bill's Wild West show as his subjects. Another Western filmmaker was Fred Balshofer, general manager for Bison Motion Pictures, an offshoot of the New York Motion Picture Company. Bison and other studios shot their films across the Hudson River, in the vicinity of Fort Lee and Coytesville, New Jersey. At the time, Fort Lee was a tiny outpost with an unpaved dirt street so dusty that twice a day workers were sent out with a horse-drawn wagon equipped with a pair of sprinklers to water down the streets. A little over a mile away, Coytesville offered dirt roads lined with trees and forested hills perfect for shooting movies: there were no electric poles or wires to have to work around. Behind Rambo's Saloon was a livery stable where movie companies could rent horses, saddles, and other necessary equipment.

Moviemaking in New Jersey grew challenging after a handful of producers agreed to acknowledge Edison as the creator of motion pictures, to produce only films that he authorized, and furthermore to relinquish their patent claims on their filmmaking. In exchange for giving the studios permission to make and distribute films in the United States using his kinetograph, a motion picture camera that used rapid, intermittent photos to capture movement, Edison raked in a bundle of royalties. The companies that fell in line with Edison—including Biograph, Lubin, Essanay, Vitagraph, Kalem, and Selig—formed their own organization, the Motion Picture Patents Company (MPPC), and tried to insist that only members of their group could produce and distribute movies. Filmmakers who chose not to belong to the organization could be prosecuted on criminal grounds and even jailed for striking out on their own.

The bullying tactics of the MPPC drove some film companies out of business. Others moved out of New York and New Jersey, far enough away to avoid the scrutiny of the trust. Most went south to warmer climes: Florida, Louisiana, New Mexico, Texas, even Cuba. Others, including Balshofer's Bison Motion Pictures, headed west to California where, it turned out, conditions were ideal for making pictures. In contrast to New Jersey's cloudy, wintry climate, Southern California's mild, sunny days seemed nothing short of miraculous. The rainy season was brief—from mid-December to mid-March—and the rainfall that did occur fell mostly at night. The remainder of the year, the sun rose brightly each morning.

The Bison company was able to shoot gun battles, stagecoach robberies, and other essential Western scenes in the hills surrounding its studio in Edendale, a neighborhood of Los Angeles now known as Echo Park and Silver Lake. The primitive technology of those early films required producers to shoot all of their scenes outside, in broad daylight, and California's climate was so accommodating that filmmakers could film indoor scenes uninterrupted. They no longer had to issue "weather permitting" calls to extras.

It turned out that filmmakers from back east were late to discover California's charms. As early as 1907, Colonel William "Bill" Selig had founded a studio in a building on Olive Street in Los Angeles that once housed a

Chinese laundry. Around that same time, filmmaker Dave Horsley bought a former tavern on the corner of Sunset Boulevard and Gower Street and turned it into a studio. In 1910 a unit of the Biograph Company started a studio in an empty car barn at the corner of Georgia and Pico streets. Four hundred and fifty miles north, the Essanay Film company was cranking out Westerns in the town of Niles.

The Bison company's cast and crew rode horses from its studio in Edendale to the Hollywood Hills, which offered plenty of curving streets ideal for movie shots. A ranch with adobe buildings west of La Brea Avenue and Hollywood Boulevard provided the perfect ambiance for the standard gun battles, stagecoach robberies, and pursuits on horseback. Another of Bison's locations was LA's Griffith Park, whose forested hills were ideal for shooting Westerns.

Edison's organization hired a spy, Joseph McCoy, whose job was to track down in and around Hollywood any filmmakers who'd refused to play ball with Edison. For a time, filmmakers hid out in Big Bear Valley, a summer resort east of Los Angeles surrounded by twenty-five miles of terrain so steep that cars couldn't begin to traverse it. To reach it, cast and crew relied on horses to carry them or pull their wagons from San Bernardino. The horses were given water and a much-needed rest halfway before climbing the remainder of the forty-one miles to Big Bear Lake. After a week's filming, the exposed negative was given to a cowboy who delivered it on horseback to the train station, and from there it was sent to Edendale to be developed.

McCoy never did determine where the movie crews disappeared to. He soon realized he was out of his element and unable to do much harm to the non-patent studios. Balshofer and two colleagues were taking an after-dinner cigarette break one evening in the lobby of the Alexandria Hotel in LA when they spotted McCoy. Balshofer greeted him good-naturedly but told him, "You're out West now, and cowboys here are a real tough bunch. They carry six-shooters, and I don't think they want to be interfered with."

Still, Balshofer hoped to avoid potential problems with Edison's organization. When wintry weather drove his company back to LA, he relocated his set to a parcel of property north of Santa Monica, near the Santa Ynez Canyon. Bison Studios built several lean-tos in the canyon; a few cowboys lived on-site, partly to take care of some horses that were kept there. Balshofer planned to fence off part of the property and hire a handful of wranglers to ride along the fringes and keep an eye out for McCoy.

As luck would have it, the Miller Brothers' 101 Ranch Wild West show was wintering a few miles away in Venice, California. Several silent films had been shot at the 101's Oklahoma ranch, and with audiences starting to abandon interest in Wild West shows in favor of Western movies, it made sense to combine the 101's offerings with Balshofer's. The Santa Monica acreage occupied by the 101 was rugged, bare bones, and hard to reach. The road from town was so muddy it was nearly impossible to navigate in winter, and when rain came, employees disembarking from the trolley had to ride on horseback to reach the hidden enclave. But the location offered Balshofer a safe place to make his movies. It helped, too, that the Millers assigned some of their most intimidating cowboys to patrol the property. Balshofer and his partner, Charles Bauman, worked out an arrangement with Joe Miller that gave them the use of some seventy-five cowboys, a couple dozen cowgirls, and thirty-five Indians, along with twenty-four oxen, a few bison, numerous horses, and all the necessary equipment, including stagecoaches and prairie schooners.

The 101's role in Hollywood expanded when Thomas Ince appeared on the scene. Ince came from a theatrical family in New York; he had entered the movie business as an actor, then worked as a production coordinator, but ultimately found his calling as a director. In 1911 Ince went to work directing Westerns for Balshofer's Bison Studios. He later set out on his own. He purchased and transformed the 101's property, installing a water system and building an entire Western town to house the actors and employees (including a separate village of tepees for the Indians). Inceville, as it came to be known, boasted ornate sets, dressing rooms, printing labs, production offices, and a commissary capable of feeding hundreds.

Ince incorporated a highly regimented method of making movies: he folded the work of a studio head, producers, directors, writers, and staff, working into a single system, under the supervision of a single general manager. The efficiency of this setup enabled Ince's studio to double its output, from one to two pictures a week, sometimes three. Almost all of the films were Westerns; in 1913 alone, Inceville cranked out more than

150 of them, helping cement the Western as a popular genre.

By now, Hollywood was overrun with wranglers who had lost their jobs when railroads took over transporting cattle long distances. On top of that, a catastrophic blizzard a quarter century earlier had decimated many herds. Scores of former wranglers, loaded guns still clamped to their holsters, would while away their days on sidewalks and at bars like Brewers and the Waterhole, located at the corner of Hollywood and Cahuenga in a section of town dubbed Gower Gulch. Universal Studios fenced in an area outside their gates where riders, derisively dubbed "corral buzzards," could bide their time hoping for work. When he needed extras, director Thomas Ince would send a car to pick up some of the cowboys and deliver them to Santa Monica, to Inceville.

Inceville made life better for everyone, including the five thousand or so horses kept there by the 101 Ranch. Trained and experienced, the horses were quality animals, ridden by equally skilled performers. Together they added oomph to Ince's movies, filling them with thrilling chase scenes. Actors who knew nothing about horses were able to learn quickly with a few lessons astride one of the 101's highly accomplished animals. The Indian performers were especially adept. A number of them had toured with the Millers' Wild West shows; some were direct descendants of fabled warriors from generations past, including several Indians who had fought in the famous Battle of the Little Bighorn. No other movie company featured actual Indians; the other studios substituted white actors adorned with black braids and artificially darkened skin.

The 101's legacy was enormous. Nearly every Western made during the first thirty years of moviemaking—among them *War on the Plains*, *The Battle of the Red Men*, and *The Deserter*—had links to the Millers or one of their connections. Back in Oklahoma, the 101 Ranch cultivated a steady bench of highly talented performers who eventually made their way to Hollywood.

For the horses, life at Inceville was infinitely better than traveling with the 101's Wild West show, which continued to journey across the United States. The train used to carry the show's performers and equipment consisted of twenty-eight cars; eight of them were set aside for the animals, and except for the time spent performing, the horses endured months squeezed in those cramped boxcars. Conditions were unnatural and unsafe. One night in 1912, a section of the train hit a spread rail in Wisconsin, smashing a handful of cars. Five prized arena horses along with several team horses perished in the accident, and thirty more suffered injuries. The Miller family simply replaced the lost horses with horses from the stockyards of Chicago. The following year, the 101 Ranch sent three train cars filled with horses and equipment to New York City and boarded them on a boat for South America. During the month-long voyage, the boat encountered several violent storms, upheaving the vessel and leaving passengers and crew—and no doubt the horses—miserably ill. In Buenos Aires, one of the show horses was found to have glanders, a contagious disease that can cause ulcers, pneumonia, fever with chills, and chest pains. The livestock inspector refused to give the rest of the horses on board the ship a clean bill of health; instead he decreed that all of them be shot and their corpses burned. The Millers followed his order, bought new horses to replace the deceased ones, and resumed their schedule.

The horses at Inceville were spared the vicissitudes of travel. The battle scenes they appeared in were jarring, but when they weren't acting out some tumultuous sequence, they were free to while away their days grazing in wide-open pastures. Not only did they lead easier lives than the 101's traveling entourage, but their working conditions were nowhere near as arduous as those of the horses who, just a couple of decades earlier, had been put to work rounding up cattle in the real West. Those horses braved a succession of hardships: broiling sun, fearsome thunderstorms, smothering billows of dust, the very real possibility of being struck by lightning—and those were just the summer conditions. Winter was worse, with shrieking, frigid winds, numbing sleet, and temperatures so glacial that trotting through the snow left the horses' feet sliced and bleeding, their nostrils clogged with ice.

3

First Came Fritz

Westerns grew in popularity, and horses were their unsung heroes. Fritz was the first, thanks to his partner, William S. Hart.

Hart came after Bronco Billy, an actor who appeared in the iconic 1903 silent classic *The Great Train Robbery* and went on to star in some four hundred short cowboy films. Billy had one major drawback, however: he had almost zero experience with horses. If a scene involved anything more than sitting astride a horse, a stunt double had to perform in his stead.

Despite his start performing Shakespeare on a New York stage, Hart was closer to the real thing. He was raised in the Dakotas, he had a lifelong infatuation with the West, and he quickly learned his way around a horse. Hart came to Los Angeles with the sole purpose in mind of acting in Western movies. He was forty-nine when he began making two-reel shorts for Ince, and he swiftly won moviegoers over by dressing in genuine-looking outfits and props and employing dusty settings to give his movies a sense of realism. By 1915 Hart was considered the most successful movie star in the United States. Now he needed a star horse who could live up to the billing.

His first choice was a jet-black gelding named Midnight, a former star of the 101 Ranch's show. Midnight was one of five horses Hart rode in 1914's *The Bargain*, the actor's first full-length movie. An anxious animal, Midnight had a notoriously hot temper; in past movies he'd broken a director's arm and an actor's leg. Fortunately Hart knew how to handle the temperamental horse and liked working with him. When the 101 declined his offer to buy Midnight, though, he began riding a considerably smaller, brown-and-white-patched pinto gelding he named Fritz.

There are competing accounts of how Fritz came to be discovered.

According to one version, the 101 purchased the horse from a Mexican who went by the name Snake Eye, who had tried to rein Fritz in by tethering him to a ball and chain on his hind leg and kicking him whenever he acted out. Fritz responded by booting another horse out of the corral. According to legend, Hart witnessed the incident and climbed over the fence to examine the insolent horse, whereupon Fritz nudged him, and a friendship was born. A second version claims that a Sioux chief named Lone Bear brought Fritz to Ince's movie ranch in 1911. Hart discovered the small horse one day when he happened upon silent-film actress Ann Little as she practiced rearing Fritz up on his hind legs. The pony nearly came down on Hart's head, but Hart was struck by his showmanship and began working with him.

However Fritz was discovered, Thomas Ince did not much care for him. Just fourteen hands tall, the pony was too short for the six-foot-two Hart, Ince believed. Prominent film producer Adolph Zukor agreed. He once scoffed that when Hart rode his pony, the actor's feet nearly touched the ground. A few Hollywood wranglers mused that Hart was too afraid to ride anything bigger. But Hart was enthralled with Fritz's stamina and skill, and under Hart's tutelage Fritz became the first celebrity pony to appear on the big screen. The little horse weighed just 990 pounds, but he was strong enough to tackle almost any assignment, and he seemed utterly fearless.

Had Fritz's coat been a solid color—black or sorrel or bay—it would have been easy to find a horse to double his risky stunts. Early movies were filmed in black and white, and most horses looked black on-screen. But the splotched pattern of Fritz's coat was as intricately shaped as a series of jigsaw puzzle pieces; it would have been nearly impossible to replicate them on another horse. As a result, Fritz was left to carry out almost all his own stunts.

Hart and Fritz were first paired in the 1915 movie *The Taking of Luke McVane*, about a man (Hart) who shoots the local sheriff out of self-defense, then risks his own life trying to patch up the sheriff's wounds. The movie was filmed in the sand dunes below Playa del Rey, near the present-day site of Los Angeles International Airport. Its climactic sequence called for the sheriff to climb onto Fritz behind Hart, for Fritz to gallop a long distance, and then, when Indians shoot Fritz, to duck behind the pony and continue the shoot-out. Despite Fritz's small stature, he managed to carry

Hart, actor Clifford Smith, who played the sheriff, and their weapons—a load Hart guessed had to weigh a combined total of 450 pounds, nearly half of Fritz's weight—for hours.

A subsequent movie called for Hart to jump Fritz through a window while Fritz dragged two villains tied to a rope. Fritz had never done anything this complicated, but Hart believed his pony was intrepid enough to give it a try. Hart had crew members remove the glass, then led the horse up to the open space to show him that no barrier existed—that he would be leaping straight through the window to the other side. The window was thirty-eight inches off the ground, barely wide and tall enough to accommodate Fritz, much less his rider, and the first time Hart tried to jump him through it, Fritz got as far as the opening and balked. Once the horse overcame his fear of the window's small size, Hart hung a sheet of cheesecloth over the open space and had him jump through that. For the final scene the crew replaced the cheesecloth with actual glass. Assuming the opening was free and clear, Fritz successfully jumped through the plate glass. He wound up with a small cut on his nose. At the sight of the pony's injury, Hart wept, overwhelmed with guilt at having tricked him.

Hart filmed most of his movies either in Newhall, California, twenty-seven miles north of Hollywood, or in the Santa Ynez Canyon, an hour's drive west. In one movie, believed to be 1918's *Riddle Gawne*, he rode Fritz up and down a twisty mountain trail that was wet and slippery from a recent rain. Fritz repeatedly stumbled and fell. In a "memoir" of Fritz written by Hart, *Told Under a White Oak Tree*, Hart recalled his words to the horse as they prepared for the stunt. "We got to do it, pardner," he told Fritz, "and that ain't the worst of it. When we get near the bottom I got to throw you and we do a houlihan or whatever comes to us because Lon Chaney, he's supposed to shoot you . . . and you go down." Fritz emerged from the stunt limping and slathered in muck up to his eyeballs. The director wanted to film a subsequent scene involving an easier ride across a flat pasture, but Hart refused to subject his horse to any more work that day.

Fritz's only flaw was his stubborn streak. To coax him into bucking, Hart would pretend to hand him a treat only to climb into the saddle instead. Each time he did so, Fritz retaliated by bucking high and hard, thrusting his legs out with all his strength. Once, he kicked scriptwriter Bert Lennon with such force that Hart flew thirty feet, landed on top of an ash heap, and was on crutches for three months. Hart was willing to oblige the pinto because Fritz more than delivered. He could fall while running. Hart "threw" him, as he called it, many times, even when it wasn't necessary. One afternoon Harry Aitken, the cofounder of Ince's Triangle Films, brought to the set a group of women who had asked to see Fritz. Hart tried to goad the pony into carrying out a few tricks, but Fritz refused to perform any of them. Determined to impress the ladies, Hart tightened up Fritz's cinch, rode him two hundred yards out, worked him up a bit, then galloped him toward the group as fast as he could and threw Fritz at their feet. The pony landed so close that Hart's head glanced one of the women's ankles.

In 1916 Inceville caught fire and suffered serious damage. Ince sold what was left of the studio to Hart, who renamed it Hartville (the property was later developed into a subdivision called Castellammare). The sale heralded an end to the Miller family's Hollywood chapter. The family gathered nearly all but 150 saddle horses that had resided at Inceville and boarded them onto ships, where they were sent to Europe to aid the Allies in World War I. Their halcyon days were over.

Despite having sold the property, Ince remained in business, and he still owned Fritz. He didn't particularly like Fritz, but he refused to sell him to Hart, rationalizing that he could keep Hart under contract indefinitely so long as Ince could offer the pony as part of the arrangement. Ince agreed to one exception, and that was to let Hart use Fritz in the 1917 movie *The Narrow Trail*, which Hart had conceived with Fritz in mind. Fritz proved his worth in that movie alone. In it, he plays the leader of a wild horse herd who, in one hair-raising scene, has to make his way across a fallen tree bridging two sides of a canyon. In the first take, Fritz navigated the curved log without any trouble. But when the cameraman asked for a second take—and asked Hart to hold Fritz still in order to get a close-up—the pony lost his footing and fell several feet, trapping Hart beneath him. Fritz remained motionless until help arrived; his hooves were positioned so close to Hart's head that, had Fritz moved, he might have seriously injured Hart. Hart later maintained that Fritz held himself completely still because he understood the peril his owner was in.

The Narrow Trail captured Fritz's magnetism and transformed him into a star in his own right. Thousands of fans wrote to him. Ince finally acquiesced: he'd give Fritz to Hart if Hart would agree to postpone a sizeable salary hike. Hart estimated the arrangement cost him $42,500, but he said it was worth every nickel. Fritz was now his. Oddly, to get back at Ince's dislike of the red pony, Hart refused to let Ince incorporate Fritz into his next fifteen pictures after that. "The little pinto never earned another dollar that Tom shared in," Hart crowed. He went so far as to take out large ads in trade papers announcing Fritz's retirement.

During his respite from filming, Fritz was kept in a barn on Washington Boulevard in LA, and he wasn't a bit happy about it. "Golly! He was mad!" Hart said. "He was fighting mad! He could not understand why he should have been cooped up for so long and see me so seldom." In the meantime, Hart rode a reliable, even-tempered gelding named Brownie in his movies. Eventually he brought Fritz back to the big screen, taking out new ads heralding the horse's comeback in the 1920 movie *Sand*. Moviegoers who had written fan letters and mailed cubes of sugar to the horse flocked to theaters to celebrate his return.

Fritz had made two close friends during his confinement: a bucking mare named Cactus Kate and a pack mule named Lisbeth, both stablemates in his barn. Back on set, Fritz refused to perform unless Kate and Lisbeth were nearby, close enough for him to take comfort in their proximity. In a scene in *Sand*, Fritz is said to have raced to the edge of a cliff, then turned to lock eyes with his friends before jumping. Two years later, filming *Travelin' On*, Fritz refused to work with a popular Hollywood monkey named Jocko until Kate was delivered to the set to calm him down. Shortly after she arrived, filming was interrupted again, this time by the rumbling sounds of a bawling mule. Lisbeth had busted out of her enclosure and sprinted a mile down busy streets to link up with her pals.

Hart listed Fritz as his costar in the movie credits, a first for an animal performer. Hart claimed Fritz could understand what he was saying to him, and critics noted that the horse did have a way of looking sympathetic when Hart spoke to him. Whatever their means of communication, it worked. Fritz jumped off cliffs with Hart. He leapt over an upended wagon in *Tumbleweeds*. It seemed there was nothing the pony wasn't willing to try, and Hart loved to show off Fritz's capabilities. Hart later claimed he never used a double for Fritz—that Fritz was the only movie horse he knew that performed every stunt himself. Nor did Hart turn to stunt doubles for himself. He carried out his own horse falls and occasionally suffered injuries as a result. It wasn't uncommon to see him hobbling around the set.

By 1924 Hart was aging and ready to retire, but there was one more movie he wanted to make. In *Singer Jim McKee* he plays a struggling miner, Jim McKee, who, with a partner, widower Buck Holden, holds up a stagecoach to collect money to support Buck's daughter, Mary. Buck is killed in the melee, and McKee escapes with Mary. The movie's climax comes when Hart, now playing a fleeing outlaw, races along the rim of a cliff.

The scene was shot at Sulphur Canyon in New Mexico. Falls had been filmed there before, but no one had ever sent a horse down the entire length of the canyon's steep sides. After Fritz got shot, he and Hart were to tumble twelve feet off the side of the cliff and roll down into a gorge 150 feet below. Hart was confident Fritz could carry out the stunt, but he worried it might injure the pony in the process. Hart and director Cliff Smith decided to fake the stunt instead. They turned to Lasky Studio's veteran mechanics, who spent five weeks constructing a horse that looked nearly identical to Fritz. The decoy's mane and tail were made of genuine horsehair, and its body contained enough springs to make its joints, even its neck, move realistically.

The cameras started rolling. Hart charged the real Fritz to the side of the cliff and pulled him into a fall. Filming stopped long enough for Hart to then lead Fritz out of the camera range so crew members could install the mechanical horse in his place. Hart then mounted the dummy horse, and the crew cut the wires holding it in place, sending actor and dummy over the edge. The edited scene was so believable that a board of censors established by the Motion Pictures Producers and Distributors organization sent for Hart to explain why in the world he would willingly imperil his beloved horse. Hart's explanation reassured industry reps, but alarmed moviegoers—unaware of the switcheroo—sent hundreds of letters protesting the move. It marked the first time audiences seemed to take notice of an animal's struggles on-screen.

Hart retired Fritz after that. The pony lived fourteen more years before succumbing in 1938. Hart buried his beloved pal at the foot of the hill below his house in Newhall, California, now a museum owned by the city of Santa Clarita. Ranch hands, some friends, and a few local children gathered around to bid Fritz farewell as a string band from the San Fernando Valley played. Hart erected a tall cobblestone monument over his grave featuring a bronze engraving of Fritz's likeness and the words: "To Bill Hart's Pinto Pony Fritz, age 31 years, a Loyal Comrade." A photo shows Hart standing next to Fritz's grave, looking utterly bereft. Hart hung a picture of Fritz over his bed and later donated a statue of himself riding Fritz to the city of Billings, Montana. It still sits high atop a hill near the airport, overlooking the Yellowstone Valley.

4

Then Came Tony

As Hart's stardom was waning, Tom Mix's celebrity was skyrocketing.

Unlike Hart, Mix was quite the dandy. He welcomed attention. At a time when the streets of Hollywood were still largely unpaved, he had his initials carved into the tire treads of his car so they would leave a trail of *TM* insignias in the dirt as he cruised around town. In contrast to Hart's authentic but bland attire, Mix paraded about in elaborate, custom-made get-ups accented with flashy diamond-filled jewelry designed to showcase his trim figure. His publicists inflated his bio, claiming Mix had been one of President Teddy Roosevelt's Rough Riders (in truth, Mix only rode in Roosevelt's inaugural parade alongside several Rough Riders). Yet no one questioned his skill as a horseman. As screenwriter Adela Rogers St. Johns put it, "Tom was as elegant on a horse as Fred Astaire on a dance floor, and that's the elegantest there is."

Mix had been a cowboy performer at the Miller family's 101 Ranch in Oklahoma when filmmaker William N. Selig came looking to shoot a Western in a natural setting. A Chicago native, Selig got into movie work in the mid-1890s. He developed the Selig Standard Camera and operated the Selig Polyscope, and his motion picture company was the first to open a studio in Southern California. By today's standards Selig's films were exceedingly short, lasting barely five minutes apiece, and the images produced by the hand-cranked cameras were so jerky they were dubbed "flickers." The movies appeared in nickelodeons, so named because they cost a nickel to watch. Upper-class Americans turned their noses up at nickelodeons, but struggling immigrants who couldn't afford to attend live performances flocked to them.

2. Early Western film star Tom Mix and his succession of horses named Tony enthralled moviegoers. "Tony" even had his own fan club. His most daring stunts were often performed by doubles. Courtesy of the Oklahoma Historical Society.

For an action sequence in the film he intended to shoot at the Miller Ranch, Selig offered the bountiful sum of $50 to any daredevil willing to ride a horse over a cliff into the swollen Salt Fork of the Arkansas River. Sensing this could be his entrance into moviedom, Mix volunteered. He rode his horse a short while to rev him up, spurred him into a fast gallop, and charged him off the thirty-foot bluff. The horse survived the fall; he swam to the other side of the river and emerged on the far shore. Mix did not fare as well. The jump broke two of his ribs and knocked out a tooth. But the important thing was that the camera caught it all on film. Mix's movie career was launched.

Ever since he was a child, Mix had yearned to be a cowboy. Growing up outside Driftwood, Pennsylvania, he learned to lasso using his mother's clothesline. He worked with horses, donkeys, and mules, teaching himself to grab hold of a galloping horse and leap onto its back. And he learned to Roman ride, a daring trick that consists of standing upright on the back of a horse that's running at full speed.

Mix joined the U.S. Army but deserted his post in 1902 and traveled west to the Oklahoma Territory with his wife, Grace. He juggled an assortment of odd jobs: bartending, teaching physical fitness in the basement of the Carnegie Library, and breaking horses for area ranches. At the 1904 World's Fair in St. Louis he met Will Rogers, who taught him to lasso three and four horses at once. Mix was on his way. Five years later he joined the Widerman Wild West Show; as part of his act, he would race into the arena on a roan-colored horse, Ol' Blue, drop to the horse's side to hide from attacking Indians, clamber back into the saddle and then somersault out of it, landing on his feet.

Not much is known about Ol' Blue except that he was thirteen when Mix began performing with him, an age when many horses were considered used up. It's likely Ol' Blue was the horse Mix rode over the cliff for Bill Selig because a year later Mix used the horse in a similar stunt. The scene was part of the movie *The Telltale Knife*. In it, Mix and another actor, Charlie Farrar, gallop their horses down the side of a mountain into the Arkansas River below, near the entrance of Grape Creek. On the day the scene was filmed, the water was gushing out of the creek so powerfully that it swept along everything in its path. Mix and Farrar were swimming their horses to a nearby sandbar when they got caught in the churning water.

Ol' Blue managed to pull himself out, but Farrar and his horse were close to drowning when a quick-thinking onlooker standing a hundred feet away managed to toss a lasso around the horse's neck and pull them ashore.

Ol' Blue is believed to have performed with Mix for the first seven years of his movie career. The horse's life ended in 1919, when he stepped into a gopher hole in his corral in Mixville, the studio where Mix made his movies, instantly breaking his leg. The roan gelding had survived all those daring stunts only to succumb to an unfortunate accident at the age of twenty-two. Distraught by the news, Mix raced to the scene and wept nonstop as his horse was euthanized. For years after, he hung lavish wreaths over Blue's grave to honor his memory.

Mix acquired a small herd of performing horses, and differences over their care eventually led to a falling-out between Mix and Selig. A consultant hired by Selig had the audacity to recommend that Mix withhold food from his horses on the days their services weren't needed on set. On top of that, Selig tried to charge Mix for the cost of boarding the horses during production. Aggravated by Selig's chintziness, Mix moved on to Fox Studios, where they agreed to give him $350 a week, pay a salary to the cowboys who worked under him, and board his horses at no cost.

Mix was looking for a horse as dependable as Ol' Blue, and he finally found him in a thoroughbred gelding he named Tony. Mix bought Tony from fellow actor and horse trainer Pat Chrisman, who'd seen Tony as a colt walking alongside a horse hauling a vegetable wagon down a street in the Los Angeles neighborhood of Edendale. The owner of the colt was looking to sell him. Chrisman bought the horse for around $14, trained him, then sold him to Mix for the marked-up price of $600.

Tony was not as big as Ol' Blue, but he had the fearlessness and showmanship Mix was looking for. He made his debut in the 1917 movie *The Heart of Texas Ryan* and went on to appear in many of Mix's films over the next fifteen years. With his solid, trim build and shiny coat—it softened in color to sorrel as he grew—his white socks accenting his hind legs and his narrow blaze, Tony was a striking horse and a constant partner to Mix. Mix's third wife, Olive, said Tony had an uncanny ability to follow his owner's commands. "When they were about to do a difficult scene, Tom would pat Tony on his nose and say, 'Now, look, Tony, here's the way we're going to do this.' And that was the way they would do it," she said. "Someone once commented that Tony must certainly have understood what Tom said to him. That was wrong, of course. But he did understand Tom's love, and that was enough."

Mix's films were shot in the Mojave Desert town of Lone Pine, California, two hundred miles north of Los Angeles, and in other Western-y locales. They were full of romance, comedy, and feverish shoot-'em-ups. Tony was adept at performing. He could untie Mix's hands, race for help if Mix was in trouble, and fend off villains and wild animals. He seemed always at the ready, and he never balked at Mix's instructions, regardless of the hazards he faced. "I always felt that Tony . . . would have bowed his head in shame rather than do anything unworthy of himself or Tom," Olive Mix said.

Director George Marshall, who worked with Mix in several films, said that Tony also carried out a number of his own horse falls, crashing through glass windows and more. "There was no imitation glass during this period either," Marshall said, "and they didn't dig up the ground to spot a fall. Wherever they were shooting, that's where you fell."

But Mix wasn't about to put Tony in any real peril. Actress Colleen Moore, who worked with Mix, said he had at least five different horses available to double for Tony—the first time a stunt horse was hired to take the place of a star horse. Tom wouldn't let Tony do dangerous stunts for fear he might break his leg, Moore said. "It was a matter of practicality, I guess, as well as love," she said. "The way Tom looked at it, there were plenty of stars around and plenty of leading ladies, but a good horse is hard to find."

For scenes involving long shots, Mix occasionally used a horse named Black Bess. For some of the riskier stunts he used Buster, a gelding who shared Tony's muscular build and sorrel coat. Buster's background is unknown, but he was big and athletic and thoroughly reliable. Makeup artists would add a white stripe down his face and dye his hind feet white to make him a dead ringer for Tony.

It was Buster, not Tony, who carried out a spectacular stunt in 1920's *The Cyclone*. The movie's plot revolves around the North-West Mounted Police, and the climactic scene called for Mix and Colleen Moore to ride Buster up several flights of stairs inside a building as, one by one, the floors beneath them collapse. The floors consisted of plaster and chicken wire, and the ability of horse and rider to emerge unharmed was nothing short of a minor miracle. In *Trailin'*, filmed the following year, it may well have been Buster doubling for Tony when Mix rode a horse across a swinging bridge. The movie's villain swings an axe and cleaves a crucial bridge support, flipping the bridge sideways and sending Mix and his horse plummeting into the water below.

In 1925's *The Great K & A Train Robbery*, Mix gallops Buster, doubling for Tony, alongside the train and leaps aboard a chugging boxcar. In another scene the two ride across a slender wooden bridge spanning the turbulent Colorado River. Another hair-raising moment occurred when, cornered inside a mansion, Mix and a fellow passenger ride Buster off a balcony into a swimming pool below.

Olive Mix claimed that Tony was jealous of Buster and would snuffle with rage whenever he spied Mix climbing into Buster's saddle. Later, as age slowed Tony down, "I actually believe he understood that Tom was trying to spare him," Olive said. As far as moviegoers were concerned, of course, Mix rode just one horse, and that was Tony. Tony was the first horse to get equal billing in movie posters, and he was cited in the titles of three of Mix's films: *Just Tony*; *Oh, You Tony!*; and *Tony Runs Wild*. During their years together millions of photos of Mix and his "Wonder Horse" circulated the world over. At the peak of Mix's career he received thousands of letters from fans every week, and thousands more were written to Tony, even when they didn't know how to reach him. Mail addressed to "Just Tony, somewhere in the USA" managed to find its way to the sorrel star.

In the 1922 movie *Sky High*, Mix races a horse doubling for Tony up a slender mule trail from the base of the Grand Canyon, skirting calamity. In another sequence, he chases his nemesis down a steep cliff. Near the bottom, the white horse Mix is riding stumbles badly, hurling himself and Mix onto the ground. Mix picks himself up, snatches the horse's reins, climbs back on him, and keeps riding. "No Western star before or since has ever taken such an accidental neck-breaking horse fall and simply continued with the scene," author Richard D. Jensen wrote in his excellent biography, *The Amazing Tom Mix*.

John Ford's 1923 movie *Three Jumps Ahead* includes Mix's most spectacular—and controversial—stunt. Mix appears to sail his horse over the Newhall Pass, a tall, narrow gap located near Newhall, California, northwest of Los Angeles. The pass is almost too tight for a stagecoach to pass through and just wide enough to make jumping its span heart-stoppingly risky. Detractors later insisted the feat involved smoke and mirrors and was pulled off by a stuntman doubling for Mix. Others claimed that Mix carried out the jump but that the actor and his horse were diminished in size by the camera to make the pass look larger. The great-niece of stuntman Ed Simpson said her uncle told her that he, Simpson, performed the stunt. Ford himself said Mix executed the jump, and Mix's biographer, Jensen, wrote that a photo of the stunt showed Mix using a ramp to raise the elevation of the side he leapt his horse from, enabling him to soar at a downward slant that made it easier to clear the chasm. However the stunt took place, Mix again used a double for Tony; by now he had insured his star horse for $20,000 and wasn't about to put him in jeopardy.

In one instance, though, Mix is believed to have ridden Tony off a train in 1923's *Eyes of the Forest*, a highly dangerous stunt. In another sequence he rides Tony as fast as he can down a trail in search of a band of thieves. The trail was set to explode mere seconds after they passed by, but a member of the crew detonated the explosion too soon. The blast caught Mix and his horse, knocked them unconscious, flung them fifty feet in the air, and left Tony with an enormous gash in his side. After a few dizzying moments Tony struggled to his feet, but Mix made him lie down again. The actor ignored his own serious injuries long enough to stitch the horse's wound shut.

Mix and Tony weren't just a phenomenon in the United States. They were equally popular overseas. To capitalize on their fame, Mix, his then-wife Victoria, and their daughter, Thomasina, rode a train from Los Angeles to New York City, Tony and his caretaker, Pat Chrisman, in tow. A cameraman for Fox Movietone News jostled with a cluster of newspaper photographers to capture Mix riding Tony up the gangplank of the London-bound ocean liner *Aquitania*. Tony stayed below deck for most of the voyage, but each day Mix brought him onto the passenger deck. During one formal dinner, Mix even rode Tony into the dining room and up the grand staircase, to the astonishment and delight of his fellow guests. In London, Edward, the Prince of Wales, dispatched a messenger to invite Tony to board at the royal stables, Tattersalls. Before their visit was over, Mix stood on Tony's back and rode him through London's famous Hyde Park, then took him by train to France, where at a benefit performance for the Children's Welfare League, he rode the horse up a flight of stairs to the balcony. "Tony seemed to enjoy the crowds as much as Tom did and he never spooked or kicked at the children, even when they ran underneath his belly and between his legs, something that would terrify many horses," Jensen wrote.

In 1927 Mix was invited to place his handprints in cement along Hollywood's Walk of Fame. Tony's hoofprints were captured too; they're still visible in the courtyard of what is now Mann's Chinese Theater. But it was all downhill from there. The following year Mix's contract with Fox expired and he set off with Tony on a vaudeville tour. The vaudeville tour helped Mix avoid the advent of "talkies." Mix had made his mark in the silent era; he'd never had to actually speak on film. He appeared in a handful of early talkies, but he wore dentures that clacked audibly when he spoke his lines. Fellow cowboy star Will Rogers joshed that Mix had nothing to worry about—that even if he couldn't speak well, Tony "could at least snort."

In 1931, though, Mix decided to give talking roles one more go. He was still recovering from a bout of peritonitis when he signed a contract with Universal to make twelve movies. By now, Tony was on his way out. In his last picture with Mix, 1932's *The Rider of Death Valley*, Tony stumbled when Mix jumped him across a small stream, and he came up limping. Later Tony tripped on a five-foot-high bank in the Mojave Desert, rolled over sideways, and landed on top of Mix, knocking him unconscious.

Tony had helped Mix earn roughly $7.5 million during their years together. He deserved to rest. The following month Mix retired the twenty-three-year-old gelding and never rode him again. Weeks later, the *New York Times* reported that Tony would be replaced by Tony Jr., a chestnut sorrel who, like Tony, had white stockings on each leg and a white diamond on his forehead. But Tony Jr. appeared in only nine of the twelve pictures Mix was slated to film. After breaking his leg in a horse fall, Mix retired from movies himself on Christmas Day, 1932. He began traveling with his own circus, including Tony Jr. in his acts. Tony Jr. retired in 1935, and after that, Mix began riding Warrior, a tall, white horse with a striking presence. Warrior's career was short-lived. When Mix died five years later at the age of sixty, he had run through most of his money and was a shadow of the movie idol he'd once been.

The faded cowboy star was driving to his ranch in Florence, Arizona, on October 12, 1940, after a night of partying at the Santa Rita Hotel in

Tucson. He was speeding on a dirt road when he happened upon an unusually slick wash. A monsoon's heavy rains had scoured out the bridge and a crew was working to restore the road when Mix came barreling through. His car dove into the ditch, causing a suitcase to fly off the shelf behind his seat, striking him in the head and breaking his neck. He died at the scene.

Their owner gone, all but one of Mix's horses and ponies were sold at auction. The lone exception was the original Tony. He was given to Mix's friend, attorney, and horseman Ivon D. Parker, who cared for the horse for the next two years as his health failed. The horse who had astounded moviegoers with his audacity lost his ability to eat dry food. The day finally came when Parker and a veterinarian led Tony to his old stall, where the vet administered a dose of chloroform and the horse died almost instantly, without any pain.

"I almost wonder if Tony didn't know what was coming early this morning," Parker commented. "I took him from my ranch in a truck and he entered it easily. On the ride to the Tom Mix estate, he looked about the country as if he knew he was getting his last view."

5

Trip Wires and More

The overwhelming popularity of Fritz and Tony helped usher in more equine stars. Silver King, a white palomino who debuted in 1924, came to be billed as "the most famous horse in the world," complete with a prima donna personality. His owner was an actor named Fred Thomson, who had noticed Silver King at an equestrian school in New York City and asked to ride him. The temperamental horse promptly tried his best to buck Thomson off. Thomson responded by heaving the horse to the ground, cinching his legs together with one end of a rope, and walloping him with the other. Despite that inauspicious start, Thomson wound up buying Silver King and teaching him multiple stunts, including how to bow, kneel, wink with one eye, and execute a stylish Spanish walk.

Silver King quickly acclimated to his star status. He was said to pitch a fit if a director substituted a double for any of his stunts, and more than once he kicked a set to pieces after the cameras were shut off. He appeared on the set of one movie wearing sunglasses. That wasn't some affectation on his owner's part: Silver King had suffered eye damage performing under the intense klieg lights that were used at the time and had to spend days in a dark stable to recuperate. He was retired in 1928 after Thomson suddenly died of tetanus after stepping on a nail in his stables.

The black Morgan stallion Rex also rose to fame. Rex was owned and tutored by Jack "Swede" Lindell, a well-regarded trainer who devised techniques for teaching horses to block out the confusing sights and sounds of movie apparatuses and focus on the assignment at hand. Lindell was looking for the setting for a movie when he discovered Rex living in solitary confinement at a detention home in Golden, Colorado—his punishment for having dragged a rider to death. Lindell rescued the horse, took him back to California, and trained him to appear in nineteen movies, often performing dramatic stunts. In 1927's *Wild Beauty*, Rex "kills" a mountain lion and attacks a rival stallion. In *Wild Blood*, he guides a bandit over a cliff. In a hilarious scene from the 1925 movie *No Man's Law*, Rex rushes to the rescue after a couple of rascally villains try to prey on a young woman who is swimming in the nude. Rearing up and bucking, Rex chases one of the men off a cliff and bumps the other over the edge with his nose.

Rex was every bit as temperamental as Silver King. In *Law of the Wild*, he charged the camera, something he was supposed to do, but instead of stopping as Lindell instructed, Rex reared up and toppled some reflectors, sending everyone on the set fleeing. For some inexplicable reason the horse had it in for one of the actors, Ernie Adams, and began chasing him. When Adams slid under a car to escape Rex, the horse fell to his knees and lunged his head sideways beneath the vehicle to try to reach him. Lindell was finally able to stop Rex by cracking his whip in the air.

Moviegoers grew accustomed to seeing star horses who had colorful personalities and were genuine partners to their cowboy costars. Gene Autry had two horses named Champion, the younger of which could smile, kiss, perform dance steps resembling the hula, rhumba, and waltz, and unravel knots. Roy Rogers's horse Little Trigger was said to be the smartest steed in Hollywood and the only one who was housebroken. (In 1944 in the lobby of the Hotel Astor in New York, he marked an *X* in the guest book by holding a pen in his mouth.) A pinto named Dice could lie down and play dead, hoist a revolver out of a holster, pick up a hat, count, and yawn on cue. His best-known performance came in the 1943 movie *It's a Great Life*. In it, Dice strolls through a hotel lobby, steps inside an elevator, backs out, and instead ascends the stairs. His star status was secured after he darted outside the studio in a fit of pique one day and was hit by a car. He wasn't seriously hurt, but hundreds of well-wishers mailed him get-well cards, telegrams, and flowers.

Star horses dazzled moviegoers. The anonymous horses brought on to do the dangerous work were easy to overlook. In the beginning their stunts weren't terribly difficult. Cowboys and Indians would first stop their horses and then tumble to the ground, executing what was referred to as a saddle fall. Stagecoach drivers assigned to wreck their wagons would bring all four of their horses to a halt and only then spill out of their seats.

Eventually, though, directors decided those action scenes looked too phony and contrived. Battle scenes would look infinitely more convincing if instead of having the riders topple over, the horses themselves could somehow be made to fall. Hart and Mix had figured out a way to throw their horses. Directors now wanted to see more horse falls take place on a bigger scale.

Stunt coordinators first devised what they called the four-hobble fall. Using the same kind of manacle that had stopped many a grazing horse from wandering off on the range, and attaching it to a cable, a stuntman could suddenly jerk the horse's feet together, crumpling him onto his side as if he'd been shot.

Yakima Canutt tweaked the concept further. Canutt was a stocky, hawk-nosed, tough-as-nails rodeo star who arrived in Hollywood when silent movies still dominated the screen. He began his career in front of the camera, starring in nearly fifty films before talkies took over. His voice was his downfall. One critic described it as "squishy soft, like a half-inflated tire," and once movies acquired sound, his acting days came to a fast halt. Behind the scenes, though, Canutt's charisma and know-how with horses proved highly useful. He schooled a young John Wayne on how to walk convincingly on-screen, how to ride in the saddle, and how to speak in a slow drawl. And in sequences too dangerous to subject Wayne to, Canutt doubled for the rising star. He wasn't afraid of anything, whether it was tearing out from behind a bush to knock the enemy off a horse or duking it out with a rival on top of an out-of-control stagecoach. Canutt so impressed Wayne that the actor once declared him "the most magnificent man in the world."

Canutt made a name for himself in *The Devil Horse* when, doubling for the actor Harry Carey Sr., he told the prop guys to tie his wrists and ankles around the horse Rex's neck and turn the two of them loose. Carey's son, Harry "Dobie" Carey Jr., said he had heard as a child that Rex killed one of his trainers while filming the serial and that Canutt insisted on riding him after that. Canutt hung from the neck of the violently defiant Rex while he did everything possible—bucking, wallowing on the ground, and swiveling rapidly—to try to throw him off.

Canutt developed a stunt where he would fall between a pair of harnessed stagecoach horses as they sped along, hang on for a bit to the wooden shaft situated between them, then drop toward the ground and quickly grab the rear axle of the coach as it sped over him, letting it drag him along. After that, he would flip over onto his stomach and make his way to the top of the stagecoach, where he would tackle the bad guy.

A similar invention of his, the "ironing board," no doubt saved a few lives. The ironing board was a narrow plank of wood positioned a foot off the ground between a team of wagon-pulling horses. If a stuntman happened to miss a jump onto the horses—for scenes in which he was trying to stop a runaway team, for example—he could fall onto the ironing board and escape being trampled.

Canutt is best known, though, for modifying a complicated device called the Running W. The idea for Running W's came from an old practice of breaking ranch horses by tethering them to a wagon with a long rope that would fling them to the ground if, in trying to escape, they bolted all the way to the rope's end. For movie purposes, a Running W consisted of two piano wires laced along the inside of a horse's front legs and attached to a leather strap encompassing each leg just above his fetlock, or ankle. A third wire was threaded up to the horse's saddle and attached to a ring held by the rider. The wire was long enough—several hundred feet or more—that the unsuspecting horse could build up a high rate of speed before his rider yanked it, jerking the horse's front feet out from under him and sending him cartwheeling to the ground. Riders often marked the spot in the dirt where the wire would come to an end. Knowing where the fall would occur made it easier for riders to pull their feet out of the stirrups and sidestep being crushed when their horse fell. Horses, though, had no control over the trip wires. Often they landed so forcefully that they broke their backs or necks and had to be put to death.

Canutt came up with a somewhat safer version. His Running W included a ring hooked to a cinch that was designed to break loose just before the horse hit the ground. The W Ring, as he called it, cut in half the force of the pull and freed the horse sooner, increasing the odds that he could catch himself before landing.

Canutt conceded that occasionally a horse that had been subjected to a Running W would refuse to run the next time wires were hooked up to him.

In the John Wayne movie *Dark Command*, one horse quickly caught on to the trick and lay down on his own as soon as he sensed the wires attached to him were about to run out. But Canutt claimed that, done correctly, Running W's were not dangerous. He maintained that he orchestrated some three hundred Running W's and never once crippled a horse.

Diana Serra Cary disagreed. A popular child star known as Baby Peggy in the early 1920s, Cary grew up listening to the stories of her father, cowboy stuntman Jack Montgomery. In her book *The Hollywood Posse: The Story of a Gallant Band of Horsemen Who Made Movie History*, she derided Running W's as "Russian Roulette on horseback" and said that, during a period when they were used daily, "the casualties among horses and riders ran higher in Hollywood than they ever had in the real West." An early executive director of the American Humane Association, Mel L. Morse, agreed. "If you have ever had the opportunity to see a Running W, you have seen an animal shaken (that is of course if the neck isn't broken)," Morse said. "The animal will stand trembling for hours afterwards and is usually not fit for anything else after it has been so used."

Trip wires were usually concealed on the big screen, but not always. In a photo taken from an action sequence of the *Three Mesquiteers* series produced by Republic Pictures in 1940, the wires are clearly visible as the horses slam to the ground on their faces. Another photo taken by the Humane Association showed a horse killed by a trip-wired fall that broke his leg. The hobbles attached to his forelegs and the wire running over his neck are discernible. "Among the spectators, a woman wept bitterly," Cary said. "She knew the horse well, for it belonged to her husband." To put the horse out of his misery, a Humane Association rep shot him.

Directors relied on two other equally treacherous tricks to make horses go down. The first was pit falls. Movie crews would dig a trench, usually eight feet square and at least two and a half feet deep, cover it with cheesecloth, branches, and leaves, then gallop a horse in its direction. The instant the unsuspecting horse encountered the pit, he would tumble and fall, frequently suffering a fatal injury.

More terrifying were tilt chutes. A horse might unwittingly allow himself to be hooked up to trip wires or sent running over a pit fall, but no horse would willingly charge off a cliff. Yet cliff-jumping provided Westerns that dramatic urgency directors were looking for—the climactic moment when

3. A horse killed by a trip wire. Note the wire attached to his front legs. Courtesy of the American Humane Association.

the good guys were able to escape their pursuers. Movie audiences would see a protagonist ride his horse to the rim of a bluff, peer down into the water below, assess the dangers involved, and, despite them, send himself and his horse over the edge. The next sequence would show hero and horse swimming safely to land. In truth, before the jump, the horse was often led onto a low wooden chute attached to a rocking platform, sometimes wrapped in metal and in any case greased heavily. Some movie crews went so far as to install a curtain at the forward end of the chute, or they would strap leather blinkers over the horse's eyes so he could be led onto the chute without balking. The blinkers were joined in the middle and connected to the bridle. To fool moviegoers, some crews painted eyes on the blinkers. A member of the crew would then raise the curtain while another tilted the chute forward. The stuntman would grab the reins and the blinkers would fling open, enabling the horse to see—too late—as he fell twenty, thirty, forty feet, sometimes farther, into the water. Edited footage made it seem as though the horse had jumped voluntarily. The reality was that many horses landed so forcefully that they broke their necks or backs and had to be shot to death. If a horse died as a result of a fall, the director would film a different horse with similar markings swimming to shore.

In *Dark Command*, Canutt took the tilt-chute concept a step further. The climactic getaway scene has Wayne and three others escaping a band of raiders by driving a supply wagon pulled by a team of horses over a bluff into a lake forty feet below. Canutt had the special effects crew build the wagon out of light balsa wood. Next they constructed two tilt chutes that together measured seventy-five feet long. The first chute, when angled, would slide the horses and wagon onto the longer chute waiting on a bluff down below. From there, the horses and the wagon would plunge into the water.

Canutt employed several measures to protect the horses. He added small cables that would release the horses from their hookups once they began their fall. He installed breakaway snaps on the inside reins. And he attached small floats at the end of each line to help keep the horses afloat in case they encountered trouble and needed to be rescued. To his amazement, the first time the stunt was performed, it took place without any problems. The devices worked so well that the stuntmen and their horses were ready to resume working half an hour later, Canutt claimed.

The movie studios lauded Canutt's efforts, as did many stunt performers. "Yak taught us the nuts and bolts of our business," stuntman Jack Williams once recalled. "The old-timers used to do stunts with a bottle of whiskey. Yak developed the methods to do them safely." In recognition of his ingenuity and "for developing safety devices to protect stunt men everywhere," the Academy of Motion Pictures awarded Canutt an honorary Oscar in 1966.

6

Ratcheting Up the Risks

By the 1920s, moviemakers began upping the ante, producing stupendous epics that put stuntmen and horses through even more reckless feats. One director in particular displayed an unusually egregious disregard for stunt performers and horses: Cecil B. DeMille, the visionary tyrant known for his outlandish extravaganzas. In his epic 1923 film *The Ten Commandments*—the silent version, not to be confused with his 1956 remake starring Charlton Heston—DeMille went all out, commandeering twenty-four square miles of California property on which to erect an Egyptian municipality, a tent city to house cast and crew, including 2,500 extras, and corrals big enough to hold three thousand horses, goats, and sheep.

The film's most perilous sequence comes when the Egyptian army battles the Israelites. Played by artillerymen, the Egyptians were decked out in gold tunics, heavy metal armor, and helmets bedecked with colorful plumes that gleamed in the sun. In the scene leading up to their confrontation, the army stages a solo charge with reckless abandon. In the middle of the skirmish, the lead chariot driven by a double for the pharaoh suddenly collapses, causing the rest of the chariots, along with the horses pulling them and their riders, to crash in its wake. The collision left a pile of injured stuntmen and lame animals, among them a team of magnificent black thoroughbred stallions DeMille had purchased in Kansas City for $10,000. Other horses ran loose, shrieking in pain, their torn flesh flapping like bloody rags. In their panicked state, several of the horses sprinted directly toward a thirty-piece orchestra DeMille had hired to play mood music in the background. The musicians kept playing until the horses, still harnessed to their chariots, careened into them, bruising the players and destroying a number of their instruments.

The following week DeMille moved the company from Santa Maria to the Mojave Desert, to Muroc Dry Lake, to film the battle scenes between the Egyptians and the Israelites. Traumatized by the bloodbath they had experienced the previous week, the cowboys hired to play the Israelites balked at DeMille's directive: he wanted them to dash their chariots down a steep cliff in an attempt to escape the Egyptian army. Ordinarily the wranglers would have carried out an assignment no matter how risky, and they would have done so with pride. But deliberately driving carriages down a precipitous bluff was too perilous. A handful of the cowboys approached the director to express concern that the sharp drop would be too dangerous to the horses and their riders. DeMille wasn't having it. His daughter Cecilia was riding her range pony nearby. DeMille beckoned the fifteen-year-old and instructed her to race down the bank as fast as she could. The teenager had no trouble speeding her pony down the hill. The director turned to the cowboys and said, "Well, if a little girl like Ciddy can do it, why can't you?"

Still, the wranglers objected. "It's one thing to bring down a single rider," they told him. "Any one of us could do that blindfolded. It's something else to have fifty to a hundred men pile off it, with chariots and teams." When they protested that the artillerymen secretly planned to deliberately ride directly over the stuntmen to prove their superiority, DeMille was undeterred. Years later he confessed that he had hoped to capitalize on the acrimony he'd detected between the actors playing the Egyptians and those playing the Israelites to inflame the tension on the big screen. No, he told the cowboys, the scene would be filmed as planned.

The wranglers returned to their colleagues, climbed into their chariots, and waited in the broiling sun. DeMille surveyed the scene, then yelled, "Ready! Camera! Action!" The artillerymen let loose their horses and careened toward the Israelites. But only a half dozen of the 275 cowboys started down the cliff toward battle. The rest stood in silent protest, watching as three or four of the chariots cartwheeled over the backs of the horses that were pulling them, miraculously avoiding injury. Their refusal to take part in the treacherous plunge ruined the sequence and infuriated

DeMille. He screamed at them through his megaphone, but the cowboys had won the day.

Stunt performers continued to report to DeMille's movie sets because they needed the work. But tensions simmered again during the making of DeMille's 1935 movie *The Crusades*, the story of King Richard the Lionheart's campaign to continue the practice of Christianity in Jerusalem. In one climactic scene, forty stuntmen decked out in helmets and armor were ordered to ride their horses four abreast across a crowded drawbridge in the path of an equal number of stuntmen portraying Saracen zealots. Under the sweltering lights of the studio, the nervous horses pranced forward apprehensively onto the ramp. There wasn't enough room to accommodate all four of them. One horse slipped and pitched over the side into a thirty-foot-deep moat, carrying his rider with him. Within minutes, three more horses and riders plummeted overboard. Two of the stuntmen, Jack Montgomery and Neal Hart, hastened their horses off the drawbridge, threw off their weapons and armor, and jumped into the moat to try to grab hold of the fallen horses. Their efforts were in vain. The steep drop had crippled every one of the animals. In their panic the horses thrashed about, injuring the men who lay in the moat beside them. A crew member handed pistols to Hart and Montgomery, who, revolted by the sickening scene in front of them, quickly put all of the horses down.

To the cowboy's way of thinking, there was nothing accidental about the accident—DeMille had deliberately jeopardized the situation to invoke the sense of urgency he desired. The director worsened matters by refusing to pay the injured stuntmen a measly $50 each in compensation. The cowboys had had enough. According to Cary, her father and several other stuntmen plotted to murder DeMille by running their horses over him before he could drop down into the camera pit at the edge of the set. When it came time to film the next sequence, seven of the riders, outfitted as knights, lowered their visors and burst out of the front lines, charging their horses as fast as they could toward DeMille. Clad in his trademark open-necked shirt, jodhpurs, and lace-up boots, the director was easy to spot. He was looking elsewhere and didn't see the riders gaining on him. Even after a member of his crew yelled at him to duck down into the pit, he might not have done so in time to escape injury.

But to the stuntmen's dismay, their plot failed. The clamor caused by their armor terrified the horses. Determined to stop the racket, the horses in the front line began bucking violently. The horses behind them, nearly seven hundred strong, also panicked and charged in the direction of the runaways, stopping only to whip around in circles trying to fling the armored riders off their backs. What was intended to be a grand assassination in the desert turned into a wild debacle, and DeMille was spared.

DeMille often turned to second unit director Arthur Rosson to orchestrate his over-the-top stunts. Another, more notorious stunt coordinator of that era was B. Reeves Eason, a robust, red-headed man with a craggy face and a reputation for recklessness. Even the risk-taker Yakima Canutt admitted that Eason had issues. "Breezy was one of the best," Canutt said, "but he had days when he drank more than he should." Despite that, directors liked Eason because he understood how to make astonishing scenes unfold, and he wasted no time on the set. For one movie, Eason shot 104 scenes in a single day, including a fight between two wild stallions.

Eason coordinated the stunt work on the 1925 silent epic *Ben-Hur*, which chronicled a Jewish man's torment by the Romans during Christ's day. The film's climax was a hair-raising chariot race. To entice stunt performers to push the envelope, Eason promised the first driver who crossed the finish line a $5,000 bonus (more than $86,000 in today's dollars). That lucrative carrot only encouraged their heedlessness.

Director Fred Niblo had forty-two cameras ready to capture the carnage, and he wasn't disappointed. The chariot drivers rounded corners at breakneck speeds, creating deadly pileups. In one particularly gruesome instance, a chariot crash left four horses fatally shattered. More stuntmen and horses suffered injuries when their chariots smashed into the rubble. By one estimate, nearly 150 horses were wounded and a half dozen were killed. "There were wrecks every day in the chariot races," Francis X. Bushman, who played the part of Messala, later recalled. "When the horses were hurt, they were not treated by a veterinarian but simply shot." Determined to make the most of the butchery, Eason positioned actors among the demolished chariots and dead horses and had them pose for publicity stills.

Years later, Eason choreographed the memorable stunt work in the 1939 Civil War masterpiece *Gone with the Wind*. Director George Cukor insisted that the scenes depicting Sherman's burning of Atlanta look as realistic as possible, and Eason was more than willing to deliver. In one sequence he had a one-horse hack driven by Yakima Canutt (doubling for Clark Gable) turn into a narrow alley where hoodlums lay in wait. Eason wanted the horse pulling the buggy to rear up and paw at the ruffians when they harassed Gable's character, Rhett Butler. The horse's owner had taught the horse to rear up on cue, but to make sure he did so at the right moment, the owner, a cowboy named Tracy Lane, placed a small hot shot under the horse's breast collar. The hot shot was comparable to the battery-powered electric prods used to herd cattle; the current was diluted because it didn't take much electricity to spur a horse.

Lane ran a wire from the hot shot to a switch under the hack seat. He lay in the bed of the hack, under a trap, waiting for Canutt to give him his cue. When Canutt turned the hack into an alley surrounded by fire, he tapped the horse with a whip, Tracy set off the hot shot, and the horse flared up just the way Eason wanted. Tracy triggered the hot shot a second time, and the horse reared again—only this time he slipped, sat down, rolled over onto his back, and thrust all four of his legs upward. The combination of the soaring flames and the sensation of the hot shot must have petrified the horse, but the stuntmen laughed it off.

Stunt performers working with horses needed to approach their work without a trace of cowardice and with enough audacity to pull off the death-defying feats a director might demand. In a day's work, a stuntman might have to fall off a racing horse, vault across a steep cliff, or let himself be dragged by a horse along the ground. The risks involved were frighteningly steep: the number of stuntmen who suffered life-changing injuries or were killed outright executing some hazardous feat was one of Hollywood's best-kept secrets. By one estimate, the career of an average stunt performer lasted just five years before he was either killed, crippled, or too worn out to continue. Studios didn't cover hospital or funeral expenses either. A victim's colleagues would pass the hat to help cover those costs.

The first stuntmen derived much of their "90-proof courage" from alcohol. Inexperienced wranglers signed on for lesser rates, hoping to break into the business. The story goes that Hoot Gibson, a former world champion cowboy, was so eager to appear in the movies that when a Universal director offered him an extra five dollars to be dragged behind a horse, he said, "Make it ten dollars and I'll let him kick me to death!"

Their joking aside, these men, along with a few women, understood the value of a good horse. Their lives, not to mention their livelihoods, depended on well-trained horses, and they were disgusted at the thought of exploiting innocent animals for the sake of ratcheting up the action on the big screen. But directors and their second unit sidekicks were less concerned about the horses' welfare than in delivering high-stakes drama. And too many cowboys were willing to crack their skulls for the princely sum of $3.00 to $7.50 a day and a bag lunch.

At least the cowboys didn't have to supply their own horses. In the early days, Universal kept dozens of horses on its back lot. Stables in and around Hollywood also delivered reliable mounts. Fat Jones's operation was the best known. Clarence Y. "Fat" Jones was still a teenager when he operated a grocery cart driven by a pair of burros. Eventually he traded the burros for a gelding named Chick, followed by another horse he named Buck. When the Pathé production company came looking for two horses for a two-reeler movie in 1912, Jones leased Chick and Buck out to them. From there, his business took off. He opened a stable near the Tom Mix studio in Edendale and later relocated his operation to what is now Griffith Park. In 1928 Jones and a partner, Leandro "Andy" Jauregui, moved again to several thousand acres they leased from Standard Oil (now Chevron) in Placerita Canyon, in the northeast corner of the San Fernando Valley. Jones built a Western set on the property and devoted much of the rest of the land to raising horses and cattle.

Jones supplied horses for many of the Western stars of the day, including William S. Hart and Tom Mix. His biggest moment came in 1930, when RKO pictures looked to him to furnish 1,100 horses and four hundred wagons for the Western *Cimarron*, which chronicled the Oklahoma Land Rush. Jauregui bought out Jones's share of the property in 1933, and Jones moved his stable closer in, to Sherman Way in North Hollywood, later relocating it again outside the adjacent town of Sun Valley, twelve miles north. He operated eleven acres of corrals and barns along with a blacksmith shop and a saddlery. Horses weren't hard to find, as ranches struggling to survive were eager to reduce their herds. The challenge was making sure the horses were skilled enough to draw wagons and carry inexperienced riders. To help with this, Jones hired a number of first-rate trainers, the best-known of whom was Swede Lindell.

Jones once said, "You can't help but like a horse that goes out and does anything you ask of him, but you don't dare get fond of them. This is strictly a business." He was known for his honesty and dependability. His stable was a de facto clearinghouse for cowboys looking for work, and some of the most famous horses of the day, including Flicka, Rex, Misty, Black Diamond, and Thunderhead, came out of his stable. Jones died in 1963 at the age of seventy, but his stable remained in operation until the mid-1970s.

Second only to Fat's stable was the Hudkins stable, originally located at the Providencia Ranch in the Hollywood Hills and later moved near the Warner Bros. studio in Burbank, on land now occupied by Forest Lawn cemetery. Brothers Ace and Art Hudkins owned the stable. Ace, Ode, and Clyde Hudkins also operated a riding academy on the property. Seeing a burgeoning market for horses in movies, the Hudkinses expanded their operation to meet the demand. They were well-regarded for their ability to supply studios with horses, horse-drawn wagons, chariots, cattle, and Western equipment.

In Hollywood's early days, the need for horses was so great that several smaller supply stables cropped up as well. George Myers and Henry Wills rented out stunt horses. Charlie Flores furnished horses to MGM studios from his stable in Culver City. His brother Joe had his own supply stable. Stable operators started their day early, before sunup. Based on the types of horses requested—a studio might call for "star" horses, "featured" horses, or extras categorized as "bit" or "mob"—wranglers would round up the horses, groom them, shoe them if necessary, clean their saddles and other necessary equipment, and transport them. In the early days when studios were makeshift operations housed in barns and other rudimentary structures, the horses would be herded down city streets to the sets. In later years, they would be loaded onto trucks and hauled to movie ranches or studios for interior shots.

Stables were expected to have on hand veteran horses experienced in movie work and younger steeds strong enough to handle arduous assignments. Chase horses, as they were called, earned the stables roughly $10 a day, a fraction of the $50 to $100 a day that a "name" horse could command. Stable operators were to keep the horses fed and in good condition. In addition to the livestock, they supplied workers experienced in maintaining the equipment and controlling the, at times, rambunctious animals.

Cowboys who arrived early to a set got to choose their horse, often an animal they had ridden before. Latecomers ran the risk of getting stuck with a lizard, stuntmen's name for an untamed horse. A lizard could cause unmitigated disaster on location. On the set of one movie, the minute the director called, "Action," an inexperienced horse stormed the cameras and lights. In a matter of seconds, he destroyed $5,000 worth of equipment and all of that day's footage.

Like many of his colleagues, Jack Montgomery, the stuntman who so despised Cecil B. DeMille, had firsthand experience in roping and riding. He'd been around horses all his life. Born in Nebraska, he was raised in Montana, where he operated a small ranch until it went under. Hungry for work, he followed several of his ranch hands to California to pursue a career in the seemingly glamorous world of stunt performing. Pretending to be a cowboy on-screen paid better than being one in real life, but Montgomery was appalled by the recklessness shown not just toward stuntmen like himself but to the animals. Especially the horses.

For his part in the 1937 Western musical *High, Wide and Handsome*, Montgomery found himself stuck with a roan-colored horse named Blue whose hooves were hideously overgrown: they extended two inches past his shoes and were so misshapen they were almost pointed. Cowboys called that condition "rocker-footed," and Montgomery was right to be alarmed. For a chase scene in which his character was part of a posse, he was told to gallop the horse full-out down a rocky canyon littered with loose shale rock. Montgomery thought about refusing the assignment, but he worried that doing so might jeopardize his chances for future work. He decided to risk it. He mounted the horse and murmured to him, "Okay, Blue, you keep your feet under you, do you hear?" He was able to keep the horse from stumbling on the shale by jerking up on his bit, which pulled the horse upward and cleared his legs from the debris. But the director, Rouben Mamoulian, chose to film the sequence again, and this time he wanted the posse to ride faster and in a tight cluster.

The men headed farther back up the canyon and began the chase a second time, fifteen horses in a single, fast-moving clump. Blue couldn't keep up. His feet were so compromised that the second he struck the rock, he tripped over his overgrown hooves, throwing Montgomery into the rocks and directly in the path of the other riders. Blue landed on top of Montgomery and rolled over him twice before he managed to get to his feet. Before anyone could stop them, three other horses ran over the stuntman. Montgomery was injured so badly that he was laid up for two months.

Stunt performers were convinced that irresponsible directors deliberately orchestrated reckless scenes so they could happily record any sensational accidents that resulted. Moreover, by treating the results as unexpected mishaps, they could avoid paying the performers adjustment checks to cover the added risks. At other times the culprit was a nearby rancher who, hoping to make a little money, would lease the studio an inexperienced horse, one that would resort to all kinds of shenanigans when anyone tried to climb in the saddle.

Trip wires weren't a secret. In his syndicated "Looking at Hollywood" column, Ed Sullivan wrote that "quite a lot of cruelty is practiced on horses. . . . It always makes me sick at my stomach to see . . . a horse flying along at full speed and suddenly catapulted to the ground by a concealed wire." But for industry workers to blow the whistle on the abuse was next to impossible. As far as Los Angeles's newspapers were concerned, movie studios were sacred cows. And no one dared risk incurring the fury of a studio head by exposing the degree of mistreatment that occurred onset. If a cowboy stuntman had succeeded in getting the word out, his career would have been over instantly.

7

Making Headway against Abuse

Two movies spurred big improvements for Hollywood horses.

The first was *The Charge of the Light Brigade*, a 1936 blockbuster starring heartthrob Australian actor Errol Flynn. Set during the Crimean War of 1853–56 and loosely based on the famous poem of the same name by Alfred, Lord Tennyson, the movie cast Flynn as a British major whose Indian ally—a potentate whose life Flynn's character had saved on a hunting trip—betrays him by siding with the enemy, Imperial Russia, and helping massacre the British stronghold at Chukoti. The film's climax involves a battle to the death by the British Twenty-Seventh Lancers Cavalry against the Russians.

Director Michael Curtiz hired second unit director Breezy Eason to coordinate the dangerous charge. Eason chose Lasky Mesa near Sonora, California, a broad valley surrounded by mountains on three sides, as the setting for the combat; the landscape there was the closest thing to India he could find. The ground was solid rock, covered with just a thin layer of dirt, but Eason didn't see that as a problem. He had his crew dig a six-hundred-foot-long furrow along one side where a car equipped with several cameras could film the riders from a low angle. To excavate the ditch, they had to blast numerous holes in the unyielding rock; the dynamite left a series of craggy edges that would prove treacherous for the stuntmen and horses assigned to replicate the charge.

From the beginning, the atmosphere was tense. The stuntmen, already unnerved by the hazardous terrain they were expected to traverse, grew even more upset when one of them, doubling Flynn, was asked to jump from a thirty-foot-high rock and land on another man who was astride a horse. The stunt might have succeeded if the sight of the leaping man's shadow hadn't frightened the horse, prompting him to step out of place. As a result, the stuntman landed directly on the horse, causing the animal to buckle under the brunt of the man's weight. The horse somehow managed to stay on his feet, but the stuntman broke his neck and died.

Although Flynn had nothing to do with the accident, some of the victim's cohorts regarded him as arrogant and decided to take their anger out on him. They got their chance right before shooting a subsequent scene when Flynn, sitting on his horse, let go of his reins to check his appearance with a mirror and a comb. The stuntmen seized the opportunity. One of them jiggled the rubber tip of his spear under the tail of Flynn's horse. Startled, the horse reared up and bucked Flynn off. The actor landed smack on his back, to the onlookers' guffaws. Flynn got to his feet, brushed off his clothes, and asked, "Which of you sons of bitches did that?" The guilty party shot back: "Want to make something of it?" A fistfight ensued, and Flynn won. The extra was carted off to the infirmary, and no one bothered Flynn after that.

Estimates vary, but by one account Eason hired 280 extras and 340 horses to carry out the charge in *Light Brigade*. Performing the dramatic falls were 38 expert stuntmen. To amplify the drama, Eason rigged as many as 125 of the horses with Running W's, guaranteeing that they would trip and fall as explosives detonated around them in the open valley. Other horses toppled into one of a half dozen eight-foot-deep concealed pits.

The stuntmen's assignments were beyond dangerous. Harrowing footage shot at ground level shows one wrangler rolling out of the way just as his horse pitches forward. The charge sequence claimed the life of a stuntman who fell off his horse and was impaled on a broken sword. One technician collapsed from sunstroke, and several riders were injured when they were thrown from their horses or fell onto the rocky ground. Nearly a dozen cowboys wound up hospitalized in critical condition.

For the horses, the sequence was even more tragic. Just as Eason had hoped, multiple scenes capture horses falling, a handful at a time. To Max Steiner's brassy, crescendoing soundtrack, one horse after another somersaults head over heels, their hind legs thrusting helplessly in the air. The charge lasts a good fifteen minutes on film and seems never-ending. Trip wires clamped around the ankles of some of the horses are visible as they lift their front legs to steady themselves after hitting the ground. Some of the horses were able to rise immediately after falling, but one ghastly scene shows riders charging down a hill past two horses who are left lying motionless on the ground. Another scene shows one horse barely able to raise his head.

Warner Bros. claimed that only two horses had to be euthanized because of stunts gone wrong, that a third horse later died of heart failure, and that a fourth horse was killed when he fell onto a sharp rock. The studio's attending veterinarian and other personnel signed affidavits to that effect. But stuntman Jack Montgomery estimated that nearly twenty-five horses broke their backs or legs and died instantly or had to be put down. He went home one night "white with dust and hollow-eyed from fatigue, pent-up anger and grief," his daughter, Diana Serra Cary, recalled. "Father knew every man," Cary said. "He also knew by sight, or had ridden himself, every chase horse that was a casualty that day." Montgomery exploded over dinner, she said. "Damned savages is what they are," he told his family. "I never saw so many good men and horses smashed up in one day in all my years in the picture business—or anywhere else for that matter."

The carnage was taking place despite the studios' pledge to abide by the Hollywood Production Code (also referred to as the Hays Code after Will Hays, the former postmaster general first hired to enforce it). Adopted in 1934 to fend off laws censoring movie content, the code mainly targeted social mores; almost as an afterthought, a single line in the code forbade cruelty to animals. The ban was widely ignored, and Flynn, for one, was incensed that performers and horses were being treated so carelessly on the set of *Light Brigade*. He confronted Curtiz about the abuse and at one point became so enraged that he physically assaulted the director. Personnel were able to pull the two men apart before either was injured, but their relationship never recovered, and in subsequent films Flynn and Curtiz only spoke to one another when absolutely necessary.

Eventually word spilled about the number of horses that were losing their lives during filming. Someone tipped off the nearby Glendale Society for the Prevention of Cruelty to Animals (SPCA), which dispatched a group of representatives to the *Light Brigade* set. One horrified SPCA witness described seeing a horse whose trip wire had run out of slack too soon swaying defenselessly, his back broken, over the edge of a pit. That same witness also described seeing the bodies of slain horses, so many of them that crews had dumped them in a specially prepared trench.

The SPCAs of Los Angeles and San Francisco joined the protests and filed charges against Warner Bros. Without running his plan by the studio's lawyers, Warner's production manager, Frank Mattison, arranged for three employees to plead guilty to animal cruelty for causing the death of three horses by way of trip wires. The legal outcome was negligible: the employees were fined just $15 apiece in court and given ten-day suspended jail sentences. But the public relations damage to the studio was significant. The Associated Press picked up the initial coverage in San Francisco's newspapers, and the story appeared in newspapers across the country. Animal lovers were appalled to learn of the senseless damage Running W's could cause. They mailed more than a thousand letters to Warner Bros. protesting the studio's callous treatment of horses.

Warner Bros. fought back. The studio's lawyer, Roy Obringer, rebutted the cruelty charges, claiming the SPCA investigator had embellished the facts. Obringer argued that in fact no horse had been injured as a result of trip wires. He met with the SPCA's local director in San Francisco to show him photos of the dead horses. They showed no evidence of trip wires, Obringer claimed, but the SPCA wasn't buying it.

Was there more to the story? Warner Bros. archives revealed that the SPCA investigator who first appeared on the scene in Sonora tried to borrow $100 from one movie official and later attempted to extort Warner Bros. employees. He wasn't successful, according to the archives, and studio personnel speculated that, in retaliation, the investigator, identified only as "Girolo," tipped off San Francisco papers about the animal cruelty allegations.

Nevertheless, the guilty pleas were on the books, so Warner Bros. turned its guns overseas to the Women's Guild of Empire in Great Britain, which had recommended boycotting *Light Brigade*. The studio sued the guild, alleging the organization had made libelous statements about animal mistreatment in the film. Warner Bros. won the lawsuit. Even so, the studio agreed to pay cowboy wranglers more money to take part in future stunts. "Straight riding" would now earn them $7.50 and the studio would pay

$3.00 to $5.00 more for every horse fall carried out. Riding a horse attached to trip wires would net a cowboy as much as $25. The wranglers detested the use of trip wires, but for many, the money was too good to turn down.

In existence since 1877, the American Humane Association (AHA) had spent decades working to improve the lives not just of children but of animals as well, chiefly horses. Early efforts concentrated on ways to humanely shoe horses and provide "homes of rest" for worn-out police- and workhorses, providing them with food, stalls, and pasture. As early as 1925 the organization established a committee to investigate the alleged cruelty in the training of animals used in films. Bolstered by public outcry, the AHA began working with the Motion Picture Producers Association to fashion guidelines for handling animals on film sets. The understanding they reached called for the Production Code Administration to review movie scripts for any scenes involving animals; if the called-for action sounded cruel in any way, a script would be referred to a small advisory group appointed by the AHA. That group, together with production code staff, would decide how to proceed. Even after a movie was produced, the advisory committee could recommend that production code administrators censor offensive scenes or delete them entirely.

Warner Bros. also adopted its own rule mandating the presence of a Humane Society representative on the set of any movie involving horse stunts. In a letter to the San Francisco SPCA, studio president Jack Warner assured the organization that Warner Bros. would never use Running W's again. He also promised that scenes involving the use of trip wires would be edited out of *Light Brigade* before the movie was released.

Animal advocates were ecstatic over the headway they'd made, but the celebration was short-lived. A month later *Light Brigade* arrived in theaters, and despite Warner's promise, none of the abusive scenes had been removed. By 1938 the American Humane Association had to admit the agreement with Hollywood had never actually been enforced. Studios were continuing to crank out movies that treated animals, mostly horses, with heedless disregard.

Animal groups revived their call for government intervention. The United Kingdom had already gone that route, implementing the Cinematograph Films (Animals) Act in 1937, which outlawed any scene that caused harm to an animal or portrayed animal suffering. The AHA was willing to propose legislation on a statewide basis if the U.S. Congress wasn't willing to ban animal mistreatment on film.

Then, in 1939, came Twentieth Century Fox's box-office bonanza *Jesse James*, which did more to bring about change. Shot in cutting-edge Technicolor—the first Western to merit that treatment—the movie starred Tyrone Power, Hollywood's most popular male actor, as the real-life James, a violent robber infamous for holding up banks, trains, and stagecoaches across the Midwest. On September 7, 1876, Jesse and his brother Frank robbed a bank in Northfield, Minnesota, during which several members of their gang were apprehended and killed. Fleeing the town, the pair found themselves two hundred miles west in Garretson, South Dakota, at the edge of a craggy, twenty-foot-wide, sixty-foot-deep canyon called Devil's Gulch, lawmen hot on their heels. Legend has it that rather than face capture, the James brothers galloped their horses toward the mouth of the canyon, stood in their saddles, spurred their horses upward, and leapt to the other side. The posse chasing them watched, dumbfounded, as they dashed away.

Whether James really did make the jump is still debated by Wild West aficionados. Regardless, Twentieth Century Fox chief Darryl Zanuck decided to intensify the drama. For the movie version, Zanuck spent a lavish $2 million to film on location in the southwestern Missouri town of Pineville. He had false fronts installed over the town's businesses and concealed its paved streets with dirt to replicate an Old West village. Now he needed a memorable climax to justify all that detail.

The script called for the detective on the hunt for James to ride into town and offer total amnesty and a $25,000 reward to whoever could capture and kill James. A member of the gang informs the detective that Jesse and Frank are planning to rob another bank. Law enforcers ambush the Jameses and shoot Jesse, but the brothers manage to escape. They hole up nearby to plot their next move.

For the movie's climax, Jesse and Frank were to jump over a cliff on horseback into the Elk River. The river offered dramatic optics, especially when the two men, chased by a posse, splatted into the water at full force. But the river was too shallow to accommodate a leap from a towering bluff, so Zanuck instructed his crew to find a more suitable jumping-off spot. They settled on Lake of the Ozarks, a deep reservoir nearly two hundred miles north that featured a seventy-foot-high cliff on one side. The right camera angle could capture the bluff and the water below and give the impression that the horses were jumping into a river.

The stunt was unbelievably dangerous. Cliff Lyons, a former rodeo cowboy who performed the jump, would be riding a horse off the equivalent of a six-and-a-half-story building. No horse would willingly acquiesce to such a hazardous feat. But the filmmakers weren't concerned about the fate of the horse, only about capturing vivid footage. The one concession second unit director Otto Brower made was to film a single horse jumping. By showing first a distance shot of the jump followed by a close-up of the same jump, the cameraman was able to make it appear as though two different horses had plunged into the water.

All that is known about the horse that was ridden off the cliff is that he was a dark bay with a wide white blaze on his face and white socks on his legs. Lyons later told Yak Canutt's son Tap that the horse was "blinkered" to prevent him from seeing anything other than what was directly in front of him. The footage doesn't show any blinkers, however. Witnesses said the film crew used a greased tilt chute to send horse and rider sliding off the cliff.

The footage of the bay's fall lasts only a few seconds, and it's sickening to watch. The instant the horse is ridden off the bluff he turns onto his back, his hind legs extended outward in a vain attempt to right himself. His bridle hovers loosely in the air and his head twists backward. For the duration of the fall, he fixes his gaze on Lyons, who is plummeting directly above him. The horse lands in the water with an enormous crash. In the movie, the camera then cuts back to the cliff where, moments later, in close-up shots, the horse's fall is shown again as though Jesse's brother Frank is making the same leap.

The next sequence shows two horses swimming leisurely toward shore on the other side of the lake. In reality the horse who'd made the jump was in trouble. While rescuers hoisted Lyons out of the water and into a boat, the horse, frantic from the trauma of his fall, began to flail about. He drowned before members of the crew could lasso him and pull him to shore.

Lyons earned $2,350 for completing the jump, a record amount for a stunt performer. But word leaked about the horse's demise, and to animal advocates—who had spent years negotiating a clampdown on animal cruelty only to see their agreements ignored—*Jesse James* was the final straw.

"We can be patient no longer," the American Humane Association wrote to the Production Code's Will Hays.

At the same time critics were praising the movie for its "consummate showmanship" and "pictorial magnificence," more than six hundred humane organizations were orchestrating a boycott. Stories describing the cruel stunt began appearing in newspapers across the United States, and fifty thousand moviegoers wrote letters of protest to Twentieth Century Fox.

Advocates encountered an even more disturbing scene in a third movie, Cecil B. DeMille's *North West Mounted Police*, about a Texas Ranger's search for a trapper wanted for murder while the trapper agitates Indians into an uprising against the Canadian government. At the instruction of second unit director Arthur Rosson, an unidentified stuntman doubling for lead actor Gary Cooper lassoed a rotary cannon called a Gatling gun while on horseback and yanked it behind him as he galloped his horse down a steep cliff toward a river. The horse's forelegs were attached to trip wires, and when the wires ran out, the horse and his rider cartwheeled nose-first down the rocky ledge, the Gatling gun hurtling behind them. Footage shows the stuntman able to stop rolling just before the ledge gives way to a precipitous drop, but the horse appears to keep tumbling. Two horses were sacrificed to capture that scene, but protestors were too focused on *Jesse James* to target DeMille's latest transgression.

Jesse James gave advocates the ammunition they were looking for. As it happened, the state of Missouri had reasonably strong animal cruelty laws, and the Missouri Humane Association was able to use them to file charges against Twentieth Century Fox. One of the advocates pushing for justice was Mel Morse, an officer of the Los Angeles SPCA who was determined to see justice served. A jowly man with combed-back hair and sympathetic eyes, Morse borrowed a car and drove across the country to that year's American Humane Association convention in Albany, New York. There he helped an officer of the organization, Richard C. Craven, craft a policy aimed at guaranteeing the safety of animals in movies. Soon afterward, the AHA created its Hollywood-based position of western regional director and named Craven to the post. A British-born former journalist, Craven had changed careers after witnessing animal cruelty in Toronto. During World

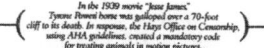

4. The outcry following the death of a horse forced to hurtle off a cliff in the 1939 movie *Jesse James* brought about a ban on cruel devices used to fall horses. Courtesy of the American Humane Association.

War I he'd helped care for horses and mules. Now with the help of three assistant inspectors, Craven began monitoring all movies involving animals.

Crusaders for humane treatment were determined to show they meant business, and finally the film industry, eager to avoid government interference, agreed to a new understanding. On December 27, 1940, the Motion Picture Producers and Distributors of America amended the Production Code to include several provisions, including an agreement that no film involving the use of Running W's would be approved for distribution.

The timing of the clampdown was fortuitous. Westerns had lost their cachet in the 1930s but were starting to make a comeback, and horses still needed to tumble to make shoot-'em-ups seem real. The art of falling horses was about to be born.

8

Learning the Ropes

If anyone had told Chuck Roberson as a boy that he would one day ride horses up on the big screen—that, what is more, he would one day be signaling those horses to purposely hit the dirt—he would have laughed at them in disbelief.

Born in 1919 to Ollie and Janniece Roberson, Chuck grew up in Joy, Texas, a wisp of a town just south of the Oklahoma border and a galaxy away from Hollywood. Northeastern Texas was wide open country in those days, an isolated stretch more populated by cows than by people. Few buildings and even fewer roads speckled the landscape. Schools were rare, and school buses were nonexistent. The easiest way for a boy to get around in those parts was on a horse.

Chuck and his younger brother, Lou, rode two to three miles back and forth to school on Rusty, the family's elderly, dependable steed. Chuck was two years older than Lou and the more experienced rider; it made sense that he held the reins. Each morning Lou would lead Rusty out of the barn and help Chuck climb onto his back. Then Lou would clamber to the top rail of the fence and wait for Chuck to ride by and pull him behind him onto the horse. The horse was outfitted with a halter and a set of reins, but no saddle. Lou would drape his arms around Chuck's waist and grab hold of Chuck's belt loops for the long bareback ride to school.

One blistering hot afternoon when school let out, the boys walked over to the hitching post where Rusty stood tethered, and Lou announced he wasn't going to ride behind Chuck anymore.

"Then you can walk home," Chuck told him.

Lou persisted, and Chuck relented. He climbed onto Rusty behind his

5. Stuntman Chuck Roberson, a master horseman considered one of the finest stunt performers Hollywood has produced. Photofest.

younger brother and held onto Lou's waist. The horse trotted slowly at first, but halfway into their ride he picked up the scent of home. Suddenly he sped off across the fields in the direction of a small opening in the fence that led to the Robersons' land.

"Whoa him up, Lou," Chuck hollered. Bending forward, he tried to grab the reins from his brother's hand, but Lou, frantic, had dropped them. Without the reins there was no way to stop the horse. When he got to the gate Rusty kicked his hind legs out, flinging both boys into a patch of bull thorns, chigger-like burrs that would be the devil to pull off of their clothes. Roberson never forgot that day; it marked the first time he had ever lost control of a horse. And even though no one but his kid brother was on hand to witness it, Chuck was humiliated beyond belief. He vowed never to fall off a horse again.

Chuck was thirteen when, in the throes of the Great Depression, his family moved to New Mexico, to a ranch sixty-six miles outside the town of Roswell. The economy was slightly better in New Mexico, and the owner of the ranch, H. L. Price, was well-known in those parts. Roberson would later describe him as "sort of a Rooster Cogburn without an eye patch." Something about young Chuck appealed to the old codger, and Price went out of his way to turn the gangly teen into an expert cowpoke. One afternoon Price decided to put Chuck to a new test. He instructed Chuck's dad, Ollie, to bring a disheveled-looking mustang out of the barn and told the teenager, "Get up on there and ride him."

Chuck stared at his dad, silently pleading for mercy. Not *this* horse, surely. The ill-tempered beast was stamping his hooves and puffing loudly. No one had ever been able to ride him for more than a few seconds, and Chuck had no reason to believe he would have any better luck reining him in.

"You ride this animal, Mutt, you'll be a full hand," Price promised, referring to Chuck by the nickname he'd given him.

Times were too lean to turn down a paying job. Ollie Roberson cautiously saddled up the horse. When he was done, he reached up and took hold of the mustang's ears to try to calm him. Chuck mounted him warily.

"You ready, son?" Ollie asked.

Chuck didn't see that he had a choice. He took the reins from his father and ground himself into the saddle. The horse stood perfectly still. Chuck prodded him with the heel of his boot. The horse still didn't move. Perplexed, Chuck relaxed his grip, and all of a sudden the horse bolted into the air with all four feet flying. He arched his back and heaved himself at the fence, trying to vault it. In two seconds flat he'd flung Chuck onto the dirt, leaving him short of breath and scrambling to grab his hat.

Get back on him, Price instructed Chuck, so Roberson dutifully climbed back on. When the mustang threw him again, Chuck mounted him a third time and a fourth time after that. Over and over he practiced until by day's end he succeeded in hanging on for six full seconds. To Chuck's immense relief, Price was satisfied with his effort. The cantankerous rancher was hoping to see some mettle in the young boy, and Chuck did not disappoint him.

Chuck never went back to school after that. Instead he stayed at the ranch as a regular hand. In a matter of months he was handling a "four-up," a wagon pulled by a team of four horses. He drove the wagon three days out at a time. At other times he would distribute salt blocks for the cattle scattered out across the range or plow ditches along the fence lines. It was tough, lonely work for a boy barely in his teens. All those hours with just himself and the horses cultivated a kinship and a deep affection for the intuitive animals, and the responsibility placed on him made Chuck grow up fast.

Eventually Chuck, his dad, and his brother left the Price ranch to work for the Flying H Ranch in New Mexico. For a time, Chuck returned to Texas to toil in the oil fields. At the age of eighteen he married and fathered a daughter named after himself, Charlene. He got a job working twelve hours a day stitching sacks for a grapefruit-packing operation. Eventually he moved his family to Culver City, California, where he got a job with the police department. The local police oversaw security at MGM Studios, which was headquartered there. Roberson was assigned to the studios' enormous lot.

His marriage didn't last, and when World War II broke out, Roberson joined the army for three years, working on a transport that carried him into the heart of the battle zones. A kamikaze attack in Okinawa left him injured and out of commission for a time, but by the end of the war Roberson had regained his strength and was back in California, where he returned to his job with the Culver City police. The following year Warner Bros. went on strike, and he was assigned to work security at that studio.

Roberson was easy-going, friendly, and unafraid of hard work. And he just happened to be in the right place at the right time. In the commissary one day he struck up a conversation with a shy horse trainer named Fred Kennedy. Kennedy was a kindred spirit. Before moving to Hollywood, he had ridden bulls and fought professionally in his native Nebraska and around the West. He was five feet nine and stocky, nothing but hard muscle, and happy to talk horses all day long. He and Roberson quickly became friends, and given Roberson's expertise with untrained horses Kennedy suggested he pursue stunt work. Republic Studios was churning out lots of cheap Westerns, Kennedy said, and could probably use someone with Roberson's ability.

It was the late 1940s, and Westerns had once again become the most popular movie genre in America. Not the most respected, perhaps—much of the movie industry turned up its collective nose at run-of-the-mill

6. Expert stuntman Fred Kennedy, a pioneer in teaching horses to fall on cue, delivers a knockout blow in the 1950 movie *Rio Grande*. Photofest.

"oaters"—but the kind most likely to draw in audiences. As a result, studios were on the lookout for wranglers who could handle a horse and weren't afraid to execute raucous action scenes.

Roberson took Kennedy's advice. He met with the studio's founder, Herbert Yates, and head wrangler Bill Jones. Plenty of would-be stunt performers claimed to have experience around horses, and Jones had devised a simple test to determine which of them were telling the truth. He walked out a large gelding paint, handed the reins to Roberson, and told him to ride the horse to the end of the movie-set street, turn around, and ride back. Roberson mounted the horse, drove him at a fast gallop to where the false storefronts ended, swung him around, and raced back. He was out of the saddle with both feet on the ground before the horse had come to a full stop, and that was all Jones needed to see.

"Report to work tomorrow morning," he said.

Roberson's first assignment was on the set of *Wyoming*, a Western starring Bill Elliott and John Carroll, about a cattle rancher forced to fend off homesteaders who'd been conned by a rustler into thinking the rancher's land was theirs to claim. Actor and fellow stuntman Ben Johnson was doubling Elliott, and Roberson watched Johnson closely in case he might be expected to carry out similar action. His chance came a couple of weeks later when filming moved four hours north to Old Kernville, a town nestled in the Sequoia National Forest. The chase sequences there involved racing horses down hillsides, tearing around thick scrub oaks, and thundering between large boulders. It was the most action Roberson had taken part in, and he was astonished at the size of his paycheck: $75 for a single day's work, more money than he'd ever seen at one time.

There's a Mexican proverb: *It is not enough for a man to know how to ride; he must also know how to fall.* Roberson had never heard this bit of wisdom, and he certainly didn't subscribe to it. He was more than a little surprised when, the next day, director Joseph Kane upped the challenge. Roberson, Kane said, I need you to ride over to that nearby ridge. When you reach the oak tree, I'm going to fire a gun, and you do a saddle fall.

Roberson was certain he had misheard his instructions. "You mean you want me to fall *off*?" he asked. He couldn't even begin to know how to deliberately topple off a horse. He'd spent years excelling at just the opposite—hanging on no matter the circumstance. But for $75 he was willing to attempt anything. When the director hollered, "Action," Roberson sent his horse galloping. At the sound of gunshot, he threw himself out of the saddle, flailing his arms and legs to add some drama to his fall. He landed with a solid thump on hard soil.

The minute Roberson staggered to his feet, Ben Johnson pulled him aside. There were gentler ways to fall off a horse, Johnson said, and Roberson's friend Fred Kennedy could show him how. The following weekend Kennedy took his new protégé to the Hudkins Brothers Movie Ranch in Burbank, where Kennedy stabled his horses. The two men saddled up a couple of mounts and headed out to a river bottom, a sandy spot where they could land softly.

Kennedy knew Roberson could ride. Now try to fall from the saddle, he said.

They started with a pliable gelding who stood patiently while Roberson practiced ejecting himself from the saddle. The trick didn't seem all that difficult, but Kennedy cautioned him. "There's a right way and a wrong way to go about this," he said. "It ain't just like a big old bullfrog jumping onto a lily pad. It's the things a fellow thinks are the most simple that'll get him killed."

For the remainder of the day Kennedy tutored Roberson in falling while his horse was trotting. Eventually he had Roberson try the same stunt while his horse cantered slowly. "Tuck your head in," Kennedy said, "and ride the stirrup right down to the ground."

Roberson practiced close to fifty falls that day. By afternoon's end he had sand in every orifice, even in his teeth, but he felt reasonably schooled in the fundamentals of his new skill. He spent the next several weekends putting himself through the drills. Before long he could fall off a horse gracefully enough that he hardly felt the wallop from landing on firm ground.

Word filtered around Hollywood that the new stuntman in town could dependably fall off a horse, and work began to flow in. Roberson purchased insurance and quickly lined up more casting calls for Indians than he could keep track of. Some mornings he would start the day at Republic's ranch in Encino, where the studio's Westerns were filmed. In the afternoons he would dash over to Paramount's ranch on Cornell Road in Agoura Hills, thirty miles west of Hollywood, to perform more saddle falls. It wasn't unusual, by the time some of the movies appeared on the big screen, for Roberson to spot himself in opposing roles in the same film: as the soldier aiming a rifle at an Indian and also as the Indian getting shot.

Before long he was assigned to a John Wayne picture, *Wake of the Red Witch*, a seafaring adventure about a long-standing hostility between the owner of a shipping company and the captain of his biggest ship. The movie didn't involve horse action of any sort. But not long after, Roberson was on the set of another Wayne picture, *The Fighting Kentuckian*, starring Wayne as a militiaman who helps French settlers in Alabama fend off a greedy land-grabber. Roberson was between scenes when he overheard director George Waggner instructing Wayne to jump from a standing position onto a tall horse tied to a hitching post.

Wayne balked at the assignment. "I sure as hell can't stand flat-footed next to a bareback horse and just hop up like I was jumping a puddle," he protested.

"Hell, I can do it," Roberson blurted out.

Everyone within earshot turned his way, startled at the temerity of this newcomer, whose second most important job was to make himself obscure on the set. But Roberson couldn't help himself: here was his chance to show his stuff.

"I can do it," he repeated.

"Well then, let's see you do it," Wayne said.

Roberson strode over to the horse and placed one hand on the ridge between the animal's shoulder blades. In a single motion he vaulted onto the horse's back. Waggner responded with the best two words Roberson could have hoped to hear: "You're hired."

Roberson could jump onto a horse, and now he'd nailed the ability to fall off one. All that was missing was a reliable horse that knew how to tumble down with him.

9

In Search of the Right Horse

Roberson rented a small house on the same street as Fred Kennedy, which made it easier to drop by and watch him train. Kennedy was not only an expert at saddle falls; he was one of the first trainers to teach horses to drop to the ground on cue. He was working with a mare in his backyard one afternoon when Roberson let himself in a side gate and climbed on top of a fence post to watch. From his seat in the saddle, Kennedy hollered over to him, "Still trying to steal my technique, Roberson? Watch this, then." He nudged his horse into a leisurely canter for a few dozen feet and then jerked his reins firmly to one side. Instantly the horse buckled and collapsed.

Roberson gave a low whistle and applauded. Kennedy tied the mare to the top rail of the fence. She was a "laying down" horse, he said—not quite ready to fall reliably. "Got to put a lot more hours on her yet."

The veteran trainer had mixed feelings about letting Roberson edge in on his turf. On the one hand Kennedy was happy to school a younger colleague in the hows and wherefores of coaxing a horse to do something as thoroughly unnatural as falling. At the same time he had no intention of revealing all his carefully honed techniques. In Roberson's presence, Kennedy might walk a horse through a few rudimentary tricks, but he'd leave it at that. If Roberson asked why he was working a horse a certain way, Kennedy would turn his back to adjust the horse's saddle and pretend as though he hadn't heard.

Roberson persisted. For the next three weeks he perched on the fence and watched as Kennedy worked his small mare. He began by having the horse lie down at the sound of his command. At first the young horse seemed unable to grasp what Kennedy was trying to show her. The day came, though, when she finally responded to his cues, and after that, Kennedy refused to put her through her paces in Roberson's presence. Despite that, Roberson picked up some vital clues about training horses for movie work. For one thing, he was struck by the gentleness with which Kennedy spoke to the mare. Not once did he lose his patience. And whenever the horse did as Kennedy asked, he thanked her with a reward.

"You can't beat anything into a child, a dog, or a horse," he told Roberson one afternoon. "These animals will do just about anything for you if you treat 'em right." It didn't hurt to have a smart horse to begin with, Kennedy added, "but it don't do no good beating hell out of a dumb one."

Applying the techniques he'd gleaned, Roberson began working with a big, strapping horse he coowned named Hot Rod to fall on command. Hot Rod was talented and learned the skill quickly, and Roberson should have hung on to him. But in a "fit of insanity," he sold his half-interest in the horse and began working instead with a petite sorrel mare he also owned, named Coco. Coco was a quarter horse, fast and smart, but at fourteen and a half hands high—fifty-eight inches, measured from the ground to the highest point between her shoulder blades, her withers—she wasn't nearly tall enough for Roberson. If it wasn't for her diminutive size, she would have made the ideal falling partner. The little mare could fall at a dead run and land precisely where Roberson directed her. Not only was she quick and accurate, but she brought a theatrical flair to her falls: she could propel her body straight up toward the sky before landing.

Stuntman Jack Williams dropped by one day in January to watch Coco carry out her stunts. He was astonished to see how spectacularly she performed. "Chuck, you've done it," he said. "I've never seen a horse fall that fast. And Lord, she didn't lie down; she jumped straight up and fell down. You've got an equine acrobat on your hands."

Williams couldn't wait to try falling Coco himself. He trotted her out a few dozen yards, whipped her around, and bolted toward Roberson. Ten feet from where Roberson stood, Williams pulled Coco's head to the side. The little horse transferred her weight from her front legs onto her left hind leg and soared into the air. She sunfished, arcing her body right and left, then flung her belly upward and fell over backward. Williams went sprawling. He got up, dusted himself off, and said, "Was that as good as I think it was?"

Even better, Roberson told him.

At five feet ten, Williams was five and a half inches shorter than Roberson, just the right height for Coco. And despite the little mare's immense talent, Roberson was ready to let someone else ride her for a change. She'd been his daughter Charlene's horse, ordinarily so gentle that Charlene could ride her bareback. But one afternoon while Charlene was riding her, Coco spied a stud horse nearby. If she hadn't been in heat, that wouldn't have been a problem; she would have ignored the other horse. This time, though, she broke into a gallop. Coco clearly wanted rid of Charlene, and in a matter of seconds she got her wish: the young girl fell and landed on her back on a rail in the wash. The fall broke Charlene's arm and two of her ribs, and that did it as far as Roberson was concerned. He vowed to find Coco a new home.

Williams was delighted with Coco. Now Roberson needed to find the right horse for himself. He'd been hired to perform stunts for *The Last Outpost*, a Western starring Ronald Reagan about a Confederate army captain charged with seizing supplies shipped east along the Santa Fe Trail before they could arrive at a Union army outpost in Arizona. The script was full of horse falls, and director Lewis R. Foster had budgeted just two stuntmen—Roberson and Williams—to handle the action. There was no time to dawdle. As quickly as possible, Roberson needed to round up a horse brave and consistent enough to ride into the thick of a staged shoot-'em-up. His performance would only be as good as the horse he brought with him, and Roberson was starting to worry that he might come up empty-handed.

Fighting a rising sense of panic, Roberson visited a trainer he knew, Frosty Royce, to see if he had any prospects. Royce assured Roberson he had the right horse. He walked to a stall at the end of his barn, opened the door, and brought out a bay gelding with a blaze in the shape of a star. A five-year-old registered quarter horse, he had undergone training for six months and was ready to go, Royce said. But one look at the diminutive horse and the nearly six-foot-four Roberson shook his head. The horse stood barely fifteen hands high, five feet in height. A man his size riding a horse that small would feel like a chimpanzee straddling a Chihuahua.

"He's not big enough for me, Frosty," Roberson said.

Reluctantly Royce mentioned another horse in his stable, a four-year-old gelding that was mostly thoroughbred with a little quarter horse mixed in. He was plenty smart, Royce said. "Flashy, too." But he wasn't trained nearly well enough to fall at a run. Royce had just begun teaching him to lie down at a walk.

Roberson glanced down the aisle of the barn. The horse Royce was referring to had thrust his head over the top of the gate at the third stall from the end and was staring back at them. He was big all right, a sorrel with a white blaze blanketing half of his face.

"Gets the tall from his daddy, I reckon, and the stocky from his mam," Royce said. "He's going to be a good one when we get him finished."

Roberson asked if he could try the horse out. Royce shrugged. He grabbed a lead rope that was hanging from a nail and walked back to the stall. He opened the door, slid a halter over the gelding's nose, and led him into the sunlight. The horse followed, his chocolate brown eyes trained on Roberson, quiet but alert. He looked muscular and sturdy, his ribcage well-rounded, his withers well-proportioned. The white stockings on three of his legs matched his blaze, and his legs looked substantial enough to offer a firm footing. More important, he exuded a sense of confidence not always evident in horses.

Something about his countenance resonated with Roberson. Besides, he was in a hurry.

"Okay, I'll take him," Roberson said.

"Suit yourself," Royce said. "He'll be $3 a day, and I want a $1,000 insurance policy on him."

Roberson agreed to the terms. The Pine-Thomas studio would be paying the freight. Roberson led the horse into his trailer, fastened the door behind him, and headed home. Production on *The Last Outpost* was scheduled to start in three weeks. He had a good instinct about the horse's potential, but at this late date he would need to pull off a small miracle to train him to fall that quickly.

Williams was waiting for him back at the house. "Good color," he said, glancing inside the trailer. "How's he fall?"

He needs a little work, Roberson mumbled.

Williams helped Roberson back the horse down the ramp. Curious about his new surroundings, the gelding pricked his ears forward but stood calmly as the two men checked him over. Are you sure he'll go? Williams pressed. Roberson grudgingly conceded that the horse had just recently learned to fall at a walking pace, nothing more. But "he seems like he'll be a quick learner," he said. "He was better than nothing, Jackie."

Roberson had no intention of admitting he hadn't actually ridden the horse yet. But he was confident the horse would perform admirably. He saddled the horse and hoisted himself onto his back. The horse immediately drew to attention, his brown eyes and strapping body attentive and ready to bolt. His heightened sense of awareness was a good sign.

Williams noticed it too. "My God," he said. "You get up on him, it's like somebody gave him a shot in the arm."

A shot in the arm. That perfectly described the vibrant energy coming off the horse. Almost as if he'd snorted cocaine. *Cocaine.* That had a racy ring to it. Plus, it sounded nicely alliterative when paired with Coco, which Roberson still had around. Cocaine it would be; Coke for short.

Some riders cued their horses by spurring them on their shoulder. Roberson adopted the method he'd learned from Fred Kennedy. That first day he taught Coke to lie down on command. Tying a rope to his left leg, he stood at Coke's left side and pulled the left rein over the saddle to the right, twisting Coke's head and neck back toward his rump. Doing so pulled Coke's left leg off balance, causing his knee to buckle and slide. Tugging the reins a bit more would cause Coke to gently fall sideways onto his left shoulder.

Coaxing the horse into falling that first time might have taken half an hour or more, but after repeating the trick enough times, Coke seemed to understand what he was expected to do. Roberson was able to remove the rope from Coke's leg and cue him to fall without it. The next step was to mount Cocaine and cue him to fall at a standstill. Over and over they repeated the drill until Coke began to fall readily. From his sire Coke had acquired the time-honored traits of a thoroughbred: grace, strength, and a desire for speed. From his quarter horse mother he carried an air of calmness, a stoic willingness to take on dauntless tasks. It helped, too, that Coke was limber in his neck, which was crucial to falling effectively. Most importantly, he seemed willing to put total faith in Roberson.

Roberson might have taken more time with Cocaine if he'd had the luxury. But with filming nearly underway, he needed to accelerate their lessons. That first day he taught Coke to lie down on command and, after that, to fall from a trot. After two and a half weeks he was falling halfway decently from a canter. The brisker his stride, the more difficult the stunt. Trotting is a two-beat gait that requires a horse to move its legs in unison in diagonal pairs: the front left leg in sync with the right hind leg, followed by the right front leg and the left hind leg. A horse can trot at that pace quite steadily, averaging eight miles an hour for hours at a stretch.

Cantering is more complicated. It's a three-beat gait, one that drives a horse forward with what sounds like three beats and a pause, the pause lasting longer the faster the horse is moving. The horse's left rear leg thrusts him onward while the other three legs advance. On the second beat, the horse's right hind leg and left front leg hit the ground simultaneously. On beat three, the horse lands on his right front leg. As cumbersome as it sounds, it's an efficient method of traveling. A horse moving at a canter can cover ten to seventeen miles an hour, twice as fast as when trotting. But to fall at that pace takes considerable skill.

The critical question was *where* Coke could fall at a gallop. It was time to find out. One afternoon Roberson tilled a wide spot in a nearby meadow to soften the dirt. He rode Cocaine out, then turned him back around and let him go. Coke sprang into action as if he understood that he needed to deliver 100 percent. When they reached the freshly plowed area, Roberson cued the horse, and even at a gallop Cocaine did not hesitate. He reared up, whirled around to his right, and landed on his left shoulder at the very spot Roberson intended.

The Last Outpost was filmed in nine locations in southern Arizona, among them the Sonoran Desert, the rugged Sierrita Mountains, and Old Tucson, an 1860s-era replica of a Western town that had been used as a movie set for more than a decade. Watching the movie, it's hard to catch more than a handful of the falls or identify who performed them. In one early scene, Ronald Reagan's character shoots an Indian who promptly jerks his horse's head hard and to the right, almost 180 degrees, prompting the horse to land in a large mud puddle and sending brown water spewing. The horse's white blaze looks identical to Cocaine's. In a subsequent battle sequence, a horse carrying an Indian rears up fully on his hind legs before collapsing into a neat coil, something Coco was expert at doing.

The movie also includes a handful of saddle falls. In one scene, one of the stuntmen—it's unclear who—dives off his horse at the foot of a steep bank, sending the horse scrambling up the side in a demonstration of agility and quick-thinking.

Roberson would later claim that over the course of three days, he and Williams carried out a combined eighty-seven horse falls—a record far surpassing anything that had come before. Their stunts occurred in the midst of a melee, as riders on horseback hollered, shot, and stabbed one another in a dusty free-for-all. Wardrobe assistants were on hand to help the two men change quickly into new outfits so they would look like different characters.

Did Cocaine and Coco really carry out all those falls? Their bodies would have been unbelievably sore at the end of the day. But at the movie's premiere in Tucson that spring, producer William Pine made a point of complimenting the "outstanding" stuntmen and horses "who had made a record eighty-seven falls in three days." To the other cowboys who were on hand, that statistic sounded incredible. They hadn't seen the likes of Cocaine, Roberson thought to himself.

For three days of work, Cocaine earned his owner a whopping $6,000. And despite being new to the game, Coke performed like a pro. Finally Roberson had found a falling horse perfectly suited for him.

10

A Debilitating Injury

Roberson was bowled over by Cocaine's ability to fall on cue. He'd dealt with more horses than he could remember, and this strong, agile gelding had a vigor and vitality he'd never encountered before. Moreover, Coke was *fast*.

Their stunt work was done for now. Roberson and Williams had the next ten days off, enough time to head back to California to check on their houses, pay bills, and catch up on business. Instead of hauling their horses nearly a thousand miles to Los Angeles and back, they found a stable where they could board them for the next week and a half. Cocaine had learned a daunting new skill in a short period of time and performed admirably under trying circumstances. Roberson didn't want to push him too hard. A few days' vacation fortified by nutritious grain and hay and he would be rested and ready to go again.

The stable the two men settled on had stalls that ran down the aisle of a long barn with access to individual runs outside. The runs were littered with more dung than Roberson would have cared to see, but the stable's manager promised him they would be cleaned first thing the following morning. At the stuntmen's request, the manager also agreed to swab the horses with a special wipe to fend off the swarms of flies that buzzed about. There was no remedy for the triple-digit temperatures and the dust that settled over the area like a sooty blanket, but Roberson felt relief knowing his horse would enjoy a good, long respite. When he and Williams drove away that morning, he glanced in the rearview mirror for one last look. Cocaine had entered the corral and plunged his nose into the water trough, cooling off from the relentless heat. Coco had lifted her head, her inquisitive eyes watching. She neighed loudly as the truck rounded the bend and disappeared from sight.

AS SOON AS ROBERSON AND WILLIAMS RETURNED TO LOS ANGELES, Roberson went looking for Coke's owner, Frosty Royce, to offer to buy the horse outright. He was disappointed to learn that Royce was out of town. Instead Roberson spent the remainder of his time off seeking out parts for upcoming Westerns, checking on his other horses, and catching up on his sleep. After a week and a half, he and Williams drove back to Tucson to resume work on *The Last Outpost*. Their first stop was the stable where they had left Cocaine and Coco to get some much-needed rest.

They spied Coco at the same spot alongside the fence where she'd stood watching them ten days earlier. Roberson had completed the sale of Coco to Williams for $400 and a television set, and Williams was eager to reunite with the horse that now belonged to him. As soon as he climbed out of the pickup and began walking in her direction, Coco raised her head in acknowledgment and nickered softly.

"You're all mine now, girl," Williams said, wrapping his arm around her chin and caressing her nose.

Cocaine, on the other hand, was nowhere to be seen. Roberson noted with annoyance that manure lay in thick clumps inside the fenced-in area. He thought he'd made it clear he wanted his horse to have clean quarters. Coke must be inside the barn then, shielding himself from the blazing Arizona sun. Roberson couldn't blame him for that.

He called out to the horse, hoping Cocaine would recognize the sound of his voice and come out to greet him. There was no response. Roberson rounded the corner to the entrance of the barn and glanced down the lengthy row of stalls to the one at the end, the one that held Cocaine. The horse was there, all right, but something about him seemed off. His head sagged low over the gate. Roberson approached him. Coke raised his head for a second, acknowledging his presence, and then dropped it again. Flies swarmed about him, and Roberson was taken aback by the vile odor that permeated from Coke's stall. The smell was revolting, like something was dead and decaying. The odor, though, was coming directly from Cocaine.

Roberson rubbed the horse's face and murmured, "What is it, fella?"

A DEBILITATING INJURY

But Coke just stood there, not moving. Roberson glanced about the barn for a halter and a lead rope. Finding none, he hollered to Williams to bring Cocaine's halter from the truck. Williams came through the barn door, took a deep breath, and said, "Whew! What died in here?"

Roberson shook his head. Sick with worry, he fumbled with Coke's halter and escorted him out into the aisleway of the barn. "Something's bad wrong," he murmured.

The light in the barn was too dark to reveal anything, so Roberson led Coke out into the barnyard. The horse hobbled badly, struggling to keep as much weight as he could off his hind legs.

Williams, following behind them, gasped audibly. "That smell. It's Cocaine's leg," he said.

The bright sunlight illuminated what the darkness inside the barn had concealed. Cocaine's left hind leg was swollen several times its size, all the way from his knee to his hoof. The swelling was so great that it had caused his skin to burst. Strips of hide were hanging like tattered ribbons from his knee. Maggots had punctured hundreds of small holes in his leg and were crawling in and out of his flesh. The smell came from the blood and pus seeping out of the sores.

"Dear God in heaven," Roberson muttered. This horse, this most promising horse, now stood before him gravely injured. "Where's the son of a bitch who owns this place?" Roberson bellowed, torn between distress and incredulous fury. He hollered again to no one in particular. "What the hell *happened*?"

Cocaine pushed his smooth, velvety nose under Roberson's arm. Tears spilled down Roberson's cheeks.

Williams offered to bring him a gun. Someone needed to end Cocaine's misery, he said.

"*Get* a gun!" Roberson yelled. "I'll shoot the dirty son of a bitch who did this to my horse."

The owner of the stable was stacking a pile of hay bales. He hurried over when he heard Roberson's shouts. In the glaring light of day Coke's wound was evident. "Sweet Mary in hell, what happened to him?" the stable owner said.

Roberson gritted his jaw. "*You tell me*," he seethed. The owner had promised to wipe the horses for flies, yet here Coke stood, covered with maggots. He'd been injured for days.

Coke dropped his head and nuzzled Roberson as the stable owner fumbled for a response. "I don't understand how this happened," he said. His stable hand had brushed the flies from Cocaine's face, and the horse seemed to be eating well, he said. The owner did a slow run back into the barn to check out Coke's stall. While he did so, Roberson called out to Williams to phone a veterinarian. The stable owner returned with a grim look on his face. There was a jagged hole in the rear wall of Coke's stall, he said. Cocaine had apparently kicked the wall and injured his leg when he pulled it back through the wood's spiked edges.

The stable owner's explanation did nothing to assuage Roberson. How could anyone not notice the putrid smell coming from Coke's injured leg, he wanted to know. By now the stable boy had joined them, looking somber and mortified. "I'm sorry, mister," the boy said. "I didn't look at his feet. I thought a cat had caught a mouse somewhere, is all."

There was no point lighting into the boy. Roberson just wanted to get help for his horse. By the time the veterinarian arrived, Roberson had led Coke to the shade of a nearby tree and begun washing his leg. The vet examined the horse for a couple of minutes before delivering the bad news. Cocaine's injury was critical, he said. It was possible to save him, but he would never be able to work again, especially as a stunt horse in the movies. Odds were likely he would limp for the rest of his days.

Roberson didn't want to hear it. Cocaine was only four—he was simply too young and too valuable. But the vet was in no mood to mince words. Your horse is hurting and in distress, he explained, and ought to be euthanized on the spot. Pressed, he conceded there was a slight chance that Coke could recover from his injury. "But it would be better my way, believe me," he said.

Roberson balked at the news. The vet was giving his professional advice, but other than assessing Coke's injury, he knew nothing about this special horse: the talent he possessed, his determination, and drive. Roberson wasn't about to see Cocaine's life ended this soon. "I want him saved," he said. The studio had a $1,000 insurance policy on Coke. That would cover the cost of transporting him to a veterinary specialist Roberson knew in

Downey, California, who was an expert in treating leg ailments in horses.

The veterinarian knew better than to argue. He pulled from his bag a huge syringe, filled it with amber-colored pain meds, and injected them into Coke's leg. Roberson watched as the horse slowly shifted his weight. Maybe it was wishful thinking, but Cocaine seemed slightly more comfortable than he'd been a few minutes earlier. It turned out the studio didn't need Roberson and Williams for more stunt work; they were free to head back home. Somberly Roberson loaded the horse onto his trailer for the eight-hour drive to Downey. The specialist there wasn't any more optimistic about Coke's chances than the first vet who had seen him. But it was clear Roberson was determined to heal this horse. He wanted to see every attempt made to rehabilitate Coke.

The following week, Roberson headed to the former Monogram Ranch in San Fernando to work on another Western, fixated on how he could save enough money to buy Cocaine from Frosty Royce. Coke had been housed at the specialist's clinic for two months when Roberson got more bad news. The company insuring Coke had sent the veterinarian a signed release instructing him to euthanize the horse. Coke was improving, the vet said, but the insurance company no longer thought it made sense to spend money trying to save him.

Roberson wasn't sure he'd heard this right.

"You mean they want to put him down because of the *vet bill*?" he said. "But you said he was getting better. Is there a chance he could be all right?"

Given enough time and the right care, the horse could recover completely, the vet explained. But the cost of rehabbing him could run into the thousands of dollars. The insurance company wasn't prepared to pay it.

Roberson pleaded with the vet to spare Cocaine. He was worth whatever it cost to bring him around. He, Roberson, would pay the veterinary bill, regardless of what it came to. The specialist didn't have a problem with that, but legally Coke belonged to the insurance company. Officials there would need to sign off on any transaction first.

Roberson phoned the insurance company. To his relief the company agreed to spare Coke's life provided Roberson paid the veterinary bill. The next morning, Roberson drove his trailer thirty miles to Downey to pick up the horse. Coke was waiting in an enclosure next to the veterinary

A DEBILITATING INJURY

hospital. He lifted his head and nickered loudly when Roberson climbed out of the truck. "Hey, Coke," Roberson called to him. The horse lifted his ears and snorted. The swelling on his injured leg was still pronounced, but it appeared to be on the mend.

The specialist went over Coke's progress. His injured leg was rife with scar tissue: large, thick, granulated outgrowths cowboys called proud flesh. The tissue was reddish-pink in tone and flat, a base upon which new skin cells could grow. If it got infected or the blood supply to it was inadequate, Coke could wind up developing more proud flesh, making it difficult for skin cells to stretch across the surface of the wound. But the combination of caustic powder and Corona ointment, used sparingly, could keep granulated tissue from growing out of hand, the veterinarian said. It wouldn't hurt to give it a try. Proud flesh could be removed surgically, a procedure that's usually painless to the horse because the scar tissue contains no nerves. But he wasn't optimistic. "You should know before you take this horse home, there is not much chance that he will be able to perform the way he did before," the vet said.

The one good piece of news was that the insurance company had paid up the $1,000 policy it had taken out on Coke. All that was owed was $73. Roberson had squirreled away enough money to pay the entire $1,000; now he'd have most of it left. He settled up with the hospital's bookkeeper, purchased a can of caustic power and some Corona ointment, led Coke into the trailer, and pulled out of the parking lot of the veterinary hospital whistling cheerfully. Despite the vet's pessimism, Roberson was confident he could rehabilitate Coke well enough to put him back in the movies.

His dad, Ollie, met them at home, looked Cocaine over, and gave a thumbs up to what he saw. There was a lot of proud flesh there, the elder Roberson agreed, but it looked as though Coke's tendons, ligaments, and bones were aligned the way they ought to be. And his pastern, the part of his leg between his fetlock and the top of his hoof, was moving the way it should. He'd seen more severe injuries many times over, Ollie said, including one horse who'd had his leg sliced all the way through by barbed wire. That horse's foot was half amputated, but once it mended, he went on to become a fine plow horse.

Roberson shook his head. He didn't need a plow horse. He needed an athletic horse, one that could fall at a full-on gallop. He asked his dad: What are the chances Coke can be that horse?

Ollie told his son what he wanted to hear. Give me three months and he'll be back at it, Ollie said.

11

Learning to Fall Again

Between jobs, Roberson worked hard at rehabilitating his new horse. Each day he and Ollie sprinkled caustic powder and dabbed ointment around Cocaine's wound and wrapped an old inner tube tightly around his leg to reduce swelling, techniques that were old-fashioned but effective. And Roberson began training his horse all over again.

Falling horses were taught their trade the same way Napoleon's army had schooled its horses in the early 1800s, when soldiers would drop their mounts to the ground and use them as shields against enemy weapons. Horses instinctively resist falling; it's one of the most unnatural things they can be asked to do. In the movies, riders can pad their own elbows, hips, and knees to cushion their falls. As a matter of routine, stuntman Hal Needham kept a bottle of Percodan on hand to ease the aches from falling. But other than refusing to carry out a dangerous stunt, horses have no means of protecting themselves. They're entirely at the mercy of their riders.

Some horses are afraid to fall. Helping them overcome their fear requires tremendous patience on the part of trainers, and that's the first thing they need to accomplish. Trainer Rodd Wolff, who has coached nine falling horses, said he starts a horse out in a familiar setting. He begins by asking the horse to execute the easiest tricks he knows, rewarding him afterward with a palm full of grain and lots of praise. At each step of teaching a horse to fall, Wolf showers the horse with approval.

"I take my time with the animal," Wolf once wrote. "Confidence is not a quality you can instill overnight. I always talk quietly and calmly to him, pet him, give him grain or a bit of carrot, make him gentle, and let him know he can trust me. I feel this phase of training is the most important.

You can apply the same approach to any horse, no matter what it is you want to teach him."

Along with praise comes repetition. Teaching a stunt is really a matter of developing a habit and practicing it daily, trainers say. Horses also need a chance to concentrate on what they're being taught. If their minds are clouded with fear, especially toward their trainer, they'll be too distracted to respond to a cue. But once a horse learns a particular trick, he almost never forgets it, even if years have gone by since he performed it last.

Critics see something inherently cruel in having a horse do something he wouldn't naturally do. William S. Hart fell his pony Fritz multiple times, but he didn't feel good about it. "Of all the stunts in pictures I regard it as the most dangerous to the horse," the actor said. "When he takes the fall, his whole weight hits on his left shoulder, and the danger is in fracturing the bone. I threw that little paint pony in almost every picture I used him in, and I am thankful that he escaped injury."

Hart expounded on his concerns in Fritz's "memoir." "All this sounds easy. Sounds like nothing at all," Hart wrote, speaking from the pony's point of view. "But to anyone that's interested, I say, don't try it. It's no fun to tear straight down a hill on slippery mud and then let go all holts and fall and have a man weighing 190 pounds under you and on top of you and all over you. And all the time you're rolling and hitting rocks and things."

Stuntman Hal Needham, who was no stranger to dangerous feats—he crashed cars, jumped off high buildings, and hung by his ankles from a biplane—wasn't a fan of falling horses on cue either. "When you train a falling horse, you really hurt him in the mouth," Needham said. "The only reason he falls is that he knows I'm going to hurt him in the mouth if he doesn't, but people who don't know horses don't see that on the screen. They can't know how much abuse that horse has gone through."

A horse that doesn't want to fall can be made to do so by yanking hard on his reins to swing his head around, then pulling harder with your other hand to swivel the horse's head into your lap, Needham explained. He preferred using Running W's to fall a horse. Needham insisted that as long as the trip wire was attached to a horse's fetlock at a 45-degree angle, the horse would turn sideways and tumble safely.

But Hart and Needham were in the minority. Most stunt performers argued that it's nearly impossible to make a horse fall if he isn't willing.

"Let me assure you of one thing," stuntwoman Martha Crawford Cantarini wrote in her memoir *Fall Girl: My Life as a Western Stunt Double*, "if ever a horse gets hurt doing this type of fall . . . King Kong would never be strong enough to make him do it again. Once taught, they do it willingly or they will never do it again." She went on to write that "if a fall has caused them pain or distress, there is little chance these days of a falling horse being pulled down in the traditional mode if they do not want to do it."

All the praise in the world couldn't convince some horses to voluntarily fall even once. Others might fall for a time only to suddenly refuse to fall ever again. A stunt performer might have no idea that a horse had decided to stop falling until he tugged the horse's reins one day to suddenly find the horse digging in his hooves, stiffening his neck, and swinging his head forward, refusing to budge. If anyone was going to go down in that scenario, it was the rider who didn't see the resistance coming.

Cueing horses to fall might not look as spontaneous as it did when they were tripped by wires. But falling of their own volition gives horses some control over their actions. Attached to trip wires, they have none. Horses land on their shoulders when they go down, but there are ways to cushion the blow. In Cocaine's day, stunt performers typically owned the horses they fell and went out of their way to keep the animals safe. They dug pliable spots in the dirt, removed any protruding rocks, and spread a thick layer of sawdust to soften the fall. They substituted hard iron stirrups with stirrups made of rubber, flexible enough not to injure the horse or rider when the horse landed on his side. They also often removed the saddle horn before a stunt to help cushion a fall.

"Think of a falling horse as an acrobat," said Petrine Mitchum, author of *Hollywood Hoofbeats: Trails Blazed Across the Silver Screen*. "They need to be athletic and fearless, and also need to have a very trusting nature. So they have to not only have a calm, strong nature but also be willing to place total trust in their trainer."

"The training is very specialized and not just anyone can do it," added Martha Crawford Cantarini. "It requires extreme patience and confidence, and the ability to read the horse and know what it is capable of, and when to push and when to back off. The trainer also has to have impeccable timing and a certain fearlessness, as well. To deliberately fall down with a 1,000-pound animal in a gallop is not for the faint of heart."

Falling horses need to have strong back muscles so they can land and roll over quickly. Done properly, falling a trained stunt horse comes with minimal risk, if any, Rodd Wolf maintained. The only real danger comes when a horse is improperly or inadequately trained, "or worse, not trained at all." In their heyday, professional falling horses were considered too valuable to risk injury. They earned money for their owners and got them lucrative work. An injured horse was an out-of-work horse. And a horse that became fearful of falling was out of work for good.

The age at which training should begin was subject to debate, but some trainers maintained that a falling horse should be around four years old. By then their bones are strong and well-developed, and it's evident whether they have the personality to perform. Trainers singled out horses that were assertive and ready to kick it into gear when the situation called for it. Even the most athletic horses, though, needed time to learn to fall. Horses spirited enough to tumble on cue typically needed a year to learn the stunt and three to four years to master it.

Cocaine happened to be the right age: four years old. The challenge now was getting him over his injury so he could fall safely again. As he had before, Roberson fitted the horse with a snaffle bit, the most conventional bit used. Made up of a mouthpiece with a D-shaped ring on either side, it rested on top of Coke's tongue and in a space between his front and back teeth and worked by applying pressure to his mouth and nose. Coke's reins were fastened to either end of the bit, laced through rings, and extended to the rider. When Roberson pulled the reins, the horse felt pressure on his gums. An equal amount of pressure on both sides of his mouth was his cue to stop. A pull to his right was his signal to turn in that direction, likewise with the left.

After three months Roberson decided it was time to put Cocaine to the test. He took a job doubling actor Rod Cameron in a Monogram Western. The swelling in Coke's leg had subsided greatly, but it hadn't disappeared, and his left hind leg had yet to grow back any hair. But Roberson needed the work. He wrapped Coke's bare leg, taped it off, painted it white to match the horse's other legs, then loaded him into a trailer and headed to location.

The script called for Roberson to race Coke down a hillside and fall him just before reaching a circle of wagon trains. Roberson inspected Coke's leg one last time before climbing into the saddle. Cocaine stepped forward and back as if he could sense Roberson's nervous energy. When the director called, "Action!" Roberson spurred him on, and Coke flew down the hill, Indians sprinting from behind. Coke was galloping so fast that for a second Roberson wondered if he could pull off a fall at the designated spot. "Good Lord, don't let this be *Rio Grande* all over again," he thought. As they approached the wagons, he transferred his weight and pulled Coke's head around. The horse whirled in the air and struck the ground, sliding twelve feet before he came to a stop beneath a wagon.

Roberson took a moment to compose himself. Cocaine had done it. He'd fallen more admirably than Roberson could have hoped. The stuntman looked up to see everyone on the sidelines standing and clapping loudly for himself and his horse. The director slapped him on the back. "That was the most spectacular fall I have ever seen, bar none," he said.

After the euphoria faded, though, Roberson was flooded with doubt. Coke had recovered enough from his injury to deliver, but maybe this was a fluke. Could a horse that survived a wound as serious as Coke's really be that good?

A few weeks later Roberson had the chance to find out. He landed a role as a stuntman in *Way of a Gaucho*, a film about a young South American cowboy sentenced to the army after killing the enemy of a friend, who deserts the military and becomes an outlaw. The movie was shot in Argentina, which meant flying Coke 6,100 miles. Roberson dyed the horse's legs and blaze reddish-brown to match the coat of the horse he was doubling. Doubling for the star of the movie, Rory Calhoun, Roberson's assignment was to race Cocaine while being chased and fall him suddenly, as if gunfire had blown him away.

The director called, "Action!" and Roberson and Coke dashed across the plains. The cameras didn't capture Coke's head being pulled to the right. They only showed Coke bursting in the air, twisting from side to side, his rust-colored mane whipping against his neck. He landed on his shoulder so hard that his hind legs kicked up toward the sky. Roberson had not yet learned to remove Coke's saddle horn; it jammed into the dirt and broke off as the horse began his slide. Immediately afterward the camera panned out to show Coke standing up and shaking himself as if he were shuddering off a fly—jolted, but unhurt. Once again, his derring-do earned Coke and Roberson a round of applause from the cast and crew. Coke's stunts weren't some accident. Despite everything he'd been through, he was a master at falling.

12

Tough Riders, Tough Horses

Their back-to-back success cemented Roberson's reputation as an expert horseman and catapulted Cocaine into the little-known world of Hollywood falling horses. Together the pair could now compete for jobs alongside an elite cadre of professionals.

The best cowboy stuntmen sincerely believed that their horses were their partners—animals who were in no small part responsible for their success. When claims arose that moviemakers were continuing to abuse horses, pioneering trainer Fred Kennedy—who had three falling horses, Trixie, Dixie, and Shanghai—rebutted the accusations by making a brief film demonstrating how falling horses were trained.

"Next time you see a horse fall in a movie, don't start shouting: 'Flying wires!' 'Cruelty!' etc.," wrote syndicated columnist Harold Heffernan. "Chances are that you will be mistaken because the days of tripping horses to fall for a scene have passed. They are animals trained to fall—just as a football player is taught to fall without hurting himself. The horse, on cue, will deftly tuck his right foreleg under him, take the fall nicely and be very happy with his reward of sugar lumps."

The American Humane Association had no objection to the practice of falling horses. By the early 1940s, AHA director Richard Craven felt comfortable that horses and other movie animals were being treated well. He defended the battle scenes depicted in *They Died with Their Boots On*, a fictionalized version of George Armstrong Custer's life and his death at the Battle of the Little Bighorn in 1876. The horses seen hitting the ground in the movie, eight or nine of them, were trained to fall, and "they are very valuable," Craven wrote in the AHA's *National Humane Review*.

"They are trained on soft, spongy ground," Craven went on to say. "There is one sure way to ruin these horses and take all the value out of them and that is to 'fall' them on hard ground and hurt them. Throw them on hard ground and you have forfeited their confidence. They distrust you, refuse to go down and their value is gone. I have talked with owners of these horses and know how anxious they are that conditions be as near perfect as possible. I have examined most of the falling horses and have yet to find a scar on one of them."

By now, Hollywood had a dozen falling horses, with trainers capable of earning as much as $500 while teaching a horse to fall and $1,000 on location to make sure rough stunts were carried out safely. "They fall in carefully prepared spaded earth and sawdust beds," reported the *Los Angeles Times*. "Nobody gets hurt—except maybe an unwary rider."

Western movies offered stuntmen and their horses plenty of work. There was an understanding in stunt circles: if you couldn't make out an actor's face during an action scene on the big screen, rest assured that a stuntman or woman had been tapped to carry out the trick.

Two stuntmen in particular stood out.

The first was Roberson's friend Jack Williams. Born in 1921 in Butte, Montana, Williams and his parents moved to Burbank, California, when he was a young boy. His mother, Paris, had already made a name for herself as a world champion trick rider in rodeos, and his father, George, had a wealth of real-life cowboy experience under his belt. Both found work performing stunts in movies.

It wasn't long before Jack joined them. At the age of four he got his first assignment, in a scene in the 1926 silent film *The Flaming Forest*, in which a man riding horseback pitched him onto a stagecoach. When he was just fifteen his dad taught him to fall horses, not just lunging forward, as most falling horses do, but backward, on horses that would rear up dramatically before they came crashing down. Williams acquired much of his expertise from watching his dad train an animal he'd dubbed "The Suicide Horse," a steed so defiant it took three years to teach him to fall.

Anything athletic, it seemed, Jack could do. He became a champion bronc rider, and while attending the University of Southern California he played on the school's polo team. He earned money from movie work on the side: as much as $225 a day falling horses, bulldogging steers, and vaulting a pair of horses over a car while he stood on their backs. Among the movies he performed in were *Daniel Boone*, *Dodge City*, and *Gone with the Wind*, where he played the tiny part of a soldier with a hair-trigger temper.

Williams left Hollywood during World War II to serve in the Coast Guard; he was a navigator on a tank landing ship, transporting troops to the Japanese-held island in the Pacific. "I was the key guy, the only one who knew where we were supposed to be," he recalled. "All my life I've tended to think in terms of picture productions, and [the Battle of Okinawa] was the greatest production I've ever seen."

The number one rule in movies, Williams learned, was to pair the right horse with the right rider. Once that happened, the rider needed to build a rapport with the horse.

"You never hurt [a horse], because he has to have confidence in you," Williams told a reporter. "He thinks you're King Kong. The minute he finds out you're not, he becomes unreliable. You do a million things right with a horse but ruin him if you do one thing wrong. Guess what the horse remembers?"

When the war ended, handsome, square-jawed Williams returned to Hollywood in *Red River*, Howard Hawks's 1948 movie about a willful rancher (John Wayne) who leads a cattle drive to Missouri with the help of a cantankerous older man (Walter Brennan) and a boy, played by Montgomery Clift. In that movie and in several other films after that, Williams quickly made a name for himself carrying out astonishing horse falls. He borrowed the technique his father had used so successfully and gave it his own spin. The sight of a horse falling on cue never failed to fascinate him.

"You have to, number one, make the horse fall and then, if there's any time, you concern yourself with your own safety," Williams said.

In Western circles he was known for his ability to perform regardless of the circumstances. More than once, Williams was called to a set to execute a horse fall no one else was able to pull off. He permitted himself a humble brag, muttering his trademark phrase "Never touched me" after carrying out a fall.

One of his best-known partners was a sorrel gelding owned by the Hudkins Brothers named Goldie. But Coco, the diminutive mare Williams bought from Roberson, was his favorite. In Coco, Williams found his soulmate. Despite her petite size, she could perform with a flair Williams had never seen before. She learned to sit, lie down, bow, and, best of all, dive to the ground on cue. Moreover, she had an uncanny way of perking up around a camera, as if she understood that its presence was her signal to go to work and do her best. Stuntman Bob Hoy began working with Williams in 1950, the same year Williams acquired Coco. "They were inseparable," Hoy recalled. "The horse had an instinct. A lot of horses will fight you when you get to the spot where they'll make the fall and won't go there. But Coco went there. She was just so great."

Coco's falling-over stunt was so startling that it drew criticism from the then western regional director for the American Humane Association. In a letter sent jointly to Williams and to movie studios dated September 18, 1954, director W. A. Young asked that stunt performers stop making their horses rear up on their hind legs until they toppled over backward. Williams, stung that anyone would even remotely accuse him of abusing Coco, promptly sued the AHA for $100,000, alleging that Young's letter had damaged his reputation, "disgraced" him, and jeopardized his right to work. The outcome of the case, filed in the Los Angeles Superior Court, is unknown.

Another champion horse-faller was Charles "Chuck" Bert Hayward. Born in 1920 to cattle ranchers in the remote sandhills of Hyannis, Nebraska, Hayward grew up surrounded by the kind of wide-open horizon that seemed to stretch forever. The countryside was dotted with occasional one-room schools and sod houses occupied by families living in almost unfathomable poverty. One native of the area, Ava Speese, recalled how her parents fashioned toothbrushes out of burnt corn cobs.

By contrast, Hayward's family did quite well. His parents, Bert and Hazel, were known for the fine-quality horses they furnished to the U.S. Cavalry stationed at Fort Robinson 120 miles away, and as a young boy Hayward helped train them. At sixteen he left home and went to work breaking horses and stacking hay. Hoping to give him a leg up, Hayward's grandparents paid his way to the Curtis Agricultural School in Nebraska. After graduating, Hayward attended business college in Omaha and toiled as a lineman until he threw his belt around a pole one day and missed, fell, and broke his back. Ineligible for the armed services because of his injury, he signed on to the merchant marines during World War II, where he worked as a medic aboard Liberty ships, massive vessels used to deliver cargo to Britain and the social union. Hayward's time on the seas instilled in him a lifelong hatred of water. "He wouldn't do a stunt in a puddle after that," his former wife, Ellen Powell, said.

When the war ended, Hayward returned to the West and the life he knew best. He worked as a cowboy at the C. C. Gentry ranch, then joined the rodeo circuit, traveling through Nebraska, South Dakota, and Wyoming. At twenty-seven he moved to California with only his ramshackle pick-up truck and $14 in his pocket. He landed in the town of Van Nuys, eleven miles north of Hollywood, where he mucked horse barns and baled hay, taking any odd job he could find.

Working at some of the stables that furnished horses for the movie business introduced Hayward to influential contacts. He knew horses—that was his calling—and the studios were looking for someone with his degree of expertise. His first film job came in 1949, when he did stunt work for the movie *Brimstone*, starring Walter Brennan as a ranch owner determined to keep homesteaders from moving in. Later that year Hayward performed in Republic's frontier-war movie *The Fighting Kentuckian* and in *She Wore a Yellow Ribbon*, the second of John Ford's Cavalry trilogy. *The Fighting Kentuckian* didn't involve any horse falls but did feature a series of wagon wrecks that could have been lethally dangerous if Hayward had been any less skilled at holding the reins.

Wiry, with a perpetual look of concentration, Hayward developed a lifelong loyalty to Ford and Wayne early on in his career. In 1950 he doubled for Wayne and performed stunts on *Rio Grande*, the same movie where Roberson botched a horse fall. During a battle scene a horse fell on top of Hayward, causing him to strike his head. He lost part of his hearing as a result of the accident and was too injured to perform for the rest of the movie. Republic Pictures wanted to stop paying Hayward after that, but Ford and Wayne wouldn't hear of it. They fought any attempt to deny Hayward his pay, and because of them the stuntman remained on the studio's payroll for the remaining three months of filming. He never forgot their kindness. "People like that—Wayne and Ford—you're part of their family," he said years later.

How or when exactly Hayward acquired Twinkle Toes, the tall, sorrel falling horse that, in industry circles, would become nearly as famous as his owner, is unclear. Like Williams, Hayward learned early that finding the right horse was important—that not just any horse could withstand the rigors of stunt work. The right horse would be able to handle any assignment that might come his way.

"Twink," as Hayward's horse was known, was an alpha male, taller than sixteen hands, with a high head, a flat hip, and a tail set a bit differently than a thoroughbred or a quarter horse. He was probably a full-bred thoroughbred with a bit of saddlebred mixed in, according to Ellen Powell. Twinkle Toes had two hind stockings and, like Cocaine, an overabundance of confidence and attitude. He was also stubborn. "He wouldn't give you anything. You had to take it," Ellen said. Falling him necessitated a rider who could take him down hard. "Otherwise, he would throw you away."

Hayward used a solid eight-inch curved bit on the horse, and Twinkle Toes's mouth was tender. Theirs was a war of wills that Hayward always won. On top of that, Hayward refrained from indulging his horse. Ellen never once saw him rewarding Twinkle Toes with a treat. "You do that, then he is nosing around" expecting more, she explained. But Hayward and Twinkle Toes shared a loyalty that was unsurpassed, Ellen said. She said Twinkle Toes would do anything Hayward asked. "He had a good horse," she affirmed. "He loved that horse. And the horse respected him and knew him."

Hayward's bond with Twinkle Toes was the secret to getting him to fall. He worked the horse at his home in the San Fernando Valley. In the early 1960s, at a time when most of the roads in the valley, even in Burbank, were unpaved, the Haywards bought two or three connecting lots on Long Ridge Road, moved a house onto their land, and kept their horses at the rear of the property, in an area about seventy feet long. "You could saddle up right there and walk down the dirt road," Ellen said. She remembered riding toward trainer Glenn Randall's barn nearby one day when she came upon a round steel ball. It turned out to be a cannonball, a vestige of California's unsettled and not-that-distant past. "It was a whole other world," she recalled. "A completely whole other world."

Twinkle Toes did Hayward's bidding, but he wasn't about to succumb to anyone else. Ellen found that out the hard way. She was no stranger to horses. She had her own quarter horse and was an experienced rider. One day she and Hayward rode to a dry creek bed nearby, and Hayward asked if she would like to fall Twinkle Toes. It sounded like a fun challenge, so

Ellen agreed to give it a go. "Be sure and take him hard," Hayward cautioned. Ellen climbed on Twinkle Toes's back and started him on a run. When the time came to fall him, she followed her husband's instructions and pulled the horse's head to the right until his nose was practically in her lap. Twinkle Toes fell, all right, but he knew he was in the hands of an uncertain rider, and he was determined to have the last word. As soon as his shoulder hit the river bottom, followed by his hip, the horse whipped Ellen off his back and into the sand. His act of aggression left her dazed and confused and lucky to have avoided a concussion.

"That was the personality of the horse," Ellen remembered. "He was a big, strong, bold horse and he knew his business. I didn't know my business and he taught me." She refused to ever ride Twinkle Toes again.

Hayward had a second falling horse named Iodine, who was tall and muscular and blessed with a more amiable personality. After crashing to the ground, Iodine would roll over on his back from one side to the other. One of his more memorable scenes occurred years later in the John Wayne movie *McLintock!* Stuntman Jerry Gatlin, a former rodeo professional, was doubling Wayne's son Patrick on Iodine in a sequence involving a tug-of-war at a picnic. As the cameras rolled, Gatlin began to fall Iodine. Chuck Roberson, doubling for one of the stars, was supposed to throw a punch at Gatlin as Iodine fell, and Gatlin's task was to stay on top of the horse as he rode him down. It was a combination of Iodine's athleticism and plain luck that enabled Gatlin to roll the horse without getting injured.

A cowboy stuntperson's calling was exceptionally dicey. Movie directors weren't about to take the chance of injuring a star actor on a risky stunt. It took a daring, often wildly heedless, human being to attempt the many tricks asked of stunt performers, especially when it came to falling horses. Stuntmen had to slip their feet out of the stirrups before the fall began in order to avoid getting twisted up with their horse. And then they had to angle away from the horse's feet to keep from getting kicked as the horse tried standing back up.

"If you didn't fall just right, you'd end up crippled," veteran stuntman Dean Smith said. "When you're going to be coming off a horse that's four and a half or five feet tall, you'd better know a little about how to land on the ground."

Smith was a lanky, affable man with a shock of hair and a smile so wide it made his eyes squint. He grew up in Breckenridge, Texas, on a ranch owned by his grandparents. Saturdays would find him at the town's movie theater watching Gene Autry, Roy Rogers, and the whole roster of cowboy stars. As a young man, Smith made a name for himself competing in track and field events. At the 1952 Olympics in Helsinki, he came in fourth in the 100-meter relay and ran the first leg of the Americans' 4x100-meter relay team, capturing the gold medal. At the University of Texas at Austin, he ran the 100-yard dash in 9.4 seconds, one-tenth of a second short of what was then the world record.

After that, Smith switched sports. He went on to play professional football for the Los Angeles Rams and the Pittsburgh Steelers, and in rodeo circles he won championships in bareback bronc riding and calf roping. While serving in the army he met an actor, James Bumgarner, who would later become known as James Garner. Back home, Garner introduced Smith in Western movie circles. Smith performed in *El Dorado*, *Big Jake*, *Rio Conchos*, *The Comancheros*, *How the West Was Won*, and many other Westerns. He also appeared in episodes of the television series *Maverick*, *Have Gun—Will Travel*, *Gunsmoke*, and *Walker, Texas Ranger*.

Stunt performers needed to know how to do slump shots, where a rider falls over as if he's been shot but remains astride the horse. Occasionally a stuntman would have to perform a "jerk off," which entailed getting yanked off his horse while riding. Stuntmen would wear hidden vests outfitted with a slender wire attached to an object stuck in the ground. The trick would be timed to enable the rider to fall into a sand pit to cushion the blow.

"You've got to give people their money's worth and make a stunt look believable. It's called 'selling the shot,'" Smith said. But "by God, you've got to be able to walk away from it," he added. "A producer couldn't hire a guy who didn't know how to ride a horse and take a fall. It's an art form."

Stunt performers took immense pride in conquering fate and showing off the knots, bruises, scrapes, and broken bones that resulted from their escapades. As stuntman Terry Leonard once said, "Most people like to think they treat their bodies like a temple. I treated mine like a South Tucson beer bar."

One of the most fearless was John "Bear" Hudkins. A nephew of the Hudkins brothers who operated one of Hollywood's best-known stables, Bear grew up in Lincoln, Nebraska, as one of ten children left fatherless at a young age. He worked to help support the family, then went west with a football scholarship to UCLA. Thanks to his uncles' connections, he quickly found work performing stunts on movie sets. The hazards of his calling became apparent when Bear was filming the 1948 John Wayne movie *Fort Apache* in Monument Valley. In a strikingly memorable scene—a sequence that was left in the movie—the horse Bear was riding toppled onto him, breaking his back. Barely thirty years old, he had to have his spine fused and was forced to stop working for a solid year while he convalesced. Once he recovered, Bear climbed back onto a horse and resumed executing the falls, transfers, and drags expected of cinematic wranglers.

Hollywood was full of daredevils like him. Boyd "Red" Morgan grew up on a farm and cattle ranch in Waurika, Oklahoma, not far from Chuck Roberson's hometown in Texas. Nicknamed for his fiery red mop, Red moved to California after high school, played football for the University of Southern California and the Washington Redskins, the Hollywood Bears, and the Birmingham Generals, and then turned to movies. He appeared in hundreds of films and TV episodes, including *Rio Lobo*, *McLintock!*, and *How the West Was Won*.

Another ace stuntman was Frank McGrath. Part Irish and part Indian, McGrath learned his horsemanship by making the rounds of small rodeos and working as a jockey at racetracks in the Midwest. When a Mexican track he was working for went out of business, he caught a freight train to California. The story goes that a movie producer happened to see McGrath leap from a train and immediately recognized his potential. McGrath later spent eight years playing the ornery cook on the TV series *Wagon Train*.

Cowgirl stunt performers were rare. One of the best was Martha Crawford Cantarini, who'd had a passion for horses ever since she was a young girl. Unbeknownst to her mother, her stepfather, Carl Crawford, would let her play hooky and steal away to the polo stables with him. He arranged a screen test for her at Twentieth Century Fox alongside a young Marilyn Monroe, but Martha had no interest in acting. Instead she found her calling doubling for some of the most famous actresses of the day—among them Eleanor Parker, Claudette Colbert, and Jean Simmons—often on horseback. And she was as skilled at falling horses as her male colleagues.

Stuntmen had toolboxes full of gear to protect them from bruising falls. Knee pads, elbow pads, and breastplates shielded key body parts. To protect their internal organs, they cinched themselves into stiff girdles. Drag pads helped shield them from scrapes when horses pulled them along the ground. Underneath their wide-brimmed cowboy hats, careful performers wore rounded safety helmets invisible to onlookers. But they couldn't have carried out half their feats without their silent partners, and falling horses had to perform without padding of any sort. Horses were absolutely essential to Western movies, and falling horses—the ones most capable of putting themselves at risk—were uncommon and highly prized. "There are basically two kinds of horses in movies: good ones and lousy ones," actor and stuntman Harry "Dobie" Carey said. "A bad horse can make the best of riders look awful."

Jerry Brown Falling Horse—the animal Chuck Roberson rode to an embarrassing, off-the-mark slide on the set of *Rio Grande*—was one of the best-known. Owned by Hudkins Brothers stables, the bay gelding had served at a cavalry post in Fort Reno, Oklahoma, during World War II. Hudkins Brothers brought him to California, where he was trained by the stuntman Jerry Brown, who named the horse after himself. Despite that *Rio Grande* gaffe, Jerry Brown the horse was gifted at falling as well as transferring, where a rider leaps from one horse onto another or onto a stagecoach. It takes guts for a horse to keep galloping while a transfer is taking place. Jerry Brown was especially adept at jumping obstacles and falling immediately afterward at the very spot his rider intended, a feat that involved an extra measure of risk. He carried out that stunt in the 1947 movie *Northwest Outpost* and again two years later in *The Fighting Kentuckian*.

Falling horses had brains—they had to in order to understand and carry out their complicated tricks. And many of them had a style all their own. Goldie, a horse belonging to Jack Williams's father, George, displayed verve and panache—he could fall over backward with a theatrical flourish—but he was so defiant that he scared the bejesus out of many of the wranglers. George Williams had the expertise to handle Goldie, but only a miracle kept Williams out of Goldie's way when the horse carried out one of his striking falls.

One of the most spirited and accomplished falling horses was Hot Rod, a thoroughbred gelding who came to stunt work by way of the racetrack. Many racehorses were pressed into service at too young an age, when their

7. Jerry Brown Falling Horse initiates one of his famous falls in the 1958 movie *Tonka*. Photofest.

tendons had not yet fully formed. Hot Rod was a victim of that practice. He was registered under the name of Salvage Goods, but by the age of four, his racing days were over, his souvenir a pair of bowed tendons. Yet he remained full of energy. Stuntman Danny Fisher bought him, trained him to fall, and renamed him Hot Rod. Fisher went on to teach Tap Canutt, a son of Yak Canutt, how to fall a horse, and Tap and Hot Rod paired up often, making their first appearance in *Hangman's Knot*, a 1952 movie starring Randolph Scott. In time, Hot Rod wound up being sold to Red Morgan, who also rode him for a number of years.

Another athletic horse was Chesterfield, owned by Danny Sands. The pair can be seen pulling off an intricate stunt in the 1948 movie *Red River*, the tale of a cattle drive along the Chisholm Trail, from Texas to Kansas. Stuntman Richard Farnsworth, doubling Montgomery Clift, is about to leap his horse over a barricade, jump off, and pull out his weapons when Sands falls Chesterfield directly in front of him. Before jumping over the barrier, Farnsworth's horse has to bound over Sands and Chesterfield. Those quick actions required of the stuntmen and their horses were extraordinary.

Bill Hart came along later with Tadpole, a reliable bay. Soon after arriving in Hollywood, Hart had the good fortune to meet Chuck Roberson, and he went on to marry Roberson's daughter, Charlene. The marriage came with a bonus: a guarantee that Hart's new father-in-law would teach him everything he knew. Hart worked on *Wanted Dead or Alive*, *Have Gun—Will Travel*, forty episodes of *Gunsmoke*, and he was cast as a regular on *Stoney Burke*, a rodeo series starring Jack Lord. Years later, in the mid-1960s, Hart loaned Tadpole out to work with Tap Canutt on the Lee Marvin movie *Cat Ballou*. Canutt needed a dependable falling horse for a scene in the film and had hoped to borrow Cocaine. But Coke was working on another film, so Roberson suggested Tadpole. On the way to location in Colorado, Tadpole went ballistic; he nearly demolished the inside of the trailer and came close to seriously injuring three other horses traveling with him. When they reached the set, wrangler Dick Webb tied the horse to a tree and tracked down Canutt to tell him his mount had arrived. But he warned Canutt that Tadpole was wound tight.

Canutt skipped lunch and went to check Tadpole out. "Expecting to see a red-eye creature with flames coming out of his mouth, I was a little surprised to find what appeared to be a reasonably sound bay horse," Canutt said. He led Tadpole around for a few minutes, then climbed into the saddle and rode him to a sandy area where the ground was soft. Canutt galloped the horse through the area once and then a second time. The third time through, "I snatched him," Canutt said. Tadpole sprang high into the air, lunging forward and high and rotating to the left. He landed on his hip, rolled completely over on his back, then stood up, uninjured and seemingly nonchalant. "I fell in love with this horse before he hit the ground," Canutt recalled. He went on to work with Tadpole many times over in the following years.

Stunt horses were usually geldings, but along with Jack Williams's Coco, stuntman David Wilding had a mare named Daisy. And Danny Fisher passed along to Tap Canutt a sorrel mare named L'Elegante. Canutt renamed her Gypsy and used her in a number of movies, including *The Last Command* (1955) and *Friendly Persuasion* (1956).

The roster of falling horses also included Baldy, a horse Frank McGrath partnered up with frequently, and Detonator, a thoroughbred gelding trained by Jim Burk. Burk was a teenager when he started training horses and entering rodeo contests. He got into stunt work with the help of his stepfather, Jimmy Loukes. Burk spent thirty years appearing in Westerns, including a dozen movies starring John Wayne, and for much of that time Detonator was right there with him.

There were Kilroy and Chug, a horse who carried out his assignments despite being blind in one eye, pot-bellied, and slower than a snail. Chug's cue to fall was not a jerk on the reins but an odd-sounding whistle emitted by his trainer, Fred Dingler. Upon hearing it, Chug would come to a sudden stop, fling his mane, drop to the ground, and play dead.

At the peak of the Western era, Hollywood had twenty-five to thirty good falling horses, fifteen or so that were truly outstanding, Roberson would later say. In hindsight's glare, the practice of cueing horses to fall is controversial. As author Jane Tompkins points out in her book *West of Everything: The Inner Life of Westerns*, horses do not perform willingly. "They have to be forced into it."

"When a man is literally in the saddle and the other animal is underneath bearing the weight, that is not a relationship among equals," Tompkins wrote. "When one being holds the reins attached to a bit in the other being's mouth, when the rider wears spurs that are meant to gore the sides of the mount to urge him to go faster, when the rider gives the commands and the horse carries them out, when the rider owns the horse, that is not a relationship among equals."

Tompkins noted something many audiences might not have realized: that the genre is "riddled with pain." Horses are goaded to cross fast-moving rivers, made to haul burdensome loads up steep banks, spurred to gallop beneath blazing suns, steered toward candy-glass windows, and expected to carry on as humans jump on and off them with no warning, she wrote. Rarely do they have any recourse but to execute their riders' commands.

Almost all of the falling horses' heroic stunts took place in the background, largely unnoticed by moviegoers except as a kind of violent backdrop that gave Westerns the air of danger and volatility that made them so popular. Westerns would have been nothing without the horses in them, but they seldom got the recognition they deserved.

Trainers would argue that horses can be taught to carry out stunts—that developing a horse's trust is far more valuable than instilling fear. In her book *Horses at Work: Harnessing Power in Industrial America*, author Ann Norton Greene wrote that horses aren't instinctively frightened of battle—conditions similar to stunt work—because they don't anticipate situations and react only when they encounter them. A horse might respond fearfully to a scenario or a noise or a smell it has been exposed to before and found frightening. But horses trained for war could be acclimated so they would not get spooked by the unexpected sights and sounds they might experience in combat. Afterward, when they would encounter trying conditions, they would rely on their trust in their rider, which was key.

A century earlier, horses in America endured far more wretched conditions. The 1846 drive across the West to take possession of upper California cost the lives of thousands of horses, some of whom became mad with thirst—edgy, volatile, and prone to galloping away—and were ultimately driven to their deaths across a landscape that was broiling in the daytime and bitterly cold at night.

During the Civil War, conditions were even worse. In 1861 the Union army procured nearly two hundred thousand horses and mules (a cross between a horse and donkey). Many never made it to their destination. Crowded into railroad cars, they would fall or get kicked, bitten, or trampled by other horses. Some of the boxcars were so inadequately ventilated that horses packed into them were smothered to death. Others traveled in railcars so unprotected from the cold that they died of exposure. The depots the trains stopped at seldom had corrals available to unload the horses, and at times they were kept in cars without food or water for days at a stretch. Conditions were no better on the ground. Horses were forced to march long distances in freezing weather with little food, regardless of wounds or illness. The roads they traveled were so primitive a horse might sink up to its knees in mud.

Horses put to service with the Confederate army faced especially brutal conditions. Bony and lethargic, their swollen withers running from open sores, those horses were often ridden until they collapsed. Author and historian Charles Francis Adams, a grandson of President John Quincy Adams, wrote: "The Air of Virginia is literally burdened today with the stench of dead horses, Federal and Confederate. You pass them on every road and find them in every field." Even mules, which were considered hardier than horses, were sometimes pressed forward until they keeled over and died. In the 1864 battle waged against the Navajos at Canyon de Chelly in present-day Arizona, horses and mules were so overtaxed that the body of one mule carrying an especially heavy load suddenly "split completely open."

American horses that escaped the horrors of war still led arduous lives. In the late 1800s and early 1900s, they provided much of the power required for everyday life. They pulled farm implements in the countryside and streetcars down city thoroughfares. They walked miles and miles on treadmills to enable farmers to thresh wheat, shell corn, grind flour, bale hay, and more. Horses consigned to those fates typically lasted three to five years before wearing out.

Horses even powered ferries and were forced to walk endlessly in small circles to turn the wheel on deck. The first commercially viable horse ferry began operating between Manhattan and Brooklyn in 1914. Powered by six to eight horses, it was big enough to ferry more than two hundred passengers across the East River in less than twenty minutes. It didn't take long for the horses supplying the power to grow dizzy or wash out. Once retired, some of them spent the rest of their days circling compulsively. British sociologist Harriet Martineau rode across the Hudson River to Albany, New York, on one of the first horse ferries and was appalled at the conditions the horses were driven to labor under. "The strongest horses, however kept up with corn, rarely survive a year of this work," she protested. Yet horse ferries continued to exist for many years.

By the mid-1950s there were just four million horses in the United States, a fraction of the thirty-four million that had existed during World War I. For urban Americans, horses had become a novelty, something to be seen only on the big screen. And in contrast to real-life horses, most of whom still toiled in the fields, movie horses appeared to have carefree, even glamorous, lives. Once cliff jumps and trip wires were abolished, movie horses appeared far better off than their workaday peers.

Other improvements began to emerge. For one thing, movie horses no longer had to walk from their stables to a film location, distances as far as thirty miles. Now they were hauled in trailers. For scenes that showed horses breaking down barn doors, busting through fences, or clearing an obstacle, studio carpenters began to use balsa wood, the kind of soft wood used in model airplanes that would fracture easily, avoiding injury. Sequences that showed horse-drawn wagons barreling along rutted trails and suddenly turning over underwent upgrades as well: a specially rigged device enabled the driver to release the horses from a wagon seconds before it upended, allowing them to escape the melee.

Several movies featured disturbing scenes that appeared to show a horse trapped in a bog or quicksand. To achieve that effect, movie crews would dig a pit with a tapered entrance and line it with wooden planks to keep the sides from caving in. Additional wooden planks would be placed at the bottom of the pit and covered with heavy matting to keep a horse from sinking in over its head. Before filling the pit with mud and topping it with peat moss to resemble a dense, oozing bog, the crew would lead a horse into the pit to demonstrate that the floor was solid and that he could be led into and out of it safely.

The 1965 movie *The Hallelujah Trail* shows a team of horses pulling a wagon that gets trapped in quicksand. Once the horses were driven onto the platform, the crew used winches to slowly lower it, making it look as if the horses and wagon were sinking. The whips used by the drivers to flagellate the horses were made of harmless cloth. In one scene, actress Lee Remick jabbed a horse with what looked like a hatpin, which was really a piece of dry spaghetti. To create a dust storm, the crew blew bentonite, a powder-like substance, in front of an enormous wind machine. Actual sand or dirt could have damaged the eyes of not just the actors but the animals too.

Stables around Hollywood began testing horses to make certain they could maintain an even temperament on location. It was especially important that a horse not panic at the sound of gunfire, a staple of Westerns. Stuntmen would acclimatize a horse by first firing a few blank shots several hundred feet away, then slowly moving in closer. Horses that could tolerate the popping sounds would be tested further. Early Westerns might show a gunman extending his arm straight out before taking aim, putting the muzzle directly over the horse's head. Now stunt performers began to protect horses' ears by packing them with cotton, and they used quarter-loads of gunpowder, just enough to create a flash; the sounds of gunfire could be magnified in the editing process. To make it appear as though they were firing black powder, wranglers greased the barrels of their guns with oil.

Many horses never did grow accustomed to the harsh sound of gunfire. Watching old Westerns, you can see them startle and panic, wheeling about in circles and looking for a fast way out as a barrel of shots rings out. Some horses could tolerate the noise at first only to eventually lose their nerve. One of Fat Jones's famous stallions, Steel, acquired an anxious twitch after too many guns were fired right next to his ears. He began tossing his head incessantly, a habit that doomed his movie career. Jones had him euthanized at the age of eighteen.

Too often in early Westerns, fights between horses were real and injurious. Now special effects crews found ways to minimize the chance of injury. When famous stallions Rex and Marky went head-to-head in the 1945 movie *Thunderhead, Son of Flicka* and the 1949 film *Sand*, crews bound their mouths shut using a special tape that didn't pull their hair. They covered the stallions' hooves with rubber slippers to lessen the impact of their kicks and pulled the horses apart when a fight got too out of hand. The camera operators "undercranked" their equipment, filming the action at a slower speed of sixteen to twenty frames a second. The fights looked more ferocious when the film was later accelerated to its normal speed. The precautions were necessary given that Rex and Marky genuinely detested one another. "Let them loose and they'd charge each other like two bull elephants," said Les Hilton, a trainer who studied under the legendary Jack "Swede" Lindell and had pulled off numerous stallion brawls.

Studios frequently used the same footage of fighting horses in subsequent movies. The Hal Roach Studios sold footage of Rex and Marky's first fight to other studios many times over for a fee of $6 a foot. Footage of horses fighting other animals was occasionally accomplished with split-screen filming. The star of the first *Red Stallion* movie was shown fighting a bear in one installment and an elk in another. In the bear scene, the horse was first filmed by itself, rearing up and swiping with its hooves. Camera operators then rewound the film and shot footage of a trained bear standing on its hind legs and swiping back. Several times a bear was seen pouncing on the horse, but it wasn't a real bear—it was stuntman Fred Kennedy in costume. The scenes involving an elk fighting with the horse were accomplished using a similar sleight of hand.

Mastering the split-screen effect required time and accuracy when it came to matching the animals up on film, and some filmmakers were more adept at achieving this than others. In the *Red Stallion* the horse is shown too far in the background—he looks unnaturally small juxtaposed against the elk. In scenes that depicted a dog being kicked by a horse and sent tumbling, filmmakers often used close-up shots and dummies. The horse's leg was often mechanical, shown kicking in close-ups with the help of a lever.

Because horses are notoriously skittish around snakes, snakes used in Westerns were also fake. Real snakes would be used for close-up shots, but if the horse was in the scene, too—especially if the horse was shown squashing the snake with its hoof—studios used mechanical rubber snakes sophisticated enough to slither and strike. The snakes even came with flickering tongues, made possible by the same mechanism that operates a clock. Whether the horses understood that the snakes were artificial is unclear.

Second unit directors came up with other clever ways to protect horses. In a memorable sequence in the 1943 film *My Friend Flicka*, a stunt double for Country Delight, the horse that portrays Flicka, appears to be severely injured after charging a barbed wire fence. In the film, Flicka is seen kicking madly at the fence even as the sharp barbs tear at her skin. To achieve that, crews substituted lengthy strands of narrow-gauge rubber to create the fence; they fashioned the barbs from harmless pieces of cork. Country Delight was given a few moments to familiarize herself with the faux fence, and after that, she was willing to charge it to get to her stablemate, who was waiting for her on the other side, out of camera range. Once that scene was shot, she lay down on cue and remained in place quietly while crew members entwined the fake barbed wire around her leg and dabbed a blood-colored substance on her coat. For the camera operator's sake, the crew filmed a strand of genuine barbed wire just above the horse's legs; the two shots were spliced together, along with sounds of a horse grunting, for realistic effect.

The second unit crew for 1949's *The Red Pony*, based on John Steinbeck's novella, pulled off a gruesome scene in which a boy's pony escapes the barn during a torrential rainstorm and develops strangles, a respiratory infection fatal to horses. The crew attached raw meat to the pony's sides and cued him to lie down, then had trained buzzards land on him and peck away at the meat. To the crew's amazement, the pony lay unfazed as the big birds carried out their assignment.

Horses often were expected to look frightened in Western movies—if, for example, they encountered a wild animal. Trainers could obtain the same expression by surprising the horse. To do that a trainer would wait until the horse was relaxed and then startle him with a sudden clattering noise. The horse would respond by raising his head, thrusting his ears forward, and widening his eyes.

Conscientious moviemakers used caution when filming unnatural combinations of animals. The 1952 movie *The Lion and the Horse* was a Warner Bros. B-Western about a cowboy who captures a wild stallion and sells it to a rodeo owner, only to steal the horse back when he learns it's being abused. A seal brown stallion named Supreme Wonder had the starring role as Wildlife in the film, which also featured a lion named Jackie. Jackie was considered gentle—if he was like most wild cats used in the movies, he would have been declawed and possibly defanged—but under ordinary circumstances the horse still would have been terrified to be around an animal that feral. To help Supreme Wonder overcome any fears, trainers housed him in a stall next to Jackie until the horse was deemed to be comfortable around the lion. In his book *Movie Horses*, author Anthony Amaral confidently states that Supreme Wonder "grew completely accustomed to his unusual neighbor," and maybe he did. But it didn't hurt that the film's location, in Mount Zion National Park outside Kanab, Utah, was at an elevation of 7,500 feet. The horses, including Supreme Wonder, were trucked there just in time to adjust to the change in altitude, but the wild animals, including Jackie, a crow called Jimmy, a squirrel named Nutcake, and a skunk dubbed One-Shot, experienced so much lethargy that they had to spend time in an oxygen tent. The climactic scenes where Wildlife fights Jackie were shot separately and edited together.

By the time he retired at the age of seventy-five, the AHA's Richard Craven had spent more than thirty years working on behalf of animals.

He had scrutinized hundreds of movies, and he genuinely believed that working conditions for animals were no longer an issue. In a story heralding his career, the *Los Angeles Times* declared that "the old days of expendable animals have gone forever." Craven's successor, Mel Morse, continued to spread that reassuring message. In a talk before the Humane Education League in LA, Morse said animal cruelty was portrayed in movies only to fit the storyline—that in reality animals were no longer handled roughly.

"Morse's humane rule is that no animal must ever be forced to do something not within his natural ability," *Good Housekeeping* magazine reported. "If an animal has to fight, jump or take a fall, it must be specially trained for the job."

Nevertheless, in many movies, horses were subjected to situations that could have frightened them badly. In one film, several horses were expected to leap over a barrier that had caught fire. The AHA required the barrier be split apart to give the horses space to jump between the sections and insisted that they be wetted down, particularly their manes and tails, before they made the jump. Even so, horses are naturally terrified of fire, and it's hard to believe they weren't petrified as they leapt across the shooting flames.

A scene in the 1945 movie *Thunderhead, Son of Flicka* was especially upsetting. Thunderhead, a white colt (played by nine different horses), is caught in a gully during a violent rain. As the water rises around him, he scrabbles frantically to climb the bank, but the soil keeps giving way. The sounds of pitiful whickering make the footage seem particularly alarming. It turns out the stormy scene was filmed inside a studio, on a set staged to look as if it was outdoors. The bank was made of a plaster mix while the bottom of the gully consisted of a thick padding covered with five inches of dirt. The rain came by way of overhead pipes that poured water down. The scene looked so authentic that moviegoers complained for years to Twentieth Century Fox about what seemed to them an obvious mistreatment of the colt. The studio reassured them that the scene was filmed on a soundstage "under very controlled—and safe—conditions." But the young horse wouldn't have known that. The distress he displayed seems disturbingly real.

A scene from the 1954 movie *Gypsy Colt*, about a treasured horse who must be taken from his young owner and sold, is equally disconcerting. The film traces the broken-hearted horse's escape from his new owners and his journey five hundred miles to return home. In one traumatic scene the star of the movie, Highland Dale (better known as the star of the television series *Fury*), appears on the verge of death, losing consciousness and collapsing in the desert. In another alarming scene the horse is chased by four motorcyclists across rock-strewn ground. Highland Dale's trainer, Ralph McCutcheon, spent three months priming the horse for those scenes, but it's difficult to imagine how easily he was able to tolerate being pursued through the desert by noisy bikes.

The 1950 movie *Francis the Talking Mule* involves the antics of a sardonic army mule and his young soldier friend Peter Stirling, played by Donald O'Connor. In a sarcastic twang perfected by character actor Chill Wills, Francis talks only to Peter, helping him out of various scrapes thanks to Francis's ability to overhear various strategies discussed by Peter's commanding officers. By the end of the movie Peter has no choice but to disclose that his consultant is none other than a mule.

Universal said the mule playing Francis was a female named Molly who had been purchased from a couple in Missouri for $350. The truth about her background was revealed decades later. Francis's real name was Judy, and the task of teaching her to "talk" rested with Les Hilton. He first tried giving Judy chewing tobacco to simulate talking. When that didn't work, he tried chewing gum, again to no avail. Finally Hilton came up with the idea of tying a nylon fish line to Judy's halter and running it under her top lip. Whenever the thread was pulled off-screen, she would curl her lips, appearing to speak. Hilton later used the same technique to get Mister Ed to look as if he was talking in the popular television series, which ran from 1958 to 1966.

There was nothing cruel about those practices. But the first *Francis* movie was such a hit that the studio called for a sequel, *Francis Goes to the Races*. Before filming could get underway, however, the studio decreed that Judy was overweight; she needed to drop 250 pounds. Her other trainer, Jimmy Phillips, thought up an unusual solution: he tied Judy to the rear of his station wagon and drove up and down the steep Hollywood Hills at fifteen miles an hour. Judy was forced to trot along behind him. She lost a hundred pounds in a week, but that wasn't enough. Phillips next cut back on her feed and replaced the filling oat hay he'd been feeding her with alfalfa. Desperate to get her to lose still more weight, Phillips also had a horse-sized sauna specially built for Judy, which sweated off another fifty pounds. Phillips pulled the mule along the Hollywood Hills for another week, but Judy had taken off all the weight she was going to. The studio gave up trying to get more pounds off her and took her as she was.

The job of the AHA's Mel Morse was to oversee the safety and well-being of some two thousand animal actors: monkeys, mules, lions, bears, wolves, llamas, camels, cats, water buffalo, skunks, panthers, chickens, cows, tigers, sheep, birds, elephants, and raccoons—but most of all horses, a thousand of them. Falling horses were the most specialized and the most valuable. They earned the most money—$300 to $500 a week on the job and $150 to $200 a week if they were undergoing training to learn a specific stunt and keeping them safe was critical. Any horse that was injured while falling would never be willing to fall again, "and that would be the end of the owner's bread and butter," Morse said.

13

Doubling for John Wayne

Stuntman Fred Kennedy had two reasons for getting hold of Roberson. First he wanted to apologize for setting Roberson up for that calamitous fall in *Rio Grande* three years earlier. Second he wanted to pass along some good news: John Wayne was about to star in a film called *Hondo*, and he needed Roberson and Cocaine to double for him and his horse.

Coke's recent performances dazzled Western moviemaking's tight-knit world. "You showed us all," Kennedy told Roberson. "It's my turn now to sit on the fence and watch you."

That's all Roberson needed to hear. He leapt at the chance to show off Coke's abilities, and getting hired for another John Wayne movie was an enormous coup. Audiences loved seeing Wayne's characters fight for their convictions. The cowboys he played all seemed to come from the same mold: they didn't go looking for conflict, but when they encountered it they didn't turn away. Wayne's characters embodied America's image of masculinity, a man capable and self-sufficient. Duke, as he was affectionately known, eschewed small talk, protected women and children, and did what he needed to do to see that justice was served. And he was brimming with charisma. Wayne had made it onto the Quigley poll of top ten film stars for three years running. He was so popular that at one point in 1949 eight different John Wayne movies—some of them re-releases—were showing in theaters across the United States. For Roberson, the opportunity to work alongside Wayne was a dream come true.

Hondo was set in the late 1800s and loosely based on *The Gift of Cochise*, a short story written by an up-and-coming writer named Louis L'Amour and published by Collier's magazine in 1952. Screenwriter James Edward

Grant had modified the plot somewhat; the movie version follows the tale of an embittered Indian scout for the U.S. Army Cavalry, Hondo Lane, who happens upon a woman and her young son fending for themselves in Apache country after the woman's husband deserted them during an Indian attack. Lane realizes that the man he killed a while back was the missing husband of the woman, Angie Lowe. Skirmishes flare up between the homesteaders, the cavalry, and the Apaches, and Lane tries to convince Angie to leave the territory. When she refuses to go, he stays behind long enough to develop a relationship with her and her son. The movie ends with the suggestion that Hondo, Angie, and the boy will journey on as a family to Hondo's ranch in California.

The role of Angie went to Geraldine Page, who was better known for her work in the theater. Ward Bond, one of Ford's favorites, played Lane's friend Buffalo Baker. The part of Lane's scraggly dog, Sam, was played by Pal, the son of the famous dog actor Lassie. To give him a bedraggled look, Pal's owner, Rudd Weatherwax, shaved the dog's coat, gave him a scruffy headpiece, and pasted a fake scar on his forehead.

Roberson took pains to make sure nothing would stand in the way of a stellar performance. Days before shooting, he secured the necessary vet checks, shots, and health certificate for Coke and trailered him just over a thousand miles from Los Angeles to Camargo, Mexico, a primitive town in the desert region just south of the U.S. border. Temperatures there hovered between 100 and 120 degrees, so hot that between scenes Weatherwax had to wrap Pal's paws with leather booties to keep them from getting burned.

Roberson would alternate doubling for Wayne with fellow stuntman Chuck Hayward. As a bonus, director John Farrow also gave Roberson bit parts as an Apache warrior and as a cavalry sergeant who is shot to death during an Indian attack. Roberson typically shied away from speaking roles—performing stunts was all he cared to do—but the extra pay didn't hurt. On top of that, he and Cocaine would handle almost all of the falling-horse scenes, with Roberson portraying both cowboys and Indians. Coke would need to be dyed different shades of brown and black to conceal the fact that the same horse was being used for so many roles.

Roberson and Coke were slated to perform the most perilous sequence in the movie, a sensational moment when Duke's character slides his horse into a shallow gully behind a rugged boulder to escape gunfire. The scene offered the perfect chance to showcase Coke's athleticism, and Roberson was eager to film it. His elation turned to dismay when he arrived on the set the morning of the shoot to discover that John Ford had flown down to watch the filming. Roberson hadn't seen Ford in the three years since *Rio Grande*, and the thought of having the surly director scrutinize him in the middle of a difficult stunt gripped him with apprehension.

"Why is Mr. Ford here?" Roberson asked fellow stuntman Frank McGrath.

"Are you kidding?" McGrath replied. "You get John Wayne and Ward Bond on a picture with Archie Stout on photography and Cliff Lyons doing second unit, and you've got most of the Old Man's company. He just come down to visit."

The next day, director Farrow decided to shoot the gully scene first to get it out of the way. Once Roberson, doubling Wayne, skidded Coke into the ravine, Duke's character was to resurface and start shooting at Apaches. Dressed identically to Wayne in cuffed pants, a brown shirt, a blue bandana around his neck, and a light tan hat, Roberson rode Coke over to inspect the gully. Its walls were narrow, and with Wayne hunkered against the back side of the boulder, waiting to leap up, there was almost no room left for Roberson to scramble out of the way once Coke executed his fall. Roberson was still strategizing how to pull off the slide when Farrow called out to him.

"Are you ready now?" the director asked.

"Sure enough," Roberson replied. He sized up the ravine once more before he and Coke trotted out of camera range. From a distance he heard the director reminding Wayne that he needed to move quickly once the fall took place. "As soon as he hits you, come up shooting," Farrow called out to him. "It has to look as though you pull the horse down and run up in one continuous motion."

Roberson glanced over at Ford. The director was slouched in his seat, watching. Roberson felt as though his entire career was at stake depending on what happened next. A thread of apprehension sank deep into his chest. "It's gonna be close," he murmured to Cocaine. "You land on me, old timer, and I'm out of the picture, and that old man's gonna classify me as a permanent ass."

Farrow called for quiet on the set and then yelled, "Roll 'em! Action!"

8. Film director John Ford (*seated right*) with character actor Harry "Dobie" Carey (*top left*) and legendary stuntman Yak Canutt (*behind right*). Photofest.

At the sound of his words, Cocaine stiffened. Roberson tipped forward in the saddle, and the horse burst into a gallop. The pair streaked toward the chasm, where Wayne was crouched behind the craggy wall. The instant they reached the outer edge of the ravine, Roberson leaned back and pulled Coke's head to the right with as much strength as he could muster, and together he and Coke skidded past a bare tree and a small shrub and disappeared from sight into the ravine. A half second later Coke's head appeared and then disappeared again, then his tail flashed into view. Right on cue, Wayne shot up over the edge of the gully as if he, and not Roberson, had been riding the horse. Wayne aimed his rifle at the enemy and began shooting.

The scene was over in a flash, but it added the jolt of adrenaline Farrow was hoping to inject. Coke had come through. There was only one hitch: the gully was so narrow that Roberson was unable to hoist his left stirrup out of the path of Coke's fall. The horse's 1,200 pounds landed on top of Roberson's ankle, and the second it did so he felt it shatter.

Oblivious to the mishap, Coke stood and sidled away a few yards, his task completed. Roberson remained hidden behind the boulder until he heard Farrow yell, "Cut!" As the crew applauded Cocaine's feat, Roberson staggered out of the camera's range, his throbbing ankle inflating inside his boot. No one seemed to notice his limp.

"How was that?" Roberson asked.

"Beautiful! Marvelous!" Farrow exclaimed. "What a fall. I've never seen anything like it."

Wayne clapped Roberson on the back. "That horse of yours is really something. One minute I think he's going to run over the top of me, and the next minute he's breathing down my boots."

Wracked with pain but ever the professional, Roberson asked the director, "You need to see it again, Mr. Farrow?"

"How could it be better?" Farrow said. The stunt was over and done. Relieved, Roberson hobbled behind a clump of sagebrush and collapsed. For weeks afterward, he wrapped the top of his short boot around his ankle and kept working. Together he and Cocaine performed nearly every fall that took place, on the side of the cavalry and as Indians too. Roberson rested only on weekends; while his fellow stuntmen partied the hours away in Camargo, he lay in bed in his tent, his ankle bolstered by pillows.

He still caroused during the week, however. The quid pro quo for working with Wayne was that stuntmen and extras were expected to be available every night to knock back a few, play a round of cards, and engage in the kind of sophomoric hijinks Wayne enjoyed. At one memorable gathering, animal trainer Rudd Weatherwax wagered his dog Pal in a poker match and lost him to Roberson. Roberson collected an IOU for the dog. An hour after that, he won another IOU from cameraman Archie Stout for $1,200. By noon the following day Roberson was up by nearly $5,000. But then Wayne pulled up a chair, and Roberson's winnings quickly disappeared.

After another late night of gambling, Roberson stumbled onto the set one morning feeling groggy and dense and thoroughly unprepared for the day's assignment. Ford and second unit director Cliff Lyons wanted Roberson and Cocaine to double Wayne and his horse in a barnyard scene where Wayne's character saddles up an untamed bronc that proceeds to buck his way around the corral, trying to throw him off. Coke's role was to play the part of the uncontrollable horse, a young steed unaccustomed to the feel of a halter around his face and the sensation of a saddle on his back. Roberson could have taken his chances with a genuinely wild horse, but he was confident Cocaine could pull off the part.

In the first take, Roberson cued Coke to rear up on his hind legs; the sounds of indignant snorts would be dubbed in later. For the bucking scenes, Roberson tightened a thin, stiff strap around Coke's flanks, a time-honored rodeo practice designed to make horses buck. Roberson signaled to Cocaine to stretch out on his side while he clutched the straps controlling the buck strap. When Lyons gave the cue, Roberson yanked tightly. The horse unfurled beneath him like coiled metal, surging with desire to escape from the strap. Each time Coke thrust out his hind legs, Roberson prodded him with his spurs, and each time Coke lurched backward, the stuntman ran the spurs down his sides. Over and around they went, orbiting about the corral once and then a second time. "The fact that the horse was broke already would make no difference; as long as that bucking strap stayed tight around his flanks, he would give me the ride of my life," Roberson said. Finally he latched onto a post and hauled himself out of the saddle, loosening the strap as he sprang. Coke had delivered the excitement the director was looking for. Lyons spent another hour capturing close-ups of Wayne riding the horse that now appeared to be broken.

Roberson and Coke spent three months in Mexico filming *Hondo*. Afterward they headed back to California. Roberson moved out of his rental house and into one in nearby Ventura. His new place was idyllic with one exception: it lacked any room for Cocaine and Coco, whom Roberson was keeping for Jack Williams. Roberson boarded the horses instead at the Ride-A-While stable run by L.C. Goss in Griffith Park. Miles of trails crisscrossed the 4,310-acre park, and horseback riding there was a popular pastime, but it's doubtful Goss rented Cocaine and Coco out to park-goers. In exchange for boarding, Goss charged Roberson 10 percent of each horse's earnings.

Roberson missed having the horses in his own backyard. Working with Coco and Cocaine each day kept them up to date on their tricks, and brushing them down afterward helped him maintain a connection with the pair. Just hearing them nicker in the pasture behind his house was a source of pleasure. Roberson later admitted that being apart from the horses must have driven him a little crazy; the day after dropping them off he married his latest girlfriend, a woman identified only as Gail. The relationship didn't last. His first marriage had ended in divorce, and this one would too.

At least his ankle was mostly healed. He and Cocaine returned to work. They performed stunts in 1954's *The Far Country*, starring Jimmy Stewart as an adventuresome cowboy who battles a dishonest lawman during a cattle drive. Next up was *The Lone Gun* with George Montgomery, about a cowboy who clashes with desperados for the hand of a rancher's daughter.

Not long after Roberson moved to the beach, stuntman Jerry Brown asked him to be a part of a benefit for orphans scheduled to take place at Devonshire Downs. Roberson had just put in six weeks of hard work. He was in no mood to haul Cocaine to a non-paying demonstration for some do-good cause. But his new bride, Gail, convinced him to take part. "Since *Hondo* was released," she told him, "*everybody* wants to see that horse."

Devonshire Downs was a horse-racing track and event facility in Northridge, California, twenty-three miles north of Hollywood. The Downs is best known for hosting the legendary three-day Newport Pop Festival in the summer of 1969, which featured the likes of Jimi Hendrix, Joe Cocker, Jethro Tull, and other famous rock bands. The racetrack and facility have since been torn down, and the property is now the site of California State University's north campus.

The benefit took place on a Sunday morning. Roberson swung by Jack Williams's place to pick him up, then drove to Goss's stables to load Cocaine and Coco into his trailer. Williams felt so strongly about Coco that Roberson couldn't help but try to have some fun with him. Chatting with Goss before retrieving their horses, Roberson and Williams watched incredulously as a heavyset customer zigzagged out toward a trail on a horse. "You should see the damned fools that ride out of here," said Goss, who was in on the joke. "Why, Jackie, you wouldn't believe what rode out on Coco this morning."

Williams whipped back at him with alarm. "Where is Coco?" he demanded.

"I rented her out about three hours ago," Goss said. "Chuck said I could do what I wanted with her when y'all wasn't using her."

Williams was beside himself. He teetered over to a fence and appeared to be fighting back tears. "I don't consider this the least bit humorous," he huffed when he found out he'd been had.

When they got to the arena, Roberson was surprised to see throngs of attendees crammed into the stands and local TV station cameras set up all along the track. A young starlet named Kim Novak was acting as emcee. Early on in the program Roberson and Williams enacted a realistic-looking brawl, which was a big hit with the crowd. The horse falls occurred later in the day, and by the time they did, Roberson's grumpy mood had disappeared. The event was giving him a chance to show off Cocaine, an opportunity he wasn't about to turn down.

Jerry Brown was also demonstrating falls with his namesake. Roberson's mishap with that horse on the set of *Rio Grande* was forever seared in his memory, but everyone else had forgotten the incident apparently. To the cowboys watching from the sidelines, Jerry Brown Falling Horse had no equal.

"Best damned falling horse around," Roberson heard one of them say.

"Never be another one like him, that's for sure."

"Yep. Best horse in the world, Jerry Brown."

Roberson couldn't believe what he was hearing. Had none of these bozos gotten word of Cocaine's exploits? He'd show them. He was mounted and ready to go when Kim Novak announced over the loudspeaker, "And now let's hear it for Chuck Roberson and his horse, Cocaine." It wasn't enough to prove the naysayers wrong. Roberson wanted to gig them a little first. He turned to the wranglers and said, "You think Jerry Brown is something. Just wait till you assholes see this!" To his colleague Jerry Brown, Roberson said, "I'm gonna show you how to fall." He dug his spurs into Cocaine and galloped him as hard as he could to the front of the speaker's stage.

"Come on, Coke, make it a good one," Roberson murmured and tugged his reins to the right. Coke thundered into the air and plunged to the ground, landing with a thud on his left shoulder. The audience let out a collective moan, certain the fall had seriously injured the horse. Only when Coke picked himself up and shook the dust off his coat did the spectators realize the fall was not an accident but instead an expertly carried-out stunt. The crowd clapped wildly, and it was all Roberson could do not to thumb his nose at the doubters on the sidelines.

Roberson steered Coke to the edge of the arena and turned to watch as stuntman Jerry Brown rode his horse toward the center. The horse stumbled slightly before going down; his fall wasn't nearly as fast and smooth as Cocaine's. And for some reason Brown was unable to lift his stirrup high enough to pull his leg out of the way. The weight of the horse collapsing on top of him crushed Brown's leg. EMTs rushed over to hoist him onto a stretcher.

Waiting for the ambulance, Brown glanced up at Roberson and Williams with a rueful grin. "I had a good job starting next week too," he said. "Stood to make 6,000 bucks, damn it." He told Williams he would recommend him for the job instead. "We kind of look alike, and if that Coco is anything close to Cocaine . . ." Brown's voice trailed off.

Roberson could have kicked himself. Mocking Brown to his face had been a mistake. If Roberson had kept his thoughts to himself, Brown might have recommended him for the job instead of Williams. "Me and my big mouth. Sorry, Jerry," Roberson told Brown.

"That's okay," Brown said. "You know, I figured that if you hadn't made such an ass out of yourself on my horse, you wouldn't be here right now."

Roberson was preparing to trailer Cocaine and Coco back up for the ride home when he realized that an awards show was about to get underway. Three years earlier, the American Humane Association had begun honoring animal actors with Picture Animal Top Star of the Year (PATSY) awards. PATSYs were highly sought after. Chosen by some 1,500 movie editors, critics, and columnists, they were considered the Academy Awards for animal performers, the closest a nonhuman could come to getting official recognition of their exploits aside from the rare hoof or paw print on Hollywood Boulevard accorded the best-known animal stars. The first ceremony, hosted by actor Ronald Reagan, honored Judy, the star of *Francis the Talking Mule*. Separate awards were given to a distinguished dog, a horse, a wild animal, and to animals lumped into a special category that included house cats, ravens, and goats. The awards came in the form of an Oscar-like statuette.

To some, the prizes seemed aimed more at the owners and trainers than the actual recipients. "I don't intend being critical, but it does seem to me that the animal winner might be better satisfied if they received a peck of oats, a well-turned banana, dog biscuits or a hunk of raw beef," columnist Merle Potter wrote. But animal trainers coveted the recognition.

In addition to the PATSY awards, awards of excellence were also handed out, along with a Craven Award in honor of AHA director Craven. That award was set aside for stunt animals who excelled in training, jumping, falling, rearing, or fighting, and they usually went to horses. Animals considered for the award had to have been trained and handled in ways that met the AHA's approval. Jerry Brown Falling Horse won the first Craven Award in 1951. Smoky, a horse owned and trained by Fat Jones, won the second award in 1952. The following year's award went to Bracket, a horse owned by the Hudkins stables.

To Roberson's surprise, the voice on the loudspeaker declared Cocaine the new winner of the Richard C. Craven Award for best performance by a stunt horse. The award meant nothing to Cocaine, of course, but Roberson was flushed with pride. That night in his house by the sea, he hung the large plaque signifying the win on his mantel, next to a photo of Wayne. There was no question now. He and Cocaine had officially made it.

14

The Searchers

The drive from Los Angeles to Monument Valley, Utah, took roughly ten hours, the majority of it along colorful Route 66 to Flagstaff, Arizona, followed by a long stretch of gravel and dirt; for Cocaine, 637 miles in all that meant shifting constantly inside a narrow trailer to withstand the endless bumps and turns, breathing in the dust kicked up from the tires, and enduring the heat of the sun beating down on the trailer's hard metal roof. Cocaine was on his way to the set of another John Ford Western.

Roberson had to credit Cocaine for getting cast in *The Searchers*. Thanks to Coke's show-stopping performance in *Hondo*, Roberson was finally able to redeem himself in Ford's eyes, and the director was ready to give him another try. Cowboy stunt performers had little chance to achieve fame, and appearing in a John Ford Western was the next best thing to having their names splashed across a theater marquee. Ford's movies were almost always box-office hits, and finding a place in his inner circle—his stock company—usually translated into steady employment, a rarity in the film industry.

Roberson had already won over John Wayne, who asked for him and Cocaine often. Roberson was sixty-three and a half inches tall and weighed 225 pounds—a half inch shorter and fifteen pounds lighter than Wayne. Roberson's hair was slightly darker and curlier than Wayne's, and in later years the stuntman would wear padding to match Wayne's girth. But the physical resemblance was so close and Roberson could imitate Wayne's stand and pigeon-toed walk so precisely that directors sometimes used him in group scenes and distance shots. Whenever a studio made a pair of boots for Wayne, they made an identical pair for Roberson also. Wayne grew to like and depend on Roberson to the point that when director John Farrow neglected to cast Roberson in one of Wayne's movies, Wayne never worked with Farrow again.

Roberson repaid the loyalty. He defended Wayne against critics who claimed the star wasn't much of a natural horseman. Wayne didn't particularly like horses, but "the Duke will ride anywhere, and he can do most anything any stuntman can do," Roberson insisted. With a star of that magnitude, he added, it just made sense to use stuntmen. "If we get hurt, they can get another guy," Roberson said. "If the Duke gets hurt, you've got maybe a three or four million dollar investment in film going down the drain."

The Searchers' story revolves around John Wayne's character, Ethan Edwards, who has barely returned home to Texas after the Civil War when his brother's family is killed by Comanche Indians. Edwards sets out to find his two nieces who were kidnapped, Lucy and Debbie, and bring them back home. Lucy turns up dead, so Ethan focuses his search on locating Debbie, played by Natalie Wood. Her adopted brother, Martin Pawley, joins Ethan in the hunt to track her down. Their journey takes years, and as time passes Martin discovers that Edwards's animosity toward the Comanches has poisoned his feelings toward his "tainted" niece. It becomes apparent that instead of saving Debbie, Ethan plans to kill her.

No other director could tell this story better than Ford. Reared in Portland, Maine, Ford moved to Hollywood with his brother, Francis, in 1914, when he was twenty years old and movies were still in their infancy. Ford quickly developed a passion for both the glamour of the business and the frenetic pace of filming. He performed as a stunt double for Francis before working his way up to assistant director at Universal. Part of his job was to oversee extras, including the wranglers whose rough livelihoods so captivated him. Along the way he also learned how to work a movie camera and various other skills, including how to detonate explosives and orchestrate horse falls using Running W's.

Early on, Ford shared a room at the Virginia Apartments with Hoot Gibson, a future star who was also new to Hollywood. Gibson was a bit player for Universal; he earned $2.50 each time he fell backward off a horse and $5.00 for getting shot out of a saddle. Enamored by Gibson's exploits, Ford bought his own saddle horse, which he dubbed Woodrow, presumably after then-president Woodrow Wilson, and began partnering with actor Harry Carey Sr. to create a progression of short, two-reel Westerns. The two-reelers took five days, six at the most, to produce. Cast and crew would ride their horses out to a location, film until the sun set, camp out in sleeping bags, and ride back to Hollywood when the picture was finished. Ford shot one two-reeler in two days, so hastily that Gibson and Carey never even bothered to dismount.

Everything about Westerns appealed to Ford, even the backstories of the out-of-work cowhands who had migrated to California to find work in films. He shared the same philosophy about the American West as historians who saw the acquisition of the sprawling landscape as an integral part of the country's fabled belief in manifest destiny. Western movies, filled with conflict and scope, depicted that creation myth better than anything, Ford believed. Audiences liked the fact that Western heroes lived uncomplicated lives; their stories offered city dwellers a temporary escape from their congested environments.

To Ford, the majesty of the western landscape was matched only by the beauty and grace depicted by horses galloping across the screen. "A running horse remains the finest subject for a motion picture camera," he said. "Is there anything more beautiful than a long shot of a man riding a horse well, or a horse racing free across a plain?"

His admiration of horses didn't necessarily mean he treated them well, however. In fact, Ford's cavalier attitude occasionally bordered on outright cruelty, at least at the start of his career. In one early film, he ordered Gibson to gallop his horse into a river whose waters were high enough to reach the horse's chest. To keep the horse from panicking when they reached the deepest section of the river, Gibson slowed his pace and turned the animal at an angle. Ford was livid. "What's the matter? You yellow?" he shouted. He ordered Gibson to bring the horse ashore, whereupon Ford climbed up on the horse himself and ran him straight into the water. Frantic, the horse reared up and fell backward on top of him. Gibson had to wade in and haul Ford out.

A more disturbing incident occurred in the winter of 1926. Ford was shooting *3 Bad Men*, starring George O'Brien and Olive Borden. The film was the tale of three outlaws rescuing a young girl whose father was killed during the Gold Rush of the 1870s. The outdoor scenes were shot in Jackson Hole, Wyoming, and temperatures there were frigid; the Teton Mountains looming in the distance were blanketed with snow. One scene called for the stuntmen doubling the desperados to swim their horses across nearby Jenny Lake, which was clogged with ice. One of the stuntmen, Pardner Jones, was too intimidated to admit that he had no idea how to swim. He asked actor George O'Brien to watch out for him as he crossed the lake.

Jones's fears were well-founded. The water was so numbingly cold that shortly after wading in, his horse fell behind the rest of the herd and began to thrash about. Suddenly the horse went under. Desperate, Jones hollered for help. O'Brien started to race into the water after him, but Ford stopped him. "I told you I don't need a lifeguard," he said with a grin.

Jones's horse surfaced for a moment only to disappear underwater a second time. By then, Jones had floated out of the saddle, and in his panic the horse accidentally kicked him in the head, knocking him unconscious. Only then did Ford allow O'Brien to plunge into the bone-chilling waters to save the stuntman. And only after the camera operators nailed the dramatic footage Ford desired did he give the go-ahead to try to save the horse. By now, though, the horse had flung himself upside down; his reins were entangled around his forelegs. Ford's brother Eddie O'Fearna and O'Brien made their way to the horse, ran a line of rope in behind his bit, and pulled him to shore, but it was too late. The horse had drowned.

Though he professed to like horses, Ford was never much of a horseman himself. Actor and stuntman Ben Johnson once said the director looked like "a sack of walnuts" in the saddle. But Ford didn't need to know how to ride a horse in order to capture one on film, and the movie industry overlooked his recklessness where animals were concerned. To Hollywood, Ford was a savior. After nosediving in popularity, Westerns enjoyed a resurgence in the late 1930s, when more sophisticated cameras and sharper sound capabilities made it possible to film outdoors once more. Ford took advantage of the new technology by going on location to make his 1939 movie *Stagecoach*. It starred a young John Wayne, featured a series of thrilling shootouts, and almost single-handedly resuscitated the Western genre.

Coming out of the Great Depression but with tensions growing around the globe, Americans were embracing their nation's bold history and yearned to see it captured on film. All of that fueled a comeback for

Western movies, and *Stagecoach* was one of the first out of the chute. Over the next decade, starring roles in 1948's *Red River* and John Ford's trilogy of movies about the cavalry—*Fort Apache* (1948), *She Wore a Yellow Ribbon* (1949), and 1950's *Rio Grande*—would secure Wayne's status as a bona fide leading man.

From the 1940s on, Westerns were as much in demand as ever. The time-honored cowboys-versus-Indians formula offered a reassuring contrast to the real-life Cold War that was escalating between the United States and the Soviet Union. Westerns portrayed America as an accomplished nation whose values were built on principled conviction and hardy independence. And because of their widespread appeal, Westerns offered a sure way for movie studios to make money. By the time filming for *The Searchers* got underway, nearly a third of the movies produced by the major studios and half of those generated by independent outfits were Westerns.

In the spring of 1955, Ford and a camera crew spent four days shooting snowy scenes for *The Searchers* in Alberta, Canada, and Gunnison, Colorado, depicting an Indian village obliterated in a raid by Custer's cavalry. One scene called for the cavalrymen and the Indians to cross a bitingly cold stream on horseback. Ford wanted the footage to convey the frozen temperatures. "If possible," the director wrote in his notes, "let's try to get the horses blowing vapor from their nostrils." It's conceivable he recruited horses from the area who would have been acclimated to the frigid March temperatures, but the horses shot in those scenes don't appear to have thick coats. If they were trailered in from LA, where they were accustomed to balmy temperatures, the freezing water would have chilled them through.

In mid-June, Ford shifted the filming to Monument Valley. Hidden away in the southeast corner of the Navajo Indian reservation, it's one of the most striking landscapes in America: a stunning tableau of orange and red sandstone mesas and obelisks offering every possible type of landscape a director could hope to find—rivers, mountains, and plains amid a stark desert backdrop. *The Searchers* was the fifth of Ford's movies to be filmed at or to feature exterior scenes from that far-flung locale. He likened the location to a Charles M. Russell painting, one that captured the West as no other setting could.

"I have been all over the world, but I consider this the most complete, beautiful and peaceful place on earth," Ford said.

The aura of authenticity came with a price. The valley was so inaccessible and primitive that it felt like a third-world country. There was no electricity or public water. The only thing remotely close to a telephone was a short-wave radio, and the only way to get the valley was by way of a partially paved road. Construction crews headed in first with nearly two dozen trucks and bulldozers used to flatten the valley floor. Workers reactivated an old well to generate a water supply, assembled enough canvas tents to house three hundred cast and crew, and built a mess hall big enough to also store the ice and food that arrived each day from Monticello, Utah. Corrals were built to hold the horses. Next to the tent village was a rudimentary airport used to fly in the director and his top stars and deliver film footage to Flagstaff each afternoon. The movie reels would be forwarded on to Los Angeles via the evening train.

The cost of transporting the director, the cast, the camera- and soundmen, the support crew, wardrobe designers, and all the extras—the food and equipment alone ran $500,000, which is $5.7 million in today's dollars—all of it necessary to capture the valley's singular ambiance, as far as Ford was concerned. Ford and most of his crew traveled most of the way there on the Santa Fe railroad's Super Chief train, complete with a diesel locomotive painted cherry red and trimmed in yellow and black, the colors of an Indian war bonnet. The entourage boarded at Union Station in LA in the evening and rode all night to Flagstaff. The next day Ford and his son Pat, the film's associate producer, flew in a small plane the remainder of the way to Monument Valley. For Cocaine and the other stunt horses, the trip was more arduous.

Roberson found the scenery as colorful, expansive, and breathtaking as Ford had promised, but at an elevation of 5,200 feet, Monument Valley was steamy by day and downright frosty by night. Ford had hoped to avoid the hottest time of year, mid- to late summer, by filming in June, when temperatures were supposed to be in the upper eighties. Instead the mercury inched past a hundred degrees most days, and a constant wind blew red dust into everyone and everything: cameras, extras, and horses.

Rain would have cooled things off but also disrupted the shoot. To keep precipitation at bay, Harry Goulding, the proprietor of the only motel in the valley, offered up the services of a Navajo medicine man named Hosteen Tso. By late afternoon each day, Ford would tell Tso the kind of weather he was looking for and Tso would "fix it up" for the next day. Ford first tested Tso's mystical talent during the filming of *Stagecoach* and had relied on him from then on. Goulding would bring Tso around to see Ford each afternoon, whereupon Ford would give the elderly man a drink of whiskey and $15. The director swore that Tso always came through; he kept the thunderstorms away. But there was nothing he could do about the high temperatures.

Roberson had no complaints. Finally he had achieved entrée into John Ford's stock company, the loose band of character actors, cowboys, and stuntmen who regularly appeared in Ford's films. When it came to a Ford movie, actors and stunt people did not ask for a role directly the way they would with most casting directors. They had to visit Ford personally, hat in hand. "When word got out that the Old Man was going to start a picture, you simply went over to the office for a visit, and he'd tell you whether you were in it or not," Dobie Carey said. Once Ford accepted an actor or a stunt performer, though, he nearly always found a way to work them into future films.

Having performed some stunt work himself early in his career, Ford had a special place in his heart for stuntmen and wranglers; he saw them as congenial performers, men and women who carried out their assignments without complaint. "They're a wonderful, kindly, gentle group of people," he said. "They're charitable, they're patriotic, and they're easy to work with."

That said, Ford had his quirks. Belonging to his stock company meant adhering to a roster of nonnegotiable rules. Once filming started, everyone down to the extras was on call from the minute Ford awoke until he called it a night. He drove cast and crew hard and tolerated no carping from any corner. And unlike Wayne, who welcomed carousing at day's end during a shoot, Ford banned workers from drinking away their aches. Ford was an alcoholic, but he didn't imbibe on the set, and he forbade everyone else from doing so altogether. If, the following morning, he found out an actor was suffering from a hangover, he would worsen the agony by making that person stand in the sun for hours at a stretch.

Despite Ford's strict rules, hijinks were common. During a break on the set of one movie, Roberson had crawled under a prop truck to take a quick nap when Ford passed by, spied the stuntman's boots sticking out, and sensed an opportunity. Ford had another stuntman tie one end of a twenty-foot-long wire to Roberson's right spur and the other end of the wire to the truck. Then he had another crew member rap on the truck and holler, "Bad Chuck—get up! Mr. Ford wants you right away!"

Roberson scrabbled out from beneath the truck and raced off—as far as the wire would let him. When he stopped suddenly, he fell flat on his face, bloodying his nose and nearly tearing his right hip out of the socket. He'd been trip-wired.

"Helluva good fall," Ford declared.

Newcomers learned that Ford liked spontaneity, and to accomplish that he frequently gave deliberately muddled instructions to the cast. Stuntman Chuck Hayward recalled how more than once, Ford, speaking to wranglers about a particular scene, would let his voice trickle off to the point of near inaudibility. "He'd head back to the camera still talking," Hayward said. "He did that on purpose, because he didn't intend that we know exactly what we were going to do. He wanted action that wasn't rehearsed."

In his biography of Ford, filmmaker and historian Peter Bogdanovich said Ford exploited cast members' fear of him as a means of bringing out their best performances. In the first take or two of a scene, "there's a sparkle, an uncertainty about it; they're not sure of their lines, and it gives you a sense of nervousness and suspense," Ford said. He was strongly opposed to rehearsing action sequences, that to do so "looks phony." The rougher the action, the better. If an actor or a horse fell accidentally, their mishap added a touch of authenticity. As screenwriter Frank S. Nugent said of Ford, "When his Redskins bite the dust, he expects to hear the thud and see the dirt spurt up."

Yet despite his chips-fall strategy, there were few accidents on the set of a Ford movie, and that's because he planned his sequences thoroughly. He spent months orchestrating his shots. Where some directors instructed their camera crews to shoot a given scene a dozen times or more, Ford was usually able to capture a scene in one take, at most two. He avoided close-ups, which would have required still more takes. He liked to let the cadence of a scene unfurl without any interruption. The result was less repeat action on the part of the stuntmen and consequently less stress on the horses.

The Searchers reunited Roberson and Cocaine with Chuck Hayward and his horse Twinkle Toes for the first time in three years. To avoid confusing the two men, Ford nicknamed Roberson "Bad Chuck"; Hayward was dubbed "Good Chuck" by default. Roberson just looked like trouble—the fun kind. He earned his sobriquet early on during the shoot when he enticed into his tent a young woman who made so much noise that by morning, word of their coupling had spread up the hill to Goulding's lodge. "I guess you had an exciting time last night," Ford told Roberson. "Next time get a quiet girl. You kept the whole camp awake."

"Hayward didn't do too badly with the girlies, either, but Ford had them labeled, so that was that," Dobie Carey said. "Besides, their looks fit their label. Roberson had a devil-may-care way about him that Ford loved. . . . Hayward was more reserved, with a quiet humor." Roberson didn't chase women, but he liked them, Charlene Roberson said. When an acquaintance once asked her if she was his wife, Charlene replied, "No, I'm too old to be his wife. I'm his daughter."

With his six-foot-four frame, his dark, curly hair, his square jaw, and his rakish demeanor, Roberson's appearance could not have contrasted more sharply with the slight but muscular Hayward. But their backgrounds and skills—as well as the talents of their stunt horses—were remarkably similar. Roberson would also play two roles in *The Searchers*: as an Apache warrior named Kloori and as a cavalry sergeant killed in an Indian attack.

Cocaine and Twinkle Toes played even more pivotal roles. Soon after Wayne's character, Ethan, arrives at his brother's house, a band of Texas Rangers gallops onto the homestead, apprehensive about Comanche raiders and the uprisings they've heard are taking place. Someone has stolen cattle from the Lars Jorgensen ranch nearby, and the Rangers intend to track down the thieves. Ethan and Debbie's adopted brother, Martin, join the posse, and forty miles out they discover Jorgensen's cattle, slaughtered senselessly. Ethan tells the men they've been duped, sidetracked into looking for the cattle so the Comanches could raid the now-defenseless homesteads.

Riding back to his brother's house, Ethan discovers the bodies of Aaron, Martha, and Ben and what's left of their scorched home. Nieces Lucy and Debbie are nowhere to be found. Ethan joins the reassembled rangers to hunt down the Comanches. The following day, the Indians zero in on the rangers, one contingent approaching from a high sandy ridge and another from the valley floor. They flank the rangers on either side.

The sequence that follows is electrifying. The captain of the rangers, the Reverend Captain Samuel Johnson Clayton, played by Ward Bond, gives the command to try to outrun the Indians, and they're off, John Wayne racing Cocaine across the desert alongside Bond, a half dozen Rangers trailing them. Chasing from behind are two dozen shouting Indians. The Rangers hurtle their horses to the San Juan River and without any hesitation plunge them into the swift-moving water to try to escape their pursuers.

The actors and stuntmen cast in those roles were instructed to ford the river with determination and drive, but no one had expected the water's current to be so powerful. The swift water came as high as the horses' thighs and nearly carried several of them away.

Those scenes were edited out of the movie, but they're included in *A Turning of the Earth*, a documentary about *The Searchers*. The outtakes show Wayne tumbling off of Cocaine and Cocaine faltering immediately afterward. As Coke clambers to right himself, Wayne dangles halfway out of the saddle, clinging to his mount.

Undaunted by the conditions, Ford stopped filming and instructed the riders to return to the shore and try again. The second attempt to ford the river wasn't any easier. As the cast of rangers neared land on the other side, the black horse carrying Ward Bond stumbled into the water and keeled over, landing nearly on top of him. The cameras kept rolling as Bond scrambled back onto his feet and grasped the horse's bridle to pull him along. The other horses sprinted past them on either side, and the horse Bond was riding laid his ears back with apprehension as the actor tugged him toward shore.

Ford kept Bond's accidental horse fall in the footage. But the fast-moving water posed too many risks—even he could see that. It bothered Ford that, amid the jostling, Roberson, portraying one of the rangers, had dropped a cherished possession, a century-old rifle the stuntman considered priceless. The water's current was so strong that instead of sinking to the bottom of the river, the rifle quickly vanished downstream. On top of that cast, crew, and horses had spent nearly nine hours filming in temperatures that topped out at nearly 120 degrees. The oppressive heat wasn't so intolerable for the humans and animals who charged in and out of the San Juan River all day; the water kept them mercifully cool. But the workers stuck on land were wilting, and Ford wanted to ease their suffering.

Relocating meant repositioning a complex collection of camera equipment. Cinematographer Winton C. Hoch was trying out a new format called VistaVision, which promised a more precise picture in wider shots, perfect for taking full advantage of Monument Valley's striking splendor. Operating the cutting-edge equipment, however, required a boatload of cumbersome gear. The caravan that rode out into the sagebrush valley included a truck with a camera crane, two horse trucks, a generator truck, a camera car, three twelve-passenger vans, a handful of jeeps, a water wagon, a hay truck, a wardrobe van, and a wagon stocked with hot meals. Ford's search for a new location to shoot the water scenes meant moving all those vehicles again.

Ford didn't mind the inconvenience. By the following morning he had staked out a more reliable alternative to the brisk-flowing San Juan. Crews hauled cameras and sound equipment three miles further out into the desert, to what looked like a large mud puddle roughly one hundred feet across and three feet deep.

"What's this?" one of the stuntmen, Terry Wilson, asked.

"This," Ford told them, "is a reservoir, gentlemen. Today, if any one of you drops his Sharps carbine into the water, it will be found. If any one of you falls off his horse, you will not drown."

It didn't matter, apparently, that the gently sloping sides of the reservoir looked vastly different from the rugged banks of the San Juan River seen in the earlier sequence. To guarantee at least a little drama in the chase scene, second unit director Wingate Smith had crews stretch a rope ankle-deep across the reservoir. The rope is visible on-screen as the Indians begin hounding the rangers across the river, but it served its purpose: the second horse from the left trips over the rope first, throwing his rider to the right as he falls with a splash. The pair land smack in the path of another Indian on a dark horse. At the same time, the horse on the far right of the screen falls, followed by two horses in the middle. The rare moviegoer familiar with falling-horse techniques would recognize what is to come as the Indians simultaneously pull their horses' heads to the right, initiating their slide. A fifth rider pulls his horse in the opposite direction to avoid colliding with horse number one.

There's something balletic about these choreographed falls. The horses struggle to stand, but the Indians who fall with them remain mired in the water as if felled by gunshot. A second wave of Indians plunging behind them retreats back to shore to reconnoiter. One Indian man rides up to the character of Scar, chief of the Nawyecka band of Comanches, to hand him a white war bonnet sprayed with eagle feathers. Instead of Wayne, the character of Scar is then seen riding the sorrel horse with three white socks and a white blaze: Cocaine.

In the next scene, the Indians charge into the river for a second time—in footage shot earlier in the San Juan. The rangers fire at them from the other side, triggering a fresh round of horse falls. As the sounds of gunshots echo back from the far side of the river, the Indians whip their horses around and charge back to shore. Then a sorrel horse with a black mane falters as he nears the water's edge, disappearing into the water headfirst and falling a second time as he starts to resurface. Another horse almost trips over him. The Indians' horses climb ashore except for one, who struggles repeatedly to right himself in the fast-moving current.

Watching these scenes, it's easy to overlook the workout Cocaine undergoes. First he powers John Wayne's character across the river. Then a couple of scenes later he carries Chief Scar, fishtailing in the water, as Roberson, doubling as Scar, dives dramatically into the river. Coke has no problem immediately righting himself after that fall. The horse's composed demeanor shines when, back on land, Wayne's character pulls a lance out of Jorgensen's senselessly slaughtered prized bull and inadvertently flicks Cocaine with the tip of the lance, not once, but twice, as he swings the weapon around. Wayne doesn't seem to realize he has struck the horse; not once does he glance back at Cocaine to see his response. Coke draws his head back but otherwise stands still.

Five years pass in the movie's timeline. Ethan and Martin track Chief Scar to the New Mexico territory. Pretending to be traders, they follow the chief into his tepee to get out of the wind. Scar shows off to them a lance decorated with the scalps of the many white people he has killed.

Behind him Ethan and Martin spy Debbie, her dark hair still in braids but no longer the little girl they remember.

Ethan and Martin exit the tepee and return to their campsite by a creek. Debbie follows them down the side of the dune to warn Martin that Scar plans to attack. Ethan pulls his gun from his holster and orders Martin to get out of the way; Ethan is intent on killing Debbie on the grounds that her years with the Comanches have permanently ruined her. Before he can shoot, he is felled by a poisonous arrow shot into his shoulder. The Comanche warrior who fired the arrow (portrayed by Roberson) is sitting astride a horse (Cocaine) at the top of the precipitously steep sand dune. In retaliation, Martin swivels around and shoots his pistol at the Indian and his horse.

What happens next is one of Coke's most memorable stunts. The horse who normally was so confident and sure-footed now needed to appear as though he had lost his balance. Cocaine begins sliding down the dune with Roberson on his back. His descent accelerates into a tumble, and he all but disappears in a cloud of red dust as he pitches forward down the dune. Roberson dives off of Coke and lands below him, somersaulting out of the way just as the big horse rolls over on his back, his legs thrust almost comically into the air. As Roberson continues to plummet, the camera captures Coke gathering his wits. Coke raises his head with an air of detachment and watches as Roberson rolls down.

There's more action in store for Cocaine. Hearing the gunshots, a war party of Comanches tops the hill and comes tearing down along the riverbank. Two Indians fall off their horses and roll into the river. That stunt might appear effortless on the part of the horses, but they had to be trained to keep their composure and continue running as their riders slid off of them. The cameras then show Roberson and Hayward, doubling for Ethan and Martin, riding Cocaine and Twinkle Toes down a shallow creek bed in the direction of a cave. The horses emerge from the creek and gallop across the desert neck-and-neck, their front legs curling gracefully in front of them, their hind legs stretched out as if they were flying—in the way that only horses can seem to do.

More than a century ago, photographer Eadweard Muybridge documented the fact that horses really do levitate when they run. Muybridge undertook his experiment at the behest of Leland Stanford, a horse breeder, governor of California, and founder of Stanford University, who wanted to prove that horses engaged in mid-gallop defied gravity. Stanford referred to that motion as "unsupported transit." On June 19, 1878, using a zoopraxiscope—a device that could make the subject in a series of still photographs look as though it was moving—Muybridge captured Stanford's mare Sallie Gardner running a 1:40 gait on the track at Palo Alto. For the slightest nanosecond the horse had all four feet off the ground as she galloped her laps.

How horses are able to race as fast as they do is a miracle of anatomy. Their fragile legs keep their bodies high above the ground, and their long strides help them to build up speed. Their legs operate as pendulums, their bones and muscles working together to enable their legs to swing forward and back. Their muscles are heaviest in their shoulders and hips, leaving their slender lower legs almost buoyant, able to extend farther and more rapidly, aided by the weight of their hooves. When a horse's front hooves strike the ground and then fold forward under his moving body, his pliable biceps help burst his legs forward. His muscles, ligaments, tendons, and joints work together to absorb the force of his hooves, at the same time emitting a shot of energy that heightens the pendulum motion.

It's breathtaking to watch Coke and Twinkle Toes demonstrate this magical and very natural movement in *The Searchers*. Pushing their hind legs off the ground to gain power, their sleek heads bob confidently in rhythm to their hoofbeats as they race toward the safety of the cave. They deliver Roberson and Hayward at the entrance and then fade from view as the Indians catch up, deliver a war cry, and begin their assault.

In the next sequence, Roberson, now doubling Scar, cues Coke to carry out a dazzling fall as Roberson first leans forward in the saddle and then back, yanking Coke's head to the right. Coke rides hard into the dirt, his head still facing backward. Immediately afterward, another rider falls off his horse but hangs on to the reins as his horse drags him, a difficult stunt for a horse to carry out. A rear shot of that fall shows the horse glancing back at his grounded rider. Movie credits don't specify who performed the stunt, but it was likely either Hayward or Frank McGrath, both of whom were experts at performing drags.

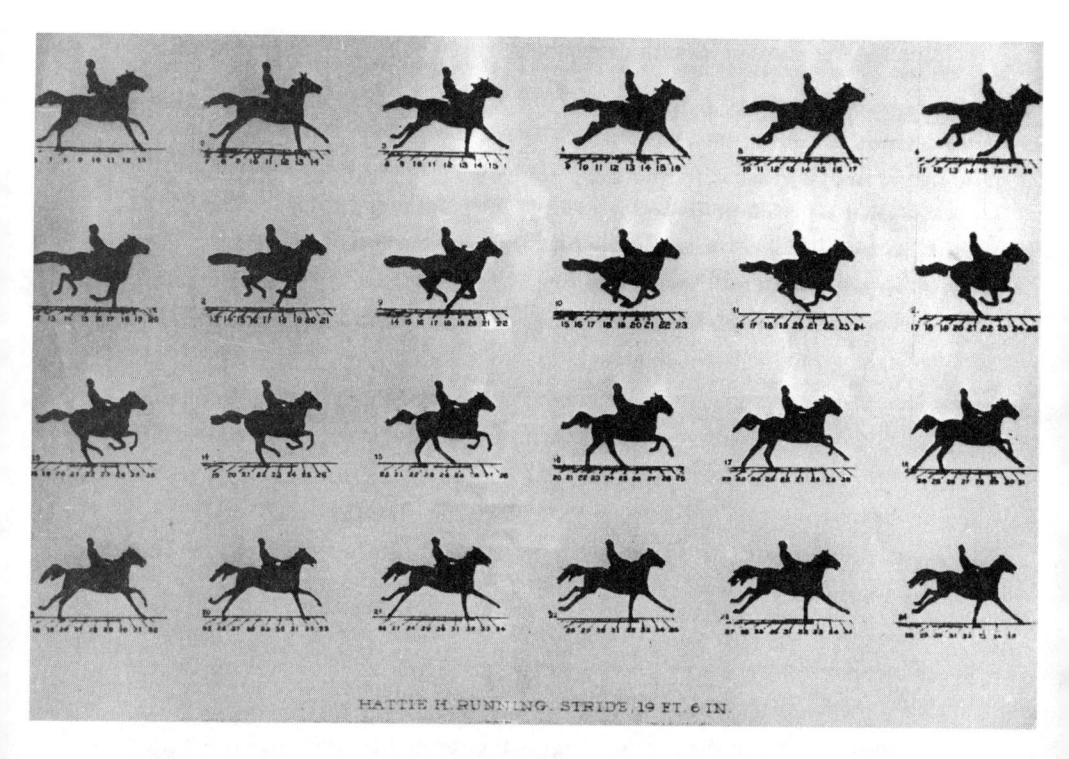

9. Photographer Eadweard Muybridge documented in 1878 that at some point while galloping, horses manage to lift all four feet off the ground. Photofest.

In his memoir, *Company of Heroes*, Dobie Carey praised the exploits of Roberson and Hayward in *The Searchers*, and he also pointed to Roberson's fall on Cocaine on the sand dune and the race to the cave as sterling examples of two expert stuntmen—and, by extension, their horses—at the peak of their trade.

"They make Duke and Jeff look so good it gives you goose bumps," Carey wrote.

Ford shot the chase to the cave sequence on the second day of filming. He was wise to get the grueling stunts out of the way early. Temperatures in Monument Valley had risen nearly twenty degrees warmer than expected for that time of year. To avoid the worst of the heat, Ford cued the cameras just as the sun rose. Even so, the long days under the sweltering rays caused several members of the cast and crew to develop sunstroke. One stuntman suffered a seizure. The suffocating heat had to have been merciless on the horses too.

The final action sequence occurs when the Texas Rangers join forces with the searchers and raid the Comanche village where Debbie lives. Martin goes looking for Debbie and finds her asleep in Scar's tent. Debbie agrees to leave with him, but before they can escape, Scar appears. Martin shoots Scar, and the rangers, hearing gunshots, rush in. Roaring with energy, their horses bolt through the village as the rangers trade shots with the Comanches. Roberson rides Coke in this sequence—except for a close-up scene where John Wayne's character, Ethan, riding Coke, enters Scar's tepee, finds him dead, scalps him, and reemerges. It's impressive to see how unruffled Cocaine remains during the jarring battle. Not once does he lay his ears back in the face of the crackling gunfire, which would have been a sign of distress. His ears remain erect, his eyes evenly observing the skirmish.

As *Searchers* fans have documented in the years since, the movie is full of inconsistencies where the horses are concerned. Early on, desperate to learn the fate of his family, Martin rides his distinctively colored buckskin horse to death (an occurrence that is mentioned but not shown). Later, when he heads out with Ethan to search for Debbie and Lucy, Martin is seen riding the same buckskin horse. In a subsequent scene, when Martin leaves the Jorgensens' home to follow Ethan, Martin's girlfriend, Laurie, loans him Sweet Face, a sorrel with a white blaze. Shortly after that, Martin and Ethan are seen riding dark horses with no blazes.

Wayne's character, Ethan, rides Cocaine throughout much of the movie, but in the scene after the village raid where, doubled by Roberson, he tangles with Martin one last time in the desert, Wayne rides a horse with four white socks and a wider blaze than Cocaine. Still later in the movie, Martin sits astride the sorrel, white-blazed Sweet Face again and Ethan is back on Coke. Wayne sits astride Cocaine in the movie's finale when he delivers Debbie to the Jorgensens' home.

Cocaine displayed a cool demeanor when necessary, but he was also high-spirited, eager to jump into the fray. That Wayne could handle his liveliness was evidence of the actor's skill. Yet Ford gave Duke a hard time about his riding ability. "When will you learn to ride a horse?" Ford griped one day. "Ride like a goddam sissy with your hand on the saddle

10. Western icon John Wayne (*right*) rode Cocaine throughout much of *The Searchers*. He had great respect for the gutsy, unflinching horse. Photofest.

horn like that. You at least should have learned to ride a horse in all those serial Westerns."

"Aw, now, Pappy," Wayne responded.

Ford kept haranguing him. "What are you? You afraid you're going to fall off or something?" He scoffed. "Look at the way you're hanging on to that horn. Geez! I can't believe you're in Westerns."

FORD WAS EXPERIENCED AT MANAGING THE UNEXPECTED; IT'S PART of what made him so effective behind the camera. But three horse-related incidents during the making of *The Searchers* left him rattled.

The governor of Utah, J. Bracken Lee, was visiting the set one day when Ford, looking to show off his stunt performers, asked a wrangler to demonstrate the proper way to execute a saddle fall. Roberson and Hayward watched from the sidelines as the inexperienced young man dutifully rode into view and suddenly pitched out of the saddle, scarcely bothering to fold his head before hitting the ground. The wrangler landed directly on his shoulder and lay there, unmoving, while his horse bolted off. Ford thought the man was merely pretending to be injured, but Roberson and Hayward could tell that he was genuinely hurt and rode out to see about him. Sure enough, the wrangler had dislocated his shoulder. Ford turned white-faced when the medic on call had to run out and attend to him.

Roberson and Hayward rejoined Ford as he was explaining to Governor Lee that injuries from horse falls were actually quite rare. To drive home his point, he ordered the two stuntmen to ride out and perform saddle falls—both of them, simultaneously. Riding Cocaine and Twinkle Toes, Roberson and Hayward trotted out fifty yards or so when Ford upped the assignment. "Wait a minute!" he yelled. "Do a horse fall!" Horse falls were more impressive because they required both horse and rider to hit the ground.

"Are we getting paid for this?" Hayward muttered to Roberson.

"Let's put it this way," Roberson said. "If we want to get paid, we do it."

Between them, they bet $10 on which of them could fall their horse first. On the count of three they spurred Cocaine and Twinkle Toes and whipped their heads to the right. Both horses landed directly in front of Ford and his guest, but Cocaine hit the ground a half second before Twinkle Toes, so Roberson won the bet. Their demonstration enabled Ford to save face with his distinguished guest.

The second incident involved the film's producer, Cornelius Vanderbilt "Sonny" Whitney. A wealthy descendant of Eli Whitney—the nineteenth-century entrepreneur best known for inventing the cotton gin—Sonny had acquired the screen rights to *The Searchers* as a favor to Ford, who struggled to pay the bills. Using Whitney's money as a foundation, Ford's business partner, Merian C. Cooper, was able to obtain additional financing and distribution rights from Warner Bros.

Whitney was pleased with his role on the money end, and eager to be a part of the goings-on, he showed up in Monument Valley with his wife, Eleanor. A polo player, he considered himself an expert with horses, and he asked Ford if he could ride alongside the wranglers as part of the raid on the Indian village.

Absolutely not, Ford told him. Too risky.

Unbeknownst to Ford, Whitney joined in the harrowing scene anyway. The sequence involved so much bedlam—including multiple horse falls as a cadre of Texas Rangers chased scores of Indian men, women, and children in and around a village of tepees while a camera truck zipped along on the sidelines—that Ford had no idea Whitney was part of the skirmish. When filming stopped, the financier rode up to Ford, basking in his boldness.

Ford let him have it. "Don't ever do that again; you could get killed out there," he said. "I know you ride polo ponies and all that, but this is a different ballgame."

"We were scared to death (Whitney) was going to break his check-writing arm," Pat Ford later quipped.

A third episode also involved the raid on the Indian camp, in a scene that showed a soldier running his horse over an Indian woman. Cast to play the part of the woman was veteran stuntman Fred Kennedy, who donned a dress and a wig to look the part. His assignment was to dart into the path of the marauding rangers so recklessly that he would appear to be struck and killed by one of the horses.

Instead of using an expert horseman to clip Kennedy, Ford gave the part to a local cowboy. The newcomer was so bowled over with excitement at the prospect of being in a movie that he forgot all about trampling Kennedy and instead raced his horse directly toward one of the cameras.

John Wayne stood watching the action from a few feet away. At the last minute the cowboy pivoted out of the camera's path and accidentally struck Wayne on his side, sending the famous star crashing. That did it for Ford. He called a halt to almost all other horse stunts in the movie after that.

A fourth incident left Roberson rethinking his carefree attitude toward his own horse.

Filming half a dozen movies in Monument Valley had established a mutual reverence between Ford and the Navajos who resided there. It wasn't just the money: Ford paid the Indians for their work, $15 a day to the men, $10 to the women, and $5 to the children, with time and a half after eight hours, plus he threw in lunch. The Navajos liked Ford's sense of humor, his patience, and the way he consulted with them at the end of each day's shooting. And they appreciated his conservative philosophy when it came to repeated takes; his efficient method of planning out scenes kept them from wearing out their horses. Nor had they forgotten that seven years earlier, after filming *She Wore a Yellow Ribbon* on their land and learning that several feet of snow had subsequently closed off access to the valley, Ford arranged for military planes to lower food to the stranded tribe.

In exchange for his munificence, Ford knew he could count on the Navajo horsemen—particularly the three Stanley brothers, along with Bob Many Mules, Harry Black Horse, Pete Grey Eyes, and Billy Yellow—to inject a dose of adrenalin and veracity to his films. The only concession he asked of them was that they use saddles, for safety's sake. Normally Indians in the time of the films' setting would have ridden bareback.

When the Fourth of July rolled around, Ford threw a party featuring barbecues, singing, fireworks, foot races, and a horse-racing contest. The Navajos looked forward most to the horse race. They were convinced that when it came to stamina, none of the movie horses could begin to outshine their own ponies. If any Hollywood horse could beat theirs, it was Cocaine. The younger Indians had watched with envy as the resilient Coke performed, and the elders told Roberson they had never seen a finer horse.

As the Independence Day festivities began to draw to a close, three young Navajo from the farthest reaches of the reservation approached Roberson and challenged him to race Cocaine against their horses. Ford witnessed the exchange and right away saw a chance to hand the Navajos a much-desired victory.

Pulling Roberson aside, Ford said, "Let them beat you, Bad Chuck."

"Aw, hell," Roberson thought. The notion of deliberately losing a race to some unkempt ponies did not sit well. But Ford wasn't giving him a choice.

"I'm telling you to lose this race, and I don't want an argument," the director said.

After Ford walked away, Roberson protested to Wayne, "I never ran a race to lose in my life." Wayne knew better, though, than to suggest that Roberson back out. "Pappy says lose, so you better come in fourth," Wayne said. Unable to keep from rubbing it in, he added, "I'm betting on the shaggy pinto with the skinny guy on top."

There was no getting around it. Roberson nodded his assent to the Indian riders. The Indians mounted their ponies and lined up next to him. One of the racers uttered something in his tribal language that sounded like an expression of disdain. The other Indian racers laughed and began trotting their ponies out across the level valley. Roberson and Coke followed from behind. When they reached what Roberson guessed was a quarter of a mile, he brought Cocaine around to a halt.

"Far enough, fellas," he shouted to his competitors.

The Indians kept riding.

"Well, okay, if you're going to be that way about it," Roberson grumbled to himself. He prodded Coke with his spurs and fell in behind the rest.

A horse can keep running for an impressive amount of time thanks to its ability to bend its lower legs tightly to gain speed without losing any energy. Part of what is so beautiful to watch about a running horse is the elegant way its head and neck rise and fall, generating momentum as the horse's pace accelerates. At a more relaxed pace, a horse's head keeps steady to save energy.

Cocaine would need to vigorously pump his head to produce the energy necessary to beat these ponies. The quarter horse in him was good for short bursts of speed but not for long distances. Each time his competitors rode another several hundred yards Roberson tried to stop, but the Indians ignored him and continued riding. After they'd trotted what looked to be a full mile, Roberson halted Coke again and hollered, "Hey, we've gone too far!" The Indians muttered something he could not hear and kept going.

Roberson's unease was building. The Indians knew Coke could beat them at a reasonable distance. Their only strategy was to exhaust him, to push him over such a long stretch that he couldn't possibly keep up. Yet even as the sun beat down, Roberson gave no thought to abandoning the race. He steered Coke so far out that by the time they finally faced back toward the finish line, he could no longer see any signs of life. The Indians waiting next to him nodded and smiled.

"This is it, boy!" Roberson shouted, patting the horse's neck.

Using sign language, one of the Indians signaled that the race would begin the second he dropped a white handkerchief on the ground. Roberson nodded that he understood. When the kerchief fell, he spurred Cocaine forward. Coke immediately jumped ahead of the Indian ponies, his long legs streaking across the dry ground as hard as he could propel them. But the sound of approaching hoofbeats was unnerving. Behind them, the Indians whooped.

At what appeared to be the halfway mark, Cocaine still led. Three-quarters of the way in he continued to lead, but fatigue was starting to set in. "Come on, Coke," Roberson called out. With an eighth of a mile left, he was still ahead. A flock of onlookers at the finish line began urging them in. Then, all at once, Coke's lead diminished. One second he was ahead by half a length, the next he led by just a neck. Roberson glimpsed Ford standing to one side, his arms crossed. The director had specifically instructed Roberson not to cross the finish line first, but Roberson could not deliberately lose this race. It simply wasn't his nature not to give his all.

By now he could hear the Indian ponies breathing heavily on either side. To hell with Ford. Roberson wanted Coke to win. He gave the horse one final push, but the desert heat had exacted a toll. With seconds to go, all three of the Indian ponies surged ahead, buzzing across the finish line just before Cocaine.

Ford had gotten his wish. Coke lost the race. Dollops of foamy sweat clung to his muscles as Roberson escorted him away from the gathering to cool him off. From a distance the stuntman watched as Ford passed out silver dollars to the winning riders and accepted their gift to him: a stretched deer hide including legs, tail, and ears. Scrawled into the deerskin was a saying: *In your travels may there be beauty behind you, beauty on both sides of you, and beauty ahead of you.*

"Given in the spirit of mutual respect and admiration and the brotherhood that you bring to our valley," tribal member John Stanley said as he presented the hide to Ford.

Afterward Ford approached Roberson to show off his gift. "Damn fine race, Bad Chuck," he said. "Perfect! My Lord, for a minute there I was afraid you were going to win. Pulled him up right at the last." Roberson stopped himself from responding. Ford left and Roberson was pulling the saddle off of Coke when Wayne strolled over to hand him a glass of iced tea.

"Smart boy," Wayne told him. "It sure looked good."

"Shoot. You think I lost the race on purpose?" Roberson said. "Those damned Indians pulled a fast one."

"He'd run until his heart busted, wouldn't he?" Wayne said, glancing over at Cocaine. "Quite a horse. But at a mile and a half—in the desert, in July, with Pappy at the finish line? I put my money on the Indian pony. Still, it was a hell of a horse race."

Roberson didn't think so. He was ashamed of himself for putting his companion through such a grueling exercise, all for the sake of Ford's ego and his own pride. He vowed never to test Coke that harshly again.

15

Doubling for the Stars

For the 1958 movie *Tonka*, Disney Studios went looking for a horse with some charisma to star in the loosely based true story of the only horse said to have survived the famous Battle of Little Bighorn. The movie's plot focuses heavily on the horse Tonka's capture by an Indian named White Bull, played by Sal Mineo, who develops a strong attachment to Tonka—so much so that he later sets the horse free to keep him from being abused by an elder cousin, Yellow Bull. Tonka is then captured and sold to the U.S. Cavalry, where he is renamed Comanche and ridden into battle by Captain Myles Keogh. Keogh is killed, and a seriously injured Comanche returns to the care of White Bull, who joins the cavalry to care for his treasured horse.

The movie revolves entirely around the character of Tonka, and after a lengthy search Disney was convinced it had found the right horse in an eight-year-old reigning champion named Canton. For the first half of the filming, near Bend, Oregon, Canton performed without any issues. Then one day he walked off the set and refused to come back. His trainer was forced to make a quick trip back to California, where he arranged to borrow the television star Flicka and bring her on board to take Canton's place. The makeup crew blotted Flicka with the same white markings as Canton, and she performed without incident. Canton was quickly retired.

Quitting work on the set was the worst thing a movie horse could do. A horse that suddenly twirled around and bolted out of sight or stood frozen in place, rebuffing any signals to perform, would force a director to halt shooting, wasting the studio's time and money. Filmmakers tolerated uncooperative horses like Silver King and Rex if the animals could otherwise be counted on to carry out a scene. Rex, the stallion who starred in dozens of movies in the 1920s and 1930s, also fought his trainer on the set, but he never quit working.

Rex's partner, Misty, was less dependable. A black thoroughbred stallion, Misty performed in seventy movies, including as Banner in *My Friend Flicka* and *Thunderhead, Son of Flicka*. But he wasn't terribly trustworthy. If filming a scene lasted longer than he liked, he simply stopped performing. His trainer, Les Hilton, learned to signal a halt to shooting whenever he sensed that Misty was reaching the end of his rope. Sometimes the opposite would happen and Misty would learn his part too well. Filming a sequence for *Thunderhead*, he was supposed to gallop to a designated spot, whereupon three wranglers would lasso him and fling him to the ground. On the third take, anticipating what the wranglers were about to do, Misty collapsed on his own before the wranglers could tackle him. The second unit crew had to film the scene with a different horse.

The horse that played Mister Ed in the popular TV series of the same name in the early 1960s, a palomino named Bamboo Harvest, was a quick learner: he could untie knots, pick up a telephone receiver, open doors, and grasp a large pencil with his mouth to write notes. But he had a stubborn streak as long as his cornsilk tail. If he was worn out from standing under the lights or simply feeling ornery, he would snort a time or two, plant his feet, and stand perfectly still, ignoring all entreaties to perform.

It didn't take much to render a horse ineligible for the big screen. On the set of 1959's *Rio Bravo*, a horse that was supposed to stand quietly at a hitching post began to protest every time a particular tune was strummed—shaking his head, baring his teeth, and pawing the ground. The third time he objected to the music he had to be removed from the set.

Falling horses were no different. Simply because a horse had fallen reliably dozens of times in the past was no guarantee that he would acquiesce the next time. Occasionally a horse known to be a dependable faller would suddenly decide not to cooperate by stiffening his legs, digging in his feet, and clenching his neck, risking genuine harm to his rider. Falling a horse was always a gamble, even with proven performers. But a volatile and unpredictable faller was too dangerous—a deal-ender.

Cocaine quickly gained a reputation for dependability. He had none of the idiosyncrasies that afflicted other falling horses. Bursts of gunfire did not seem to faze him. Given the right prompt, he could fall or play dead on the spot. Roberson could execute a transfer—slowing down to leap off of Coke onto a roaring steam engine, for example—and Coke would continue running as if nothing had happened. Some horses, either out of ignorance or indifference, would step on their riders in the process of rising to their feet after falling. Coke never did.

Unlike other stunt horses, who tended to be high-strung, Cocaine had a docile disposition—that is, until Roberson climbed on his back. In an instant Coke's boldness and energy shot to the fore. At the sound of "Action!" his ears pricked, his eyes lit with excitement, and he was ready to go. To load him into a trailer, all Roberson had to do was click his tongue, and Coke climbed aboard willingly.

"He had a desire to please," Roberson said. "He seemed to enjoy doing things right for me. A word of praise seemed to light up those big, brown eyes of his, and I got as attached to him as to any horse I had ever ridden."

Word of Cocaine's expertise spread fast. Western directors began to request him for their movies, and Roberson dyed Coke's coat numerous times depending on the role he was to portray. For his prominent part as the feisty stallion in *The Wonderful Country*, it wasn't enough to spray Coke with Streaks N Tips, the temporary colorant preferred by makeup artists. Except for a tiny white star left on his blaze, Roberson had to dye every inch of Coke coal black.

Released in 1959, *The Wonderful Country* starred Robert Mitchum as Martin Brady, an American gunman banished to Mexico for having slain his father's assassin. The movie was filmed in Durango, Mexico, a backwoods expanse where roads consisted of simple cobblestone or dirt trails. Roberson trailered Coke the 1,460 miles from their home in the San Fernando Valley. Greeting them were hundred-degree temperatures, but thankfully the stables set aside for the horses were made of adobe, which helped deflect the heat. Cocaine was pressed into performing every feat possible: plenty of falls, of course, but also drags and transfers and lay-downs. In addition to his full plate of stunts, Roberson was given a speaking role or two. He spent his evenings mentally counting up the money he was going to make from the film.

The final days of shooting were especially demanding. Roberson doubled for Mitchum in a scene where his horse, played by Coke, falls and breaks a leg and has to be fatally shot. Coke needed to lie immobile long enough to

11. Chuck Roberson doubled for Robert Mitchum in the 1959 movie *The Wonderful Country*. Cocaine's coat was dyed black for this scene. Courtesy of John Hagner's Hollywood Stuntmen's Hall of Fame.

look dead. And since the dye job that concealed his sorrel coat was starting to wear off, Roberson had to stain it all over again.

After a boisterous wrap-up party, the cast and crew headed home to California. Roberson loaded Cocaine and two other horses into a trailer and sped along Mexico's dusty desert. He was hot, tired, and anxious to get the horses home and assumed he'd have no problem crossing back into the United States. When the inspector on duty at the border asked to see the horses' papers, Roberson pulled out the necessary documents describing the three horses and listing their ages, figuring he would be back on the road in a matter of minutes. The inspector riffled through the papers before glancing up with a skeptical look on his face.

"These papers say you cross the border with two sorrels and one bay horse," he said. "I see only one red horse, señor, one bay, and one horse as black as midnight. We cannot permit you to cross over with different horses than your papers say you bring into Mexico."

Roberson tried to explain. He'd been working on a movie, he said. In truth, he told the man, the black horse, Cocaine, had a sorrel coat. "We had to dye him black" for his role.

"The black horse is not on the paper," the inspector insisted. "Have you sold a red one and hope to play tricks here at the border? I cannot permit it."

By now several other inspectors had joined the first one, and it dawned on Roberson that if he was unable to prove his case, the officials were prepared to impound all three horses. Stifling his exasperation, he pulled the trailer to the side of the main gate, unloaded Cocaine in the hot sun, gathered the inspectors around, and parted some of Coke's hair to prove to them that underneath the black coloring his roots really were red. But the dye job was still fresh. To Roberson's dismay, he'd stained Coke's coat so thoroughly that none of the horse's natural color was evident.

"I'm telling you we had to dye him black." Roberson was pleading at this point. "It just hasn't been long enough to grow out."

The inspectors weren't convinced and might have delayed him indefinitely if Roberson hadn't suddenly remembered that he still had half a gallon of dye stored somewhere in the trailer. While one inspector held sternly to Cocaine's halter, Roberson rummaged through his belongings. Sure enough, the can of dye was tucked away beneath a saddle. He produced it with a mixture of vindication and anxiety. The inspectors discussed the matter for another twenty minutes before deciding to let him continue on. On the U.S. side of the border, Roberson got out of his truck and let out a few shouts of relief before resuming the drive home.

It happened that some of the best falling horses—Coke, Twinkle Toes, and Coco—all had sorrel coats with white blazes. In fact, directors began to recruit horses with sorrel coats and white blazes like Cocaine's—and like Jack Williams's Coco and Chuck Hayward's Twinkle Toes—to make it that much easier to swap in a stunt horse for risky scenes. Roberson would frequently use dye to alter the width of Coke's blaze to match that of the horse he was subbing for. Only an astute moviegoer might have noticed that a character riding up on a sorrel horse with a white blaze was a tip-off that a horse fall was imminent.

In the 1950s and early 1960s, thanks to their talented steeds, Roberson, Chuck Hayward, and Jack Williams were able to find constant work in A-Westerns, B-Westerns, and, between Roberson and Hayward, nearly all the films featuring John Wayne, who by now had become the biggest movie star in the world.

Jack Williams appeared in fifty-five movies and television shows, most of them Westerns, often with Coco. Chuck Hayward performed in thirty-seven movies or TV shows, most of them with Twink; Hayward doubled for John Wayne, Yul Brynner, Stuart Whitman, Chill Wills, and Steve McQueen, among many others. Roberson appeared in ninety-three movies or television episodes. Among them was Wayne's 1963 movie *McLintock!*, a romantic comedy about an aging rancher who finds himself fighting off a variety of interlopers, including his ex-wife, who arrives back on the scene to claim custody of their daughter. In a sequence involving an egg race, Roberson climbs atop a horse (Cocaine) and holds him steady. Coke looks as though he's ready to gallop away, but he follows Roberson's direction and restrains himself, bobbing his head furiously to keep himself in check.

Roberson was known for his expert horsemanship, and Coke's exploits made him stand out even more. He doubled for some of Hollywood's leading stars in an array of the era's most memorable films: Clark Gable, Gary Cooper, Rock Hudson, Jeff Chandler, Burt Lancaster, Charlton Heston, Joel McCrea, Stewart Granger, Richard Boone, George Kennedy, Ronald Reagan, Rory Calhoun, Macdonald Carey, Robert Ryan, Van Heflin, and Fred MacMurray. He appeared in a string of top Westerns, among them *The Lusty Men*, *Two Rode Together*, and *The Far Country*, a number of B-Westerns, including *Lightning Guns*, *Frontier Outpost*, *Western Renegades*, and *Fort Dodge Stampede*, and nearly all of John Wayne's cowboy flicks.

A few times Cocaine, Coco, and Twinkle Toes all performed in the same movie. That happened with 1961's *The Comancheros*, in 1964 with *Cheyenne Autumn*, and with 1965's *The Sons of Katie Elder*. Cocaine came face-to-face with Coco in the 1962 movie *How the West Was Won*. Roberson, riding Cocaine, plays a cowboy who comes up against an Indian played by

Jack Williams. Coco easily steals the show. Roberson's character shoots Williams's, whereupon Coco rears up and falls backward as Williams hits the dirt beside her. With the cameras filming, Coco flutters her legs in the air, and then—in a startling scene—she starts to roll slowly over the top of Williams. Williams continued to lie still as Coco's massive weight squashed him. Roberson was convinced the stunt had killed him. Finally director Henry Hathaway yelled, "Cut!" and shouted, "Lord! Why didn't he move?"

"Because you didn't yell cut!" an uninjured Williams shouted back.

Roberson and Hayward were friendly rivals, each capable of executing daring deeds astride a horse. For a time, Hayward lived a few houses away from Roberson's place in Sun Valley, California. The two men competed even on their off days. One afternoon while practicing in his front yard, Roberson accidentally fell off a horse, a perfectly normal occurrence during training. Still, he glanced up quickly to see if Hayward had spied his tumble. To his relief, he hadn't.

The biggest display of falling horses took place during the filming of John Wayne's pet project, *The Alamo*. Wayne had long been enamored with that 1836 battle, a decisive event in Texas's struggle for independence from Mexico. The skirmish began when some two hundred volunteer soldiers, including popular frontiersman Davy Crockett, took over the Alamo, a former Franciscan mission located in present-day San Antonio. Mexican general Antonio López de Santa Anna, backed by thousands of Mexican soldiers, attacked the fort and, thirteen days into the siege, slaughtered the Texans and gained control. The carnage galvanized many Texans, as well as other Americans, to join the Texan Army. Forty-six days later they defeated the Mexicans. Wayne was determined to convey the heroic deeds of Davy Crockett and his volunteer army, and he nearly went broke producing a film he believed would pay a worthy salute to the cause.

In the interest of authenticity, Wayne decided to film the movie in Texas. He found the ideal spot on a ranch just north of the town of Brackettville, a few miles from the Mexico border. Owned by a man named Happy Shahan, the ranch covered more than twenty thousand acres of mesquite and sagebrush, and it offered the plains, valleys, and streams needed to capture Texas's solitary feel. Crews hired by Wayne spent two years there building a replica of the Alamo and a vintage street representing Old San Antonio. The property was so remote that workers had to dig wells to guarantee a water supply, install electrical cables, and flatten a landing strip long and wide enough to accommodate the private planes that would fly Wayne and his cohorts in and out.

Wayne hadn't scrimped on the location, and he wasn't about to cut corners on the horses. Hundreds were needed for the battle scene. It was wrangler Bill Jones's job to acquire and train them. Jones scouted the entire state of Texas and parts of Missouri, Arkansas, Oklahoma, New Mexico, Arizona, and California to find enough horses at a price Wayne was willing to pay. By one account, Jones purchased seven hundred horses and leased another seven hundred, paying an average of $200 apiece. A few of the horses came from the Fort Smith Livestock Auction in Arkansas and likely escaped a trip to the slaughterhouse. Crews erected five hundred acres of stock corrals to hold the horses and stocked up on tens of thousands of dollars' worth of feed. Veterinarians were brought in to vaccinate the horses for pleuropneumonia, otherwise known as shipping fever, once they arrived.

Jones hired fifteen local wranglers to school the extras in horseback riding and break the horses to the point that they could carry on amid loud distractions. The wranglers had their work cut out for them. One of them described some of the horses as "damn old crazy animals . . . bucking sons of a guns . . . rank sons of bitches." The horses were untrained and unaccustomed to the gunshots and other harsh noises typical of Western sets, and many of them were flat-out wild. To acclimatize their mounts to the explosive sounds of gunshots and cannon fire, trainers would periodically shoot blank pistols and detonate blasts of dynamite near their corrals. The horses also needed to learn to ignore intense lights and to step over and around the cameras, cables, and fallen bodies they would encounter during filming. And they needed to learn to pull wagons and caissons alongside other horses and mules, six to a team. Wrangler Buddy Sherwood used a tranquil mule from East Texas to help calm the untrained horses and mules.

The extras hired to ride the animals—nearly a thousand of whom were brought over the border from Mexico—were similarly inexperienced. The Mexican riders commuted fifty miles to the set, riding in double-decker buses from the city of Piedras Negras. They had to start out in the pre-dawn darkness to arrive at the ranch by sunrise. The horses were up early, too, by 3:00 a.m., so they would be saddled and waiting when the riders arrived at dawn.

Wranglers rode the horses all day long to break them in. The Mexican riders brought with them McClellan saddles, created by U.S. Army officer George B. McClellan just before the Civil War. Designed more simply and less expensively than the prevailing saddles of the day, McClellan saddles felt lighter on a horse but were durable enough to carry a rider. The Mexican version, though, came with iron stirrups that were harder on the horses than the wooden stirrups originally used. On top of that, the horses had to contend with the soldiers' swords, which jostled about as they rode, randomly striking the horses on their flanks.

Coordinating the action scenes was second unit director Cliff Lyons, who'd never encountered a stunt he considered too perilous to attempt. One of Lyons's best attributes was his finely honed bullshit detector. He assumed, correctly, that of the hundreds of would-be cowboys who showed up to win parts as extras, few had any idea how to ride a horse. "All right, cowboys," Lyons told them. "Riding for a goddam picture ain't like shooing a goddamn cow out of the goddamn garden. Let's see how many of you cowboys can cut it." Mother, as the stuntmen called him, put the fledgling riders to the test by having them gallop their horses down a slope as fast as they could go. The extras auditioned ten at a time, and as they started out, Lyons would stand among them, whipping the horses and pounding so hard on the extras that they would fall out of their saddles.

"Mother made a hell of a lot of infantrymen that day and humbled many a cow chaser," one stuntman recalled. As wrangler John Plunker Sheedy said in John Farkis's exhaustive book *Not Thinkin'... Just Rememberin'... The Making of John Wayne's "The Alamo,"* some of the extras had no idea how to ride a horse, but "they put them on a horse anyway. We got a lot of free falls out of that deal."

Lyons spent months plotting the horse falls and other stunts, and back in Hollywood he spread the word that Wayne's movie needed seasoned falling horses—the best in the field. Lyons had in mind a knockout sequence where fourteen riders portraying Mexican soldiers would gallop their horses into the face of cannon fire, jump their mounts over a four-foot-high barricade separating the chapel from the mission's front gate, then fall to the ground as though they'd been struck. It was a jaw-dropping stunt that needed to be timed perfectly to achieve the desired effect. It was crucial that all the action occur in a single scene, and to accomplish that would require carefully choreographed timing. The braver horses would need to lead the way to serve as role models for the more timid mounts.

It didn't take much coaxing to interest moviedom's best Western stunt performers. Wayne was offering a base salary of $325 a week and $200 on top of that each time a horse fall was involved. Nearly all of Hollywood's most skilled horses and riders signed up, including Roberson and Cocaine; Chuck Hayward and Twinkle Toes; Jack Williams and Coco; Tap Canutt and Gypsy; Red Morgan and Hot Rod; and Jim Burk and Detonator. Joining them were veteran stuntmen Leroy Johnson, Bob Morgan, Dean Smith, Billie Williams, Joe Canutt, Bill Hart, Tom Hennesy, Bear Hudkins, Gil Perkins, and Ted White.

To soften the falls, crews raked away rocks and brush from the spots where the horses were to land, and they spread two feet of sand at the base of the palisade wall. Stuntmen were issued soft rubber stirrups covered in leather to protect the sides of the horses when they fell. As an extra precaution, Wayne insisted the entire set be gone over each morning to make certain no rattlesnakes lurked in the brush. On cooler days the snakes would slither out into the open to keep warm.

For days leading up to the filming, the stuntmen practiced their timing, first by themselves and later in pairs. The jagged edge of the palisade unnerved several of the horses; when the time came to leap over it, they shrank back with fright. To overcome their hesitation, the crew laid wooden planks on the top of the palisade to even out the edges. And because not all of the horses could jump as high as others, Lyons had his crew build a ramp on the back side of the wall that would shorten the drop. Cameras were set up on the opposite side to capture the falls head-on. Filmed at the right angle, the horses would appear to be leaping higher than they really were.

Lyons wasn't fond of retakes—he preferred to nail a sequence the first go around—but to film the group jump from different angles it was necessary to carry out the falls twice. Roberson and Cocaine were to lead the way, and because of that, Roberson felt immense pressure not to bungle the stunt. "Basically, if the first horse and rider was good, the rest could screw up," he figured.

Lyons's instructions weren't the easiest to follow. Before one sequence, he called all of the stuntmen together at the top of a rise. "Bad Chuck, you lead out," Lyons started. "The rest of you guys follow Bad Chuck here, and I want you to come down this goddam hill, dammit, and I want you to *DAMN*! I mean I really want to see you, *Damn*! I mean, *Goddammit*! I want you to, *DAMN*!" With that Lyons clapped his hands, steered his horse around, and rode away. The stuntmen had no idea what any of that meant. Dean Smith pointed his thumb at Roberson. "Bad Chuck here's the only one who can understand him." And indeed, Roberson did. "Follow me, boys," he said. "All he wants us to do is ride nice and easy down the hill and through the gate of the mission."

On the big screen, the sequence looks flawless. Led by Cocaine, the horses leap over the palisade in two rows, sailing over a lineup of Texan soldiers who are crouched against the barrier. Schooled in falling, the horses crash to the ground as dictated, one by one. A moviegoer would have had to look closely to notice that the heads of the horses are whipped to the right a split second before they begin their descent, the telltale sign that their falls were not spontaneous but instead carefully choreographed.

The sequence is over in seconds, but it perfectly captures the havoc Wayne sought to convey. It set a record for the number of horses who had carried out a group fall; previously the largest number to do so was eight. The stunt may have been harder on the riders than on their mounts, though. One rider cracked a rib, and several others suffered cuts and bruises. Stuntman Jack Young was seriously injured during filming.

Young had taught his horse, an unidentified mare, to stagger and fall when he touched her nose with the toe of his boot. Ordinarily the horse would fall slowly, giving Young enough time to pull his boot out of the stirrup before his horse landed on the ground. This time, though, Young made the mistake of pulling on the reins and kicking the horse's nose a second too soon. The mare fell instantly, catching Young's boot in the stirrup. He landed directly in the path of the other horses, all of them flailing wildly in their attempts to right themselves after having tumbled. One of the horses kicked Young in the head, knocking him out and rendering his body completely limp. The fact that Young was out cold while he was getting tossed about like a rag doll probably kept him from being killed. As it was, he spent seventeen days in a coma and needed six months to recuperate from a broken back, a fractured skull, and numerous broken bones. As soon as he was able to work again, his agent booked him a part in the film *Two Rode Together*. But Young never enjoyed horse-falling again. In an interview when he was eighty-five years old, he said of horses: "I hate the (bleeping) things."

Stuntman Jim Burk later admitted he learned an important lesson doing that palisade jump. As soon as he leapt his horse Detonator over the barricade, Burk tried to fall him. But Detonator hadn't yet landed on all four feet, and he ignored Burk's cues. Once the horse had all four feet on the ground Burk tried to take him down again, and this time Detonator fell as he was instructed to do. The American Humane Association later declared that falling a horse immediately after jumping over a wall was too dangerous and consequently banned the practice.

Wayne was considerate of the cast members and stuntmen he'd performed with so often, but he was indifferent toward horses. One morning Wayne rode out on horseback with assistant director Robert Relyea to inspect possible locations for filming. While out, a spectator stopped Wayne to ask for his autograph. The interruption irritated the star, and when his horse, who was standing behind him, suddenly bent down and bit him on his rear, Wayne's annoyance morphed into anger. He wheeled around, drew back his right shoulder, and clouted the horse between the eyes. The stunned horse dropped his head slowly and began to crumple. Perhaps regretting his move, Wayne knelt in front of the horse, wrapped his hands around the animal's shoulders, and helped lift him back on his feet, but he continued to lock eyes with him as if daring him to bite him again.

Nor did Wayne mind putting the horses, as well as his best stuntmen, through a few gratuitous paces. Director John Ford had been itching to help direct *The Alamo*—given the lackluster reviews it later received, it might have been a good thing if he had—but Wayne was equally determined not to let him. Wayne knew that if Ford directed even one scene of the movie, word would spread that *The Alamo* was Ford's film and not his. But Ford was too curious; he couldn't stay away. Two weeks after production began, he arrived on the set and immediately began second-guessing Wayne. "Jesus Christ, Duke, that's not the way to do it," Ford would say. Desperate to appease Ford but also determined to maintain control over his own project, Wayne turned to his chief camera operator,

William Clothier, for advice. Give Ford a second unit to direct, Clothier suggested.

Wayne gathered his best stuntmen together and explained the situation. Go along with whatever Ford asks of you, he told them. "Whatever he shoots, I'm telling you now, none of that will be in the picture." Wayne then convinced Ford that second unit director Lyons had far too many action scenes to oversee and could really use Ford's help. Ford wasn't terribly excited at the prospect of directing an action sequence, but he agreed to it.

A photo taken shortly afterward captured two rows of stuntmen, some standing, some kneeling in the dirt, dutifully taking instructions from Ford. In the days to come the stuntmen had to put their horses through numerous stunts solely to mollify the irascible director. Clothier later estimated it cost $250,000 to let Ford direct the superfluous scenes.

Roberson had a small speaking role as a Tennessee volunteer who accompanied Davy Crockett to the Alamo. At one point the character he plays asks, "Do that mean what I think it do?" Whereupon a younger man answers, "It do!" Months later Roberson happened to be in Chicago for a showing of *The Alamo* when he overheard a patron question Wayne's ability to produce, direct, and star in the film. "Damn right, he did it all himself," Roberson intervened. "He's a helluva guy."

The tension broke when the other man recognized him. "You're what's his name," the man said. "You're that mean-what-I-think-it-do."

"It do," Roberson replied.

Wayne's slavish devotion to *The Alamo*—"Fourteen years in the making!" the trailer boasted—failed to make it a hit. Critics panned the movie. "Interminable," one said.

ALONG WITH COCAINE, ROBERSON HAD TRUCKED ANOTHER HORSE to Texas. His name was Hondo; Roberson had brought him home from the movie of the same name and attempted to train him, without much success. Hondo wasn't working out on *The Alamo* set either. Multiple stuntmen tried to fall him, and each time the horse would plant his feet and refuse to budge. Or he would circle around and around as if he were contemplating falling, but he'd never actually fall. Exasperated, Roberson vowed to get rid of the horse. By the time he returned to California, he had both Cocaine,

Hondo, and a third horse that had performed as an extra. Roberson thought the third horse had the potential to become an expert faller.

Stuntman Hal Needham was interested in Hondo and in the second horse too. Roberson was still living at his oceanfront property in Ventura, but he kept his horses in Sun Valley, where he had a house, a barn, a corral, and five acres of hilly pasture for his horses to roam. He rented out to Needham his house at the front of the property. On weekends Needham invited friends over to practice stunts, such as falling out of a tree in the backyard, testing motorcycle feats, and engaging in pretend fights. The stuntmen also worked on tricks involving horses. Roberson's yard had plenty of sand so the horses could fall without getting hurt.

Needham brought Roberson's unnamed horse from Texas out for a test ride and felt an instant liking to him: the horse seemed intelligent and capable, plus he was sweet-tempered. He had just one bad habit, and that was a tendency to ride alongside a fence or a building so narrowly that a rider who wasn't keeping close watch might wind up getting his leg crushed. Tugging on the horse's reins to pull him away from the obstacle had the opposite effect; the horse would respond by running faster and closing in even more tightly against the fence.

Charlene, Roberson's daughter, made a name for herself as Hollywood's first female makeup artist, and she happened to live in a house at the rear of the property, behind the house Needham was renting. Needham had such a gregarious personality that Charlene couldn't help but like him, but she didn't think much of his style of training. Trying to master horse falls, she said, Needham would practice falling the same horse over and over. When he grew tired of tumbling, he would turn the horse over to another stuntman who would fall the same horse multiple times more. "If *you're* tired, think about the horse," Charlene thought to herself.

Roberson dropped by occasionally to watch the action, and he, too, must have disapproved of what he saw, because after a time he stopped letting Needham work his horses. Later, after Charlene married stuntman Bill Hart and Hart asked Roberson for tips on getting horses to fall, Roberson declined to let him practice on his mounts. Instead he told Hart, "Next time I'm going to do a job, you can come watch me."

Charlene Roberson spoke of the love her dad had for animals and the tenderness he felt toward them. She offered as an example the time

Charlene's daughter Theda got a pet raccoon. Roberson built a big outdoor cage for the wild animal and was annoyed when he came home one day to find Theda had left no water in the cage. That happened a second time—no water in the cage. The third time it happened, Charlene came home to find Theda herself sitting in the cage, crying. "Like baseball, three times and you're out," Roberson admonished his granddaughter. Theda learned her lesson and never let the raccoon go without water again.

Despite his misgivings, Roberson sold Honda and the unnamed horse to Needham, who spent the next eight months working with them. Needham broke Alamo—the name he gave his new horse—of his fence-riding habit and taught both him and Hondo not only to fall but also to rear and jump, something not all falling horses could do. Needham saw in both horses the hot blood and speed needed to perform. He went on to claim that he trained two of the greatest stunt horses in movie history.

One film Needham performed in called for him to rush headlong at the enemy, guns a-blazing, then vault his horse over a log and fall him. The horse in question was Hondo, and there was considerable speculation on the set that in the face of all that gunfire, Hondo would freeze up and refuse to fall. Needham was confident Hondo would perform, however, and the horse did not disappoint. "He charged into the rifle fire, jumped the log, and fell right on the designated spot," Needham said. "Hondo made believers of them, and he also got us a lot of jobs as word spread about how spectacular he was."

The fiery Hondo learned his lessons well. All Needham had to do was raise his right hand to pull on the rein and the horse would hit the ground. That became an issue when Needham performed with Honda in John Wayne's 1967 movie *The War Wagon*. Wayne was about to film a sequence that required him to ride a horse into town when he spied Needham exercising Hondo on the outskirts of the set and asked if he might use him in the scene. Flattered, Needham dismounted and handed Wayne the reins. The star actor was circling Hondo, getting adjusted to him, when he spotted his wife, Pilar, a few yards away. Wayne raised his right hand to wave at Pilar, and the next thing he knew, he and Hondo had hit the dirt. Wayne was uninjured, but those few minutes astride Hondo were enough. "That horse is a danger to mankind," he muttered as he handed back the reins.

Needham was clearly enamored with his horses. In a memoir he described galloping Alamo to a designated spot and cueing him to fall. The horse went down as instructed while Needham rolled off of him, barreled over a couple of times, and then sat up on the ground. Afterward he recalled, "Alamo came up behind me and leaned his head on my shoulder. I scratched him affectionately under the chin."

But tragedy occurred in *Little Big Man*, the 1970 movie starring Dustin Hoffman and Faye Dunaway. The film recounts an elderly man's reminiscences of growing up with Indians and fighting with General Custer. Serving as a stuntman and second unit director, Needham was asked by director Arthur Penn to gallop Hondo as fast as possible off a hillside for one scene. The pair were halfway down the hill when Hondo stepped in a gopher hole and fell, breaking his leg.

"We were way out in the country," Needham remembered. "They said if you don't get a vet out here and verify that he has a broken leg, then you can't collect the insurance on him. And I said, it's going to take two hours to get a vet out here. I don't want that horse to lay there suffering. Get me a gun." A member of the crew, Billy Burton, produced a firearm, but Needham couldn't bring himself to pull the trigger. He handed the gun back to Burton and asked him to put an end to Hondo's suffering. Distraught, Needham turned and walked away. Seconds later the sound of the gunshot rang out. "I was devastated and started to cry in front of the whole crew," Needham recalled. "Don't tell me grown men don't cry."

16

Aging and Still Falling

By the mid-1950s, television began to supersede the silver screen as the most popular medium for Westerns. TV Westerns followed on the heels of radio's Saturday Afternoon Matinee, a showcase for Western series that had cultivated legions of young fans. The programs were initially aimed at children—*Hopalong Cassidy* was the first to air, in 1949—but by 1955 shows like *Gunsmoke* and *Bonanza* were attracting adult viewers by the millions, and by 1959 there were thirty Westerns on television. At one point eight of the top ten television shows were Westerns: *Gunsmoke*; *Wagon Train*; *Have Gun—Will Travel*; *The Rifleman*; *Maverick*; *The Life and Legend of Wyatt Earp*; *Zane Grey Theatre*; and *Wanted Dead or Alive*. The only non-Westerns to attract similar numbers of viewers were *The Lucy-Desi Comedy Hour* and *The Danny Thomas Show*. Sales of toys with some connection to Western TV shows were expected to reach $125 million that year, more than $1 billion in today's dollars.

In addition to the series, networks frequently aired B-Westerns, and viewers couldn't get enough. Americans living in the 1940s and 1950s were just a generation or two removed from the Wild West era of the late 1800s, and TV Westerns delivered a reassuring sense of morality, a comforting throwback to a time in the nation's history that many viewers perceived as simpler and therefore better. "America grew too fast, and we have lost something in the process," motivational researcher Ernest Dichter told *Time* magazine in an attempt to explain Westerns' overwhelming following. "The Western story offers us a way to return to the soil, a chance to redefine our roots."

The popularity of television Westerns had a dampening effect on Western movies, however. To shoot a Western for the big screen, a studio had to lease trained horses, hire riders, and maintain backlots or rent movie ranches big enough to accommodate the inevitable shoot-outs. A TV series could be filmed for half the cost. TV shows were shot in black and white, and they had fewer calls for stunt horses, partly because of the cost involved but also because many of the shows were filmed on relatively small lots. (Watch an episode of *Gunsmoke*; it's surprising how contained the action is, on just a handful of sets.) Still, studios continued to crank out plenty of B-Westerns. A number were filmed at Universal Studios in Burbank, but many other movies and TV shows were produced in the foothills of the San Fernando and Simi valleys, wide open stretches north of Los Angeles abundant with the sagebrush, coulees, and striking outcroppings that gave the productions the feel of the real West.

Almost all the movie ranches were located within thirty miles of the major studios. There was a reason for that: union workers were guaranteed extra pay if they worked out of town, the definition of "out of town" being more than thirty miles out. Studios maneuvered around having to pay the extra wages by buying up ranches within that thirty-mile range. In the early days of television, cast members and stunt performers would wait in the parking lot of a Standard Oil gas station on the corner of Ventura Boulevard and Sepulveda Boulevard in Sherman Oaks—now the site of a huge shopping mall, just off I-405—for the studios' stretch limos to hum along and give them a ride. The limos would arrive by 6:00 a.m. with signs in the righthand corner of the windshield denoting which Westerns they were assigned to pick up cast and crew for. By the time they got to the West Valley, to places like Thousand Oaks and Iverson's ranch in Canoga Park, the horses were saddled and waiting to go. Other ranches used for filming included the Apacheland Movie Ranch near the Superstition Mountains; the Big Sky Movie Ranch located in the Simi Valley; the Iverson Movie Ranch and the Spahn Movie Ranch north of Chatsworth; the Bell Moving Picture Ranch in the Simi Hills; the Corriganville Movie Ranch in the Simi Valley; the Lasky Movie Ranch in the San Fernando Valley; the Monogram Ranch, later renamed the Melody Ranch, near Newhall; and the Paramount Ranch in the Santa Monica Mountains near Agoura Hills. Wildfires nearly destroyed the Paramount Ranch in the fall of 2018.

Iverson's ranch was especially sought after because of its distinctive outthrusts of rocks. "All the low-budget Westerns were made at Iverson's," actor and stuntman Dobie Carey said. "Many times, you'd be in the middle of a dialogue scene and gunshots would ruin the take. They'd be coming from another company just over the hill. Sometimes there would be three shows shooting there on the same day." Regardless of which ranch was used, Roberson's Sun Valley property was conveniently close by. He could easily trailer Cocaine to a set.

By 1964 Roberson had reached his mid-forties and Cocaine was twenty years old, a time in their lives when each might have been expected to slow down. But the two remained in high demand. John Wayne continued to hire the pair to double him and his horse. "The sixties were full of horse falls, saddle falls, high falls and screen fights," Roberson said, and Cocaine performed as energetically as ever.

In Western circles, Roberson had gained renown as a first-class "pound-grounder," willing to attempt just about anything. For the 1950 movie *The Eagle and the Hawk*, filmed near Sedona, Arizona, he allowed himself to be tied between a pair of wild horses—his hands tethered to their manes, his feet fastened to their tails—as they galloped across a field. The stunt cost him two broken ribs and a fair amount of skin. Because Roberson was willing to try anything, he had sought out the fastest falling horse in Hollywood, and Coke delivered: he could fall while charging thirty-five miles an hour. For one scene he landed so resoundingly that he threw Roberson forty-five feet.

The good times weren't always so good. One especially upsetting event occurred during the shooting of John Ford's *The Horse Soldiers*. The movie is based on an 1863 Civil War encounter dubbed Grierson's Raid, where a Union colonel, Benjamin Grierson, led his troops deep into Confederate country to wipe out a railroad line carrying supplies to Vicksburg. The tactic deflated the Confederate army and was regarded as one of the Union army's most ingenious coups. The movie called for a series of horse falls, and Fred Kennedy, the veteran trainer who had helped invent the stunt, confided in Roberson that he hoped to nail a part and that he planned to retire after the movie was shot. Ford, though, felt that Kennedy was out of shape and too old at forty-eight to be diving off a tumbling horse. Instead Ford assigned Kennedy the role of a trooper tasked with looking after the character of Miss Hannah Hunter, played by Constance Towers. Kennedy persisted, though, and Ford finally consented to let him also perform a saddle fall while doubling actor William Holden. "A Christmas present for Fred," Ford explained to an aide.

Filming began in late October of 1958 in Louisiana. The scene involving Kennedy's fall would be shot along the Homochitto River near Natchitoches. Even at his age, a saddle fall should have been simple enough for Kennedy to pull off. After all, he was an expert at both falling horses and falling off of horses and had performed both stunts for years.

The cameras were put in place. Ford instructed Kennedy to remain on the ground once he fell. Constance Towers would rush to his side and throw herself on him. Kennedy was not to move until he heard Ford say the word "Cut." At the sound of "Action," Kennedy rode the horse into a swampy area as instructed and fell precisely where he was supposed to, but he landed oddly; his head was twisted backward. Actor Walter Reed, who was riding behind Kennedy, later said Kennedy's horse was spooked by the sight of a campfire nearby, prompting him to shy away in the opposite direction, changing the arc of Kennedy's fall and causing him to land on his head. As the cameras continued to roll, Towers ran in and flung herself on Kennedy, only to recoil in alarm when she realized he was seriously hurt. The fall had broken Kennedy's neck. He died on the way to the hospital.

Fellow stuntmen later divulged that this wasn't Kennedy's first neck injury; he'd broken his neck two years earlier. It's possible that even though the first break healed, it left him vulnerable to further harm.

Ford is said to have kept the scene depicting Kennedy's fall in the final version of the film (if he did so, it's not obvious). But the director was so overcome by Kennedy's death that he stopped filming in Louisiana soon after that. He returned to California and eventually shot the last battle scene in the San Fernando Valley. The movie was supposed to end with the Union troops celebrating their victory. Instead Ford chose to go with a new ending in which John Wayne's character bids farewell to William Holden's, who elects to stay behind with the wounded soldiers, dooming himself to capture.

Second unit director Cliff Lyons objected to the softer approach. When Ford cautioned the stuntmen, "Boys, take it easy," Lyons protested that riding roughly was what they'd been paid to do. But Ford prevailed. In one of the final scenes, the Union troops gallop across a bridge without incident. "Not one guy fell off the saddle," screenwriter John Lee Mahin later lamented. "I didn't know what the hell was the matter."

Back home, Roberson was waiting for the return of his colleagues, figuring they would throw a party to celebrate the movie's wrap. It was left to Hal Needham to deliver an envelope from Wayne informing Roberson that Kennedy was dead. He was stunned by the news but not 100 percent surprised. "Fred was too damn old for it," Roberson told his friends. "He knew he was too goddam old, and he should have quit while he was ahead. It's for damn sure I'll get out when I feel my reflexes going."

Kennedy's death made headlines across the country; several newspapers even published a series of photos showing the stuntman in mid-fall and lying face up, his face scrunched in agony. Months later, when the film was released, the press kit for *The Horse Soldiers* boasted about the movie's numerous casualties, including four broken legs and three broken arms—"some of the wildest riding to ever hit the screen"—but made no mention of Kennedy's demise.

Ford, though, had not forgotten. He took Kennedy's death hard. An inveterate alcoholic, Ford had followed his doctor's orders and abstained from drinking while *The Horse Soldiers* was being shot. But he typically capped off the end of a shoot by disappearing on a binge. This time, mired in grief, he really tied one on. Kennedy's death ended Ford's enthusiasm for horse falls. The director renowned for making some of Hollywood's most beloved Westerns would go on to film several more, but he incorporated few if any horse falls in them.

COCAINE HAD COME A LONG WAY FROM HIS INJURY IN TUCSON WHEN the veterinarian had predicted he would never perform again. But in 1962 he encountered danger off the set again. Roberson was working on assignment elsewhere in the San Fernando Valley when he got word that a wildfire had started in the part of Sun Valley that ran along La Tuna Canyon, near his house. Frantic that he couldn't be there himself to try to keep the fire at bay, Roberson phoned Charlene and told her to let the horses out. "Are you sure, Daddy?" Charlene asked. "What if they get run over?" "They'll be safer on the streets," Roberson replied.

Charlene was three months pregnant with her first baby. Neighbors were heeding the mandate to evacuate, and Charlene wanted to flee too. Her first thought was of her unborn child. But her dad had issued marching orders, and she knew better than to argue. She ran out of the house. From the backyard where Cocaine and the other horses were kept, she could see embers fluttering over the bone-dry hill, and she knew what that meant. The horses also knew that danger was afoot. They pawed the ground and trumpeted their fear, Cocaine shrieking the loudest.

Charlene raced to the front of the yard and flung open the gate to the street. Coke was the first horse to bolt out, the others close behind. Charlene watched as the horses hightailed it down Penrose Street, their manes flapping. With the horses out of the line of fire, she turned her attention to her father's second instruction: to climb on top of the house and hose down the roof. She was apprehensive as she scaled the ladder, and wetting the roof seemed to take forever. The water pressure in the hose was as weak as a stream of urine.

Fortunately, in a matter of minutes the danger subsided. The winds changed direction and Roberson's property was spared. Later that day, as soon as he arrived home, Roberson set out on foot in search of the horses. An hour later he returned riding Cocaine bareback, the other horses trailing from behind. Coke knew better than to wander far, and the other horses had followed his lead.

A few years later the city of Los Angeles constructed a twenty-foot-wide concrete and fenced-in wash that cut through the middle of Roberson's property. Gone were the days when his horses could meander out of the backyard and up the grassy hill, free to roam; the new ditch separated the yard from the pastureland. Still, as unattractive as it was, the wash offered one big advantage: it protected Roberson's house and yard from fire. Several times in the years since, flames have burned right up to the wash and stopped there, unable to leap over the manmade ravine. "I didn't want the wash," Charlene said, "but it's probably saved the place two or three times."

Cocaine even survived the dangers of radiation dust.

The Conqueror, a 1956 movie produced by Hollywood tycoon Howard Hughes, told the story of a tempestuous romance between a Mongol warrior chief played by John Wayne and the daughter of his sworn nemesis, played by Susan Hayward and popular Mexican star Pedro Armendáriz. The movie featured a record number of horse falls, 119 of them, performed by a half dozen expert stunt performers, including Roberson and Coke. But the movie is best remembered for the dangers its location posed to cast and crew. The exterior scenes were shot in the desert town of St. George, Utah, which happened to be 137 miles downwind from where the U.S. government was conducting a series of above-ground nuclear weapons tests.

From 1951 to 1962 federal scientists set off more than a hundred such tests; the year before filming of *The Conqueror* began, eleven above-ground tests occurred, coating the dunes and gorges surrounding St. George with toxic dust. Officials insisted the blasts posed no health hazard, but thousands of sheep grazing nearby died in the aftermath of one explosion. Hughes shot on location there for four months, and later, for reshoots, he had sixty tons of the soil hauled to California to match the Utah landscape. Roberson and Cocaine performed numerous falls in the contaminated dirt.

Over the following twenty-six years, 92 of the 220 cast and crew who worked on *The Conqueror* developed cancer, and half of them died from the disease. Pedro Armendáriz's cancer was diagnosed in 1960. He committed suicide in 1963. Director Dick Powell succumbed that same year. Wayne first suffered lung cancer (possibly a result of his heavy cigarette habit) and ultimately died of stomach cancer in 1979. Susan Hayward developed brain cancer and died in 1975; she was just fifty-seven. Cancer also killed actress Agnes Moorehead. Wayne's sons, Michael and Patrick, both survived cancer scares.

While a direct connection between fallout radiation and individual cases of cancer has been impossible to prove, the number of cases was highly suspicious. Typically among a group of people that size, only thirty-odd cases of cancer would develop, according to Robert Pendleton, a professor of biology at the University of Utah. Yet Cocaine did not appear to suffer from exposure to the contaminated dirt, and neither did Roberson, at least for some time. But by the early 1970s, as deaths among other cast and crew began to climb, Hughes spent $12 million buying every copy of the film he could find. He was said to have spent his last years watching the movie over and over. Hughes may have been the only one watching. *The Conqueror* made one list of the fifty worst films of all time, and after his death Wayne was sarcastically awarded a Golden Turkey for his portrayal.

Ellen Powell, the daughter of director Richard Powell and actress Joan Blondell, accompanied her father to St. George and remembers being dazzled by Chuck Roberson's flirtatious personality and his derring-do astride Cocaine. Charlene Roberson was there also, and years later she vividly remembered the sixteenth birthday party thrown for Ellen in St. George. John Wayne's oldest son, Michael, had asked Charlene to accompany him to the soiree, but the studio thought it would be more appropriate for Michael to escort Ellen. Charlene was so annoyed by this turn of events that she filled a burlap sack with horse manure, tied a large red bow around it, and gave it to Ellen as a birthday present. "I hope you didn't put your name on it," a mortified Roberson said when he found out about the gag gift. "First and last," his daughter shot back.

Charlene's fall from Coco years earlier had instilled in her a fear of horses. She wanted to please her dad, so she didn't object when he asked her to feed and water the horses each day, spray them for flies, shovel their manure, and pick the thistles out of the sand. But she finally confessed that Cocaine intimidated her. "When I feed him, he runs up to me like he's going to bite me," Charlene told her dad. Not only that but Cocaine would snort indignantly, blowing snot all over her.

Roberson thought about it for a minute. "Are you feeding him first?" he asked. Charlene said that she wasn't. "You have to feed him first. He expects it," Roberson explained. Charlene followed his advice, and Coke stopped charging her.

Charlene lost her fear of Cocaine, but she remained jealous of the horse in those early years. Cocaine was such a favorite of her dad's, and Roberson seemed to go out of his way to accommodate the horse's desires. He smoothed Vaseline around Coke's eyes to keep away flies, and he stipulated that Coke be fed oats and hay, a better quality of feed than the other horses got. Roberson boasted about Cocaine's level of intelligence. The other horses would swallow avocados grown on the property whole, pits and all, only to experience stomach upset. Coke was smart enough to spit out the pit.

Roberson had no patience for Charlene's resentment of his best-loved horse. As a teenager she complained once about having to care for the horses, and Roberson threw it back at her. "That fancy dress you're wearing?" he said. "Cocaine paid for that."

Charlene had a change of heart after a veterinarian came to the house one misty evening to give Cocaine his shots. Roberson was out on assignment, but he was scheduled to trailer Coke to Mexico the following morning, and he needed to line up the necessary vaccinations. The veterinarian didn't care for stuntmen or stunt horses, and the first thing he announced when he arrived was that Cocaine had better be tied up and waiting. He wasn't; he was wandering freely about the yard. But Charlene knew how important it was for Coke to get his shots, so she assured the vet that she could rope him. How she hoped to accomplish this, she had no idea. In the darkness Charlene went to fetch a lariat—a rope tied into a permanent loop, called a hondo knot. She beckoned to Cocaine, slowly approached him, and, hoping for the best, tossed the lariat in his direction. To her astonishment Coke walked straight toward the loop and thrust his head inside.

Charlene was beyond relieved; Cocaine had made her job easy. She no longer felt bitterly toward him. From then on, as far as she was concerned, Coke was family.

17

The Return of Cruelty

If only the story could end there. Trip wires banished. Falling horses trained to land safely. All's well.

For a time, anyway, that appeared to be the case. By the early 1960s, moviemakers seemed to understand that animals should be treated compassionately. At the very least they grasped the need to abide by standards established by the American Humane Association. The AHA had five field representatives supervising the use of animals in movies—stables around Hollywood still had more than a thousand horses ready to lease out—and filmmakers seemed willing to acquiesce to the organization's protocols.

When Harold Melniker took over as head of the AHA's western office in 1962, he thought the bad old ways were gone for good. Trim and tan, with a headful of gray hair swept back and tucked behind his ears, Melniker was handsome enough to play the lead in feature films himself. He'd come to Los Angeles twenty-four years earlier after working as a lawyer in New York. California's sunny warmth appealed to him. Melniker handled legal affairs first for MGM and then RKO, and he represented both studios in discussions with the AHA. The Humane Association was so impressed by Melniker's manner that it offered him its most prominent post. Melniker "is not getting West coast-lawyer rich" at his job, one newspaper reported, but he relished being out from under a studio's thumb, overseeing work he felt made a difference.

Studios preparing to film a movie with animals knew to send Melniker a script in advance. If he spotted any action he deemed unacceptable, he would note that in his comments, along with suggestions for working around the scene in question or eliminating it entirely. The animals' safety was foremost in Melniker's mind. Where Westerns were concerned, Melniker recommended using quarter-load ammunition to soften the sound of gunshots; louder versions could always be added during editing. He might suggest simulating an action instead of using live animals. Or he'd tell the studios they needed to use trained animals. Trained falling horses were clearly preferable to inexperienced steeds who had no inkling how to fall on cue.

Melniker would assign one of his field representatives to witness the filming of a movie from start to finish. For movies shot out of state, the rep packed a large suitcase because he'd need to be on hand however many weeks the shooting took. His job was to make sure the horses and cattle on location were watered, fed, sheltered, given ample time to rest, and weren't subjected to any action that might result in injury. If any animals were limping, the rep would see to it that they were taken out of the lineup. If the hay hauled in for the horses was low-grade, he would insist on a better quality of feed. If horses were being trucked twenty miles away to a location that had no drinking supply, the rep made sure a water truck came along too.

One of the AHA's reps, Jack Shannon, had come to California forty years earlier, delivering a truck full of steers to market. He happened onto a Western set and quickly decided he'd rather ride a horse in the movies than across a pasture back home on the family ranch. He worked as a wrangler and stuntman, occasionally acting alongside the likes of William S. Hart, Tom Mix, Hoot Gibson, and Hopalong Cassidy. Shannon liked the fact that his work with the AHA gave him a voice where the treatment of horses was concerned.

The *Los Angeles Times* followed Shannon around for a day, from the set of a new ABC David Carradine Western called *Shane*, which was shot in the San Fernando Valley north of Hollywood, to the set of NBC's *Bonanza*. Shannon's third stop was the set of the Henry Fonda movie *Welcome to Hard Times*, which was partially filmed at the Conejo Ranch in Thousand Oaks.

Stunt riders could carry out as many falls as they cared to, but the AHA now stipulated that falling horses be limited to just two falls a day. "(The rider's) getting paid for it, and he can say no, or demand an extra hundred bucks, but the horse doesn't have those options," Melniker said. It was important that horses and cattle not be worn out from running, that the ground they were expected to cross wasn't hazardous, and that the second unit director had enough wranglers on hand to keep matters under control. Shannon watched to make sure actors and extras weren't jerking a horse's reins too hard or spurring him too often or too forcefully.

"There's an occasional performer who thinks yanking a horse to a halt is the greatest bit of acting since Stanislavski," Melniker commented. Shannon saw the same tendency. "Some of these actors they bring out of New York these days don't know a horse's got a heart and lungs—they think he's got a motor inside him like a sports car," he said.

AHA reps learned to brace for the unexpected. For one movie, a studio leased five hundred horses from nearby riding academies. Before filming started, the rep assigned to the shoot discovered that some of the horses had saddle sores; the stables had worked them too hard. At his insistence the horses were sent back and replaced with healthier animals.

The AHA's authority to intervene in those scenarios convinced Melniker that the system was working. He'd hashed out guidelines with the studios, and they were following them. His reps felt accepted on movie sets. Studios paid a rep's travel and living expenses for out-of-town locations, but not his salary. "That gives us the freedom to be completely independent and objective," Melniker said. Best of all, he was happy to report that Running W's were "positively forbidden now."

The AHA okayed certain practices that would be considered unacceptable today. The organization had no issue with letting a veterinarian sedate an animal that needed to play dead if an animal trained to lie still couldn't be found. (The AHA stipulated that sedation not take place until the exact moment it was needed and that an experienced veterinarian remain on set until the animal regained consciousness.) In a memorable scene in the 1965 movie *Cat Ballou*, a gray horse named Smokey leans against a building with his front legs crossed, snoozing along with his rider, Lee Marvin. The horse didn't just happen to doze off; he was drugged. And the PATSY awards given out with great fanfare by the Humane Association included recognition for chimpanzees, wild animals who—it's now understood—have to be beaten into submission to perform. A chimpanzee's all-teeth-bared smile is actually a grimace, a sign of fear and distress.

But Melniker soon realized the disadvantages of his job. For one thing, his field reps had an unreasonable amount of ground to cover. In 1965

12. The horse in this scene from the 1965 movie *Cat Ballou* was drugged to look as if he was dozing. Photofest.

alone, animals and birds made 19,540 appearances in movies and TV, including 10,144 appearances by horses, the animal most frequently used on-screen. Yet there was no way Humane Association reps could be on hand for every sequence involving horses, and some directors learned simply to postpone risky action scenes until the AHA rep had left the set. It wasn't unheard of for a director to ask a rep point-blank to leave if the rep objected too strongly to a problematic scene. Even when the reps stayed in place, they could only suggest that a director follow the proper guidelines. They lacked any authority to enforce their recommendations.

Added to that, Hollywood's Production Code—or Hay's Code—was starting to lose steam. The code's ban on profanity, nudity, and sex seemed ridiculously passé at a time when social mores were relaxing on those fronts. Among the code's many can't-do's was an edict forbidding a couple to kiss with open mouths. Romantic scenes required actresses to keep one foot on the floor. The code had been modified several times over the years to allow once-taboo topics like adultery, prostitution, and miscegenation to be addressed on-screen, and films that contained racy language were starting to win approval.

Threats to the American movie industry rose from other corners. A decade and a half earlier the U.S. Supreme Court had ruled that studios violated anti-trust laws by owning and operating their own theaters. As a result, studios were forced to sell off their theaters, ending their convenient practice of distributing their own movies. No longer tied to studios, theater owners could now decide to show foreign films that weren't bound by the Production Code—movies that could, and did, offer racier content. Director Otto Preminger and Ingmar Bergman's films routinely violated the code, and other foreign-made films challenged conventional ideas about subject matters like homosexuality, which the code strictly forbade.

Television posed an even greater threat. For the first time Americans could watch programs from the comfort of their living rooms, without paying an admission fee. TV shows had to follow strict guidelines as far as content was concerned, and television producers and directors were more willing to comply with the Production Code. The networks depended on licenses granted to them by the Federal Communications Commission; they had no desire to air some controversial sequence that might invite the scrutiny of the FCC or a committee of Congress.

Increasingly, though, movie studios felt freed from those same constraints. Desperate to win back audiences and seeing how much more permissive foreign movies were, Hollywood producers began making more risqué movies designed to keep audiences in their seats. Billy Wilder's 1959 film *Some Like It Hot*, starring Tony Curtis and Marilyn Monroe, became a huge hit despite the fact that it failed to obtain a certificate of approval, diminishing further the code's sway.

In 1952 the U.S. Supreme Court dealt another blow. The high court overturned a 1915 ruling that said movies were not entitled to the U.S. Constitution's protection of free speech. In fact, the court ruled, movies *were* entitled to free speech protection. Then, in 1966, MGM released the film *Blow-Up* despite production code officials giving it a definitive thumbs down in light of the movie's unmistakably suggestive content. When *Blow-Up* took off at the box office, other studios began turning out provocative subject matter too. The Production Code had lost its influence.

Finally in 1966 the Motion Picture Association of America tossed out the Production Code and replaced it with a bulleted list of guidelines. Masterminding the change was Jack Valenti, a slightly built man with intense dark eyes and a can-do demeanor who, before moving to California to head the MPAA, had spent years as an aide and confidante to President Lyndon B. Johnson. Valenti viewed the code as an outdated and unnecessary form of censorship and an "iron-fisted moral arbiter" whose influence was eroding in the wake of America's rapidly changing cultural and political mores. "I didn't like the Hays Code, and I was determined to throw it over the side, the sooner the better," Valenti said.

The new guidelines asked studios to adhere to community standards of good taste when it came to sex and violence but didn't mandate that they do so. Movies that crossed the boundaries might be denied a seal of approval, but Valenti knew that withholding the official okay didn't pose much of a threat. Foreign and independent producers were under no compunction to abide by the new code. Why should American-made movies have to?

The death of the Production Code ushered in a new golden age of filmmaking, a time when movies veered from traditional formulas to more challenging and realistic storylines. The treatment of animals on-screen suffered as a result, however. One of the MPAA's eleven new tenets declared that "excessive cruelty to animals shall not be portrayed and animals shall not be treated inhumanely." The difference—and this was key—was that studios were no longer required to submit their scripts to the American Humane Association or allow AHA reps on their sets. The guidelines were strictly voluntary. And foreign filmmakers, as well as American filmmakers who were producing movies overseas, saw no reason to abide by them.

As far as movie animals were concerned, the demise of the Production

Code could not have come at a worse time. Movies, Westerns included, were starting to reflect a 180-degree change in American culture that began with the assassination of President John F. Kennedy in 1963. Up to that point, filmmakers were still turning out optimistic, often guileless portrayals of Western expansion, with clearly drawn good guys and bad guys, and the good guys nearly always won. Kennedy's assassination, followed by the polarizing Vietnam War, changed everything. The nation's dispirited tone was reflected in a new wave of films that upended the long-held myth of American superiority. Western protagonists no longer stood willing to battle on the side of right, even if it cost them their lives. In just a few years, Westerns rolled out by European filmmakers introduced a world of indiscriminate bloodshed, one in which the heroic gunslinger was searching to define himself. These new protagonists could no longer be expected to save the day.

Gone were the early studio titans, the Mayers, the Cohns, the Warners, the Zukors, and the Schencks, who had been willing to work with the AHA. The major studios continued to submit scripts in advance, but there was no guarantee they would abide by the AHA's requests. To cut costs, producers began filming movies abroad, where actors and stunt performers could be hired less expensively and filming could take place conveniently out of sight of the humane reps. A producer shooting a movie in Spain might discover that he couldn't find a trained falling horse to shoot a scene. Instead of cutting the sequence, he would often resort to using trip wires. Second unit directors often had no objection to using cruel and archaic Running W's. In fact, many of them claimed that trip wires were completely safe.

The treatment of horses fell victim to the rough new climate, as the 1962 movie *Taras Bulba* exemplified. A 1500s-era spectacle chronicling the Cossack freedom fighters' war against the Poles, *Taras Bulba* starred Yul Brynner as a Cossack trying to teach his two sons (one of them played by Tony Curtis) to learn the ways of the Poles so they could turn around and help defeat them. The movie was partially shot in California, but the battle scenes were filmed in Argentina, out of sight of the American Humane Association. Included was an enormous combat sequence involving nine thousand horses and ten to twelve thousand soldiers wildly brandishing swords as they plowed into the enemy. So many horses fell that they piled on top of one another. In one scene, a blast takes place just as a soldier rides past on his horse. The horse skids across the grass as he falls. Another rider jumps a horse over a cannon at the exact moment it's lit. That horse may well have been Cocaine. Roberson later said he fell Cocaine fifteen times in a single afternoon on the *Taras Bulba* set.

Filmmakers never admitted to mistreating animals. When director J. Lee Thompson showed *Taras Bulba* in Chicago, one newspaper account of his visit made light of the action sequences and the fact that Argentine gauchos had been hired to fall off the horses in the battle scenes. "After the showing, all gathered around Thompson to inquire anxiously if any harm befell the horses," the reporter wrote. "They were given the proper assurances, of course. What is needed, we think, is a Society for the Prevention of Cruelty to Actors."

The same year Valenti did away with the Production Code, Columbia Pictures released *Alvarez Kelly*. Based on the true story of the Beefsteak Raid of 1864, when a Confederate major general stole a herd of cattle destined for Union troops, *Alvarez Kelly* stars William Holden as the cattleman who reluctantly agrees to help steer the stolen herd out of Union hands toward to the rebel capital of Richmond, Virginia. The film was shot in and around Baton Rouge, Louisiana, and it contains a couple of noteworthy horse falls.

In an early scene meant to show the ineptitude of Confederate soldiers around livestock, stuntman Mickey Gilbert and his brother-in-law, Little Joe Yrigoyen, simultaneously fall their horses, Gypsy and Rebel, after nearly colliding with one another head-on. Gilbert and Yrigoyen had practiced the stunt repeatedly at Gilbert's ranch before trying it on-screen. The scene was impressive, and the horses, trained to fall, landed safely. A later sequence shows stuntman Jack Williams falling his mare Coco in her signature rearing-back fashion during a cattle drive—with the added twist that this time she falls backward onto the downside of a bank sloping to a creek. The stunt is astonishing. Williams tries to clamber out of Coco's way, but her hind end rolls over him as she struggles to stop her fall, finally coming to a rest at the edge of the water. She rises to her feet immediately afterward, uninjured.

Another stunt in *Alvarez Kelly* went terribly awry, though, in a scene that didn't make the final cut. Gilbert was racing his horse Gypsy alongside the cattle when his character was shot by a man positioned high up in a tree.

Gilbert was rigged to catch his foot in a stirrup when he fell out of the saddle, whereupon he would be dragged along the ground next to Gypsy's rear leg. Underneath his stunt vest was a nylon strap tied to a release unit, which in turn was tied to the stirrup. The release unit also had a cable that Gilbert could jerk at any point to release himself from his horse.

Everything went as planned, at first. When Gilbert's father-in-law, stunt coordinator Big Joe Yrigoyen, called out, "Action!" a stuntman perched in the tree fired a fake shot at Gilbert, and Gilbert pressed a button setting off his squib (blood packet). Gilbert dived off his horse, and Gypsy dragged him forty feet or so as planned when suddenly a steer veered directly in front of her, causing her to turn sharply to the right. Trained to stay on course, the horse quickly straightened herself out, but the swerve caused Gilbert's left thigh to crash into her right hind leg just below her ankle, snapping her bone. As soon as Gilbert saw Gypsy hobbling on three legs, he pulled the release cable; freed from the weight of the stuntman, the horse crumpled to the ground. Gilbert rushed to Gypsy's side and held her head in his lap, talking to her to try to soothe her, but nothing could be done. Yrigoyen had to put her down. "It was a terrible ending to such a wild camera shot," Gilbert said. "My father-in-law and I shared a lot of tears over Gypsy's unfortunate end."

The AHA might have been able to stop that stunt had a rep been allowed on location.

The industry's Valenti was aware of the growing violence in movies and also that the U.S. Supreme Court had recently affirmed the right of states, cities, and counties to ban films they believed should not be seen by children. Dozens of local governments—including Dallas, Detroit, Birmingham, and Chicago—had established censorship boards designed to weed out objectionable movies. Moviemakers needed to do more than attach a "for mature audiences" warning in their ads. In 1968 the MPAA created its own rating system designed to warn parents that a given film might contain offensive language, sex, violence, and/or the simulated use of illegal drugs. The ratings were simplified by letters: G stood for general audiences, M for mature content, R for restricted (those under seventeen were not admitted without an adult), and X for sexually explicit matter. (PG-13, meant for moviegoers thirteen and older, was included later.) The National Association of Theatre Owners agreed to abide by the system.

THE RETURN OF CRUELTY

Still, moviemakers were ratcheting up the shock factor—anything to win back audiences. In 1969's *Butch Cassidy and the Sundance Kid*, director George Roy Hill filmed a scene showing Butch and Sundance (played by Paul Newman and Robert Redford) jumping their horses from a moving railroad car. The crew built a ramp on the other side of the car so the horses could get a head start as they raced through the car. The stunt was pulled off successfully, but it could easily have gone awry.

Harold Melniker was still determined to put an end to the irresponsible behavior. In 1970, under his direction, the American Humane Association began issuing its own movie ratings. To eliminate any confusion over what the ratings meant, Melniker kept things simple: either a film would be deemed acceptable or it wouldn't. There were three reasons why a movie might earn a thumbs down: if animals were killed during filming, if they were mistreated, or if they were used in an objectionable way. An acceptable rating meant the filmmakers had allowed animal advocates on the set and had abided by AHA guidelines. A movie shot overseas could qualify for an acceptable rating if a responsible, qualified source was able to certify that all animal action and animal handling complied with established U.S. humane standards.

The Humane Association planned to periodically distribute lists of acceptable and unacceptable movies, hoping that if a movie was deemed unacceptable, moviegoers would not only refuse to see it but also be moved to protest its showing at local theaters. Melniker's fondest desire was that filmmakers shooting movies overseas would stop mistreating and killing animals and that, in time, the ratings program could be discontinued.

"We think one way to bring about change is to try to reduce the number of tickets sold," Melniker said. "If it hurts [a producer's] pocketbook, even the independent producer filming outside the U.S. may have a second thought when he casually says 'Let's use a trip.'"

The first year the AHA issued ratings, *Dirty Dingus Magee*, *The Wild Country*, and—despite the death of Hal Needham's horse Hondo—*Little Big Man* all qualified as acceptable for their treatment of animals.

The use of Running W's was the American Humane Association's biggest concern. Movies made in the United States had stopped incorporating trip wires a generation earlier. Now the cruel devices were back, especially in films made overseas. Falling horses weren't as prevalent as they had once been, now that the popularity of Westerns had tapered off. Those who were still available, like Cocaine, didn't come cheap, and too many directors simply weren't willing to pay what it took to hire them to perform.

For the rare moviegoer who knew what to look for, it was easy to spot a horse fallen by a trip wire. "If you see a galloping horse suddenly and abruptly go to the ground in a headlong, nose-first crash, you have seen a Running W trip, and it is totally inexcusable," Melniker said.

The Production Code would have prevented such a practice, and had it still been in place, authorities could have ordered a disturbing sequence to be deleted from a movie or refused to let it be shown in theaters. But the code had been abolished, so moviemakers were under no legal obligation to protect horses from Running W's, tilt chutes, or other such devices. Under the Motion Picture Association's new rating system, a sequence came under fire only if an animal was shown to be obviously injured. And even if that were the case, the review board's only recourse was to assign a film a more restrictive rating, something the MPAA was reluctant to ever do.

Over the next four years, the Humane Association gave thumbs down to a number of movies for horse-trips, including *Soldier Blue*, *The Hunting Party*, *Lawman*, *Valdez Is Coming*, *The Culpepper Cattle Co.*, *Chato's Land*, and *Scalawag*. Most producers openly admitted to Melniker that they had used Running W's in their battle scenes. They did so, they said, because they believed the practice was safe, that the odds of causing injury to the horses were about a million to one. Melniker argued in vain that regardless of the chances, no animal should be subjected to the risk of injury.

In 1972 the AHA added another layer of messaging by issuing its first "No Animals Were Harmed" tagline to a movie, *The Doberman Gang*, hoping other filmmakers would aspire to earn the tagline too. But the careless treatment of animals continued. *The Culpepper Cattle Co.*, about a young boy's coming of age on the range, includes a very obvious horse-trip: the victim is shown galloping one second and crashing straight down the next. "We couldn't eliminate that spill," producer Paul Helmick said. "It kills a one-legged cowboy the audience grows to love and is essential to the plot." In response to complaints, the studio added footage purportedly showing the horse that had been tripped rising to his feet, uninjured. But it's impossible to tell if the horse that was tripped was the same horse shown walking away, Melniker argued. Nor was there any guarantee that the next horse to be tripped would be lucky enough to emerge unscathed.

Chato's Land stars Charles Bronson as a half-Apache man who finds himself the target of a posse after he shoots the local sheriff in self-defense. When posse members rape his wife in revenge, Chato tracks them down and begins killing them one by one. In one scene the villains are riding across the desert when one of the horses goes down headfirst, a sign that he had no idea what was coming. It would have been easy to use a trained falling horse to carry out that fall. Instead trip wires were used. In another scene a horse ridden by one of Bronson's enemies falls rapidly at the sound of gunshot. The horse is able to turn his head slightly to the right so that he lands on the side of his face, but he was clearly caught off guard. As he rolls over with his legs in the air, the wire attachments are visible on his front legs. In a third scene Bronson's Chato "shoots" one of the runaway horses from atop a cliff. The horse, clearly taken by surprise, goes down knees and nose first, his neck bending backward as his face hits flat against the rocky dirt, his hind legs struggling to keep the rest of his body from falling. The camera turns away just as the horse begins to lift his head.

After the *New York Times* published a piece detailing some of the gratuitous killing of animals in movies, the MPAA received 1,400 letters condemning animal abuse. Hoping to fend off criticism, Valenti met with top officials at four humane organizations and vowed to abolish the inhumane treatment of animals. He encouraged filmmakers to cooperate with the American Humane Association by allowing its representatives back on their sets. "I am convinced that voluntary and cooperative efforts will produce salutary results. No abuse of animals should be tolerated," Valenti said. But Mel Morse left the meeting disgusted. He said Valenti made it clear the responsibility for enforcing anti-cruelty laws would rest with the states in which the films were being made. In reality, Morse said, no one on a set was likely to lodge a complaint for fear of losing future employment. And even if someone did speak up, few animal welfare offices around the country were capable of fielding complaints involving movie productions. "A horse looks injured, but the director says, 'Heck, he's just bruised. Look, he can still walk.' Three days later the horse dies," Morse said.

By 1975 the time-honored guidelines for handling horses seemed completely derailed. The American Humane Association had been unhappy with the mistreatment of horses in *Scalawag*, a 1973 Paramount film directed by Kirk Douglas, a Western version of Robert Louis Stevenson's *Treasure Island*. Several horses were tripped, including one horse that somersaulted head over heels, almost landing on the man riding him, and another nearly got trampled by horses speeding behind him down a cliff.

Now Douglas had come out with another movie, *Posse*, the tale of a U.S. marshal who, looking to gain political popularity, heads a group of vigilantes determined to track down an infamous bank robber. The movie association rated the film G for general audiences, but the AHA rated it as unacceptable, in part because of a disturbing scene that showed a horse falling off a cliff and into a river after being "shot." The horse narrowly missed the river's other rocky side and landed in the water headfirst. In another scene a horse jumps out of a railroad boxcar below, landing head-first and somersaulting. It's unclear whether the boxcar was moving when the horse leapt from it. Either way the fall was hazardous, and the AHA was upset. Douglas, though, wasn't a bit contrite. In fact, he was angered by the unacceptable rating.

"It's infringing on my livelihood," Douglas protested to one newspaper. "I have made fifty-five movies and never once has there been an animal hurt in any one of them. I depend upon the expert advice of my stuntmen."

The 1975 movie *The Wind and the Lion*, starring Sean Connery and Candice Bergen, also drew protests. Shot in Spain, the movie tells the semi-true story of an incident in 1904 when Berber forces in Morocco kidnapped an American woman and her two children. The opening sequence shows Sean Connery and a team of bandits smashing their horses through fences and tumbling sensationally, thanks to trip wires attached to their legs. In the climactic battle sequence, a dozen or more horses also stumble dramatically. Explosions take place at the very moment horses gallop by. After one such blast, two horses go down, tripped by wires. One comes to his feet again, barely avoiding stepping on his rider, who is still on the ground. In another scene a horse fall executed by a trained stunt horse occurs, followed by two very obvious trips, and then a third scene of a white horse that barely has time to tuck his head before hitting the ground. The trip-wired falls just keep coming.

Mickey Gilbert was one of the stuntmen hired for the film. "I can't tell you how many horse falls I did," he said. Instead of Running W's, he said, the crew used complicated "toe-tappers," interconnecting cables that were threaded down the back of, and then taped to, a horse's forelegs, then passed between the horse's shoes and its hooves, with washers anchored at the front of the hooves to keep the cables in place. Separate cables were attached between the horse's front legs, and from there a single cable continued up the horse's side to a handle the rider could pull when he wanted the horse to fall. Once activated, the cables would pin the horse's front feet up against his chest, forcing him to go down on his knees. The cables were practically invisible, so the falls looked natural. In one pivotal sequence in the movie, the stuntmen yanked the cables of the toe-tappers just as metal casings filled with pieces of cork were detonated, showering the set with debris. It looked as if the explosives had felled the horses.

Toe-tappers were also used in *The Wind and the Lion*'s opening kidnapping sequence, which shows two horses crashing through a latticework wall and jumping over three-foot-high brick walls. The husband of Bergen's character pulls out a gun and "shoots" the first horse. The animal's knees crumple, and he hits the ground full-on, his body splayed out, his hind legs thrust in the air. Two more horses plow through a gate. The rider of one is shot, and the horse crashes. Another horse blasts over the latticework wall. Then come two more horses, one of them a chestnut wearing a headband that's dangling so low it threatens to obscure his vision. The horse with the headband is shot and falls, skidding on his knees and landing on his head.

Still another stunt shows a rider blasting his horse through a glass wall from inside the ambassador's mansion. Crew members planned to use breakaway glass in the wall, but stunt coordinator Terry Leonard couldn't convince the first horse to go near the glass. The horse might not have been spooked if he'd first been trained to walk through cellophane flaps, but Leonard decided to try something else. According to Gilbert, Leonard sliced a ping-pong ball in half, painted each half to look like an eyeball, and fastened them over the eyes of the horse, blinding him. "Sometimes you've gotta do what you've gotta do," Gilbert recalled Leonard saying when Gilbert questioned the efficacy of the stunt. Leonard ran the blinded horse toward the wall, and unable to see the glass, the horse dutifully jumped through it. But the ground on the other side was lower—something he hadn't anticipated. The horse stumbled and fell, throwing Leonard over his head.

"Terry got the shot he'd wanted to get," Gilbert wrote years later, "but that sequence always bothered me a bit.... It seemed to me that there would've been a way to get it that was easier on, and safer for, the animal."

It's unclear whether Leonard was describing the same scene in an interview years later when he said that he'd pulled off the stunt the first time, but that the cameraman missed it and he had to do it again. The second time around, the horse flipped over in the air and landed on top of him. Leonard broke his nose and fractured his collarbone performing those stunts. It wasn't until a year later that he discovered he had also broken his sixth thoracic vertebrae.

Leonard vehemently denied ever mishandling horses. "I'm all for taking care of animals and treating them properly, and not abusing them," he said in a 2012 interview. "We monitor their temperature; we don't run them when we don't need to. When they start to sweat and overheat like a car radiator, we swap them out, we cool them off, get another horse in there. I'm way ahead of the humane department, or any animal rights people ... don't bag on me and make me look like a bad guy because I'm hurting animals. There's no way. God damn." Director John Milius insisted that not one horse was killed or injured filming *The Wind and the Lion*. But the AHA's Melniker called his claim "completely spurious and absurd on its face."

"I've never seen so much unconscionable handling of animals in a motion picture," Melniker lamented. "It has become obvious that the industry is unable to handle the situation itself."

Melniker didn't hold the actors performing in these reckless movies responsible for the mistreatment. Either they weren't aware of the risks involved in horse-tripping or they had been reassured that what they were witnessing was standard procedure, Melniker said. What the stars weren't told was that trip wires were often inflicted on an "ND," a "non-descript" or "killer" horse who was destined for the slaughterhouse regardless of whether he survived the trip, Melniker explained. "And even if he does get up, maybe he's lost three or four teeth. And sometimes the horse may have broken his leg or neck."

Years earlier, Mel Morse had helped Richard Craven write the policy banning trip wires, tilt chutes, and pit falls. In 1940 Morse left the AHA to head up the training of war dogs in World War II; he cross-bred Airedales, German shepherds, and American bull terriers to develop a unique type of combat dog. When the war ended, Morse returned to the AHA, where he succeeded Richard Craven as head of the organization's West Coast office. Morse worked with television producers to adhere to humane standards in their shows, and he helped launch the AHA's PATSY awards. Eventually he became general manager of the AHA based out of Albany, New York. When the stress of constant travel began to wear him out, Morse gave up that job and returned to California, where he wound up as executive secretary and director of the Marin County Humane Society. He remained very much involved in the treatment of animals in movies, however, especially after the Production Code was abolished. "The movie industry has just walked away from any humanitarian responsibilities," he protested.

The old code had forbidden animal mistreatment in the course of filming. The new guidelines applied only to action that wound up being used in the film. "If an animal is actually killed making a movie, the scene stays right in the film. That's the whole point, you see," Morse said. "They want to use that scene of the animal going off a cliff. . . . In the old days, we could demand the scene be dropped. Today all we can do is try to get the film a more restrictive rating, but that hardly ever happens."

Morse was upset by sequences involving bullfights or rodeos, scenes that required continuous action to capture the action on film. He claimed second unit directors would shove itchy salve up the rectums of the animals to make sure they bucked continuously. But he felt a special loathing for the practice of tripping horses. He also criticized his former employer, the AHA, claiming that instead of trying to force the deletion of cruel scenes from movies, the organization merely listed them in its publications.

It's unclear why Morse was so disparaging of the AHA's efforts. The organization's ratings garnered widespread publicity, at least for the first few years. And the AHA's Melniker was plenty vocal about his unhappiness over the mistreatment of animals on film—any form of mistreatment, not just trip wires. For example, to get a horse to play dead it wasn't uncommon for filmmakers to sedate the horse for twenty minutes, then for another twenty minutes, then twenty minutes after that. By the time the final retake was shot, the horse had sometimes been narcotized to death. The Humane Association eventually banned the use of sedatives.

Eventually animal advocates tried a bold new approach. A California state senator who represented Hollywood, David A. Roberti, introduced legislation backed by another outfit, the Fund for Animals, which would require filmmakers whose movies featured animals to either file a sworn statement from the producer or director that no animal was abused or killed, or obtain a certificate from the AHA verifying the animals had been treated humanely. If it was later discovered that animals were in fact mistreated or killed, the person signing the affidavit would be charged with a felony.

Theater owners would be held culpable too. Under the proposed state law, any exhibitor who sold or charged admission to a noncertified movie would be committing a misdemeanor. To oversee matters, the state of California would create a new agency, the Commission for the Protection of Animals, to make certain that noncompliant movies were not distributed in that state. The bill would require organizations or individuals who suspected animal abuse to demonstrate that the scenes in question involved inhumane treatment. If they succeeded in doing so, the state attorney general could then investigate. The legislation would not ban scenes portraying violence to animals so long as the animals were not subjected to pain or injury during the filming.

Roberti's bill was extraordinary. Never before had there been any such attempt to rein in filmmakers who handled animals recklessly. The MPAA's Valenti argued that laws were already on the books prohibiting the mistreatment of animals on and off the set. Roberti's bill was in essence censorship, a violation of the First Amendment's protection of freedom of speech, Valenti maintained. To require distributors to prove themselves innocent of a charge was a violation of due process, he said. Roberti countered that movies featuring the torture and killing of animals clearly showed the film industry was incapable of policing itself, especially in the case of movies made outside the United States.

The bill first went before California's Senate Judiciary Committee, where a host of actors, stunt performers, and animal trainers described scenes involving deliberately staged cockfights, the heedless slaughtering of livestock, and the reviled practice of horse-tripping. Among the witnesses was actor Richard Basehart, who said trip wires wound up killing three horses used in a movie he had worked on in Spain. (It was unclear which movie he was referring to. Basehart appeared in two Westerns shot in Spain—*Chato's Land* and *The Savage Guns*.) "What was lost was not just the dignity of the horses but the dignity of us and we have precious little to spare," Basehart said.

Film director Stanley Kramer and actor Glenn Ford also testified before the committee. "I have been in 187 films and I know whereof I speak when I say the animals desperately need this protection," Ford said. Poet and songwriter Rod McKuen, who'd started a Foundation for Animal Concern, said he'd seen more than two dozen films in the previous six months that included abuse, and not just of horses. In one movie, a cat was tortured and dissected by children, he said. In another, crew members pushed seven mules off a cliff so camera operators could fully capture the death of one. In still a third, dogs were shot in the head and left to die. If Roberti's bill failed to pass, McKuen said, he vowed to launch a campaign urging filmmakers to make their movies outside California.

The panel heard not just from celebrities but from stunt performers, wranglers, animal trainers, camera operators, and "ramrods," the crew members in charge of animal action. The president of the cameramans' union told the committee his organization unanimously supported Roberti's bill. The head of the Stuntmen's Association of Motion Pictures, representing 111 stunt performers, said 99 percent of the group's members favored the Roberti bill.

The legislature's judiciary committee approved Roberti's bill by a vote of 7–1 and sent it on to the Senate Committee on Finance to weigh the cost of operating the proposed animal cruelty commission. The finance committee approved the bill as did the full Senate, by a vote of 26–4. Now the California State Assembly needed to pass the legislation as well, and here is where Valenti's organization must have gone into overdrive lobbying against its passage. In the end, the legislation failed to make it out of an assembly committee. It was rejected by a single vote. Proponents vowed to continue fighting for its passage. In the meantime they encouraged writers, actors, directors, and other involved parties to refuse to work on any film involving the mistreatment of animals. But no such statute has ever been signed into law.

It wasn't until 1980, when *Heaven's Gate* was released, that animal mistreatment in movies surged to the forefront again. Set in the late 1800s, the movie chronicles the story of a sheriff who tries to defend some 250 immigrant farmers and families from cattle barons intent on killing them in order to seize control of their land. The movie stars Jeff Bridges, Kris Kristofferson, Christopher Walken, and Isabelle Huppert and was directed by Michael Cimino, who had recently won best picture and best director Oscars for his 1978 masterpiece *The Deer Hunter*.

Cimino was obsessive to a fault with his films. He spent months selecting the location of various scenes, choosing each character's wardrobe, and even picking out the horses he wanted to use. And he insisted on having full control. He turned down numerous requests from the AHA to post an inspector on the set of *Heaven's Gate*, which was shot at Glacier National Park in Montana, and he forbade any outsiders on the set. Once filming ended, the reason for all the secrecy began to seep out, including numerous reports that Running W's had been used and that five horses had died; one was blown up with dynamite. Crew members were instructed to bleed several horses from the neck so makeup artists could smear the actors with genuine blood. On top of that, Cimino treated a number of unshod ponies harshly: for one scene, they were filmed disembarking from a railroad boxcar nearly two dozen times, a rough exercise that left some of the animals, many of them thin and in poor condition, with bleeding feet. The ponies were so exhausted that by the end of the day the film crew beat them to get them back into the boxcar.

The AHA circulated a press release worldwide itemizing the cruelty on the set and asking moviegoers to boycott the film. Convincing people to stay away wasn't terribly difficult. Despite its staggering $36 million price tag and even when cut to three hours in length, the movie was a colossal failure, both critically and at the box office. But one good thing did come about as a result of *Heaven's Gate*: the AHA petitioned the Screen Actors Guild to get involved in the escalating problem of animal abuse, and it did. The following year the guild, together with the Alliance of Motion Picture and Television Producers, signed a contract stipulating that studios would submit scripts to the AHA for films involving animals and allow Humane Association inspectors renewed access onto their sets. Running W's were not outlawed, however, and no penalties were set forth if moviemakers failed to honor the new arrangement.

The negligent treatment of horses saddened many of the veteran stunt performers. "So many horses contributed to a film industry that did not reward them," stuntwoman Martha Crawford Cantarini wrote. "They were my teachers. Their insight was real and they taught me a valuable lesson, that as we strive to learn the best ways to motivate our horses, they are motivating us to be the best we can be. So much credit for the success of the Westerns belongs to the horses."

18

Out to Pasture

By 1970 the popularity of television Westerns had begun a steep decline. Parental advocate organizations were protesting the old-fashioned violence and stereotyping of Indians depicted in the shoot-'em-ups, and viewers lost interest in their simplistic and formulaic plots. For a decade or more, audiences couldn't get enough of *Rawhide*'s Rowdy Yates (played by heartthrob Clint Eastwood) and *The Virginian*'s Trampas (played by Doug McClure). Now suddenly they were over it. Besides, advertisers had caught on to the fact that Westerns appealed by and large to older viewers, mostly men. The networks' most desirable audience—young women—had no desire to watch gun-toting marshals and barroom brawls. *Gunsmoke* and *Death Valley Days*, the last two traditional Westerns shown on TV, ended their runs in 1975.

Western movies were still being made, however, and the best ones were still turning to expert falling horses to add dynamism and verve. Chuck Hayward's Twinkle Toes was slowing down, but he continued to perform. Arguably his most important role was a segment that featured him on ABC News. The story came at the end of the broadcast on May 7, 1976, and focused on the mistreatment of horses in Western films. "There's a right way to handle horse stunts and there's a wrong way," news anchor Harry Reasoner started off by saying. "A replacement for a dead horse is fifty dollars cheaper than hiring a horse who knows what he's doing." He then turned the segment over to reporter Roger Caras, who spoke directly into the camera as he stood next to Hayward and Twinkle Toes, the horse's face now white with age.

"Twinkle Toes is old enough to vote," Caras said. "He's never been hurt.

He's never gone lame, although he's done hundreds of stunts. Because he and his rider are professionals."

Next the cameras turned to Hayward, who had mounted Twinkle Toes and was walking him slowly. "Are you sure you're ready? Sure you got everything on?" Caras said. Hayward nodded and barely turned Twinkle Toes's head to the right when he went down, his left front leg bending slightly as he made his descent.

The secret behind that stunt, Caras explained, was "years and years of training behind what looks so easy here."

"The trouble is not all producers want to pay a professional's fee, and a lot of unsuspecting horses have been deliberately tripped and killed by hobbles and wire devices," Caras said. He then threw a fake punch at the horse and Hayward fell Twinkle Toes again. The stuntman patted Twinkle Toes when he got back on his feet.

Reporter Caras ticked off the safety measures put in place to cushion Twinkle Toes's fall. Stirrups made of four-ply tires were to collapse when the horse fell against them. The saddle horn was removed. Flat saddles and cantles (the upturned back of the saddle) were introduced to help support the rider's spine. The next scene showed a different stuntman, George Wilbur, falling Hayward's gentler horse, Iodine. Iodine went down fast, rolled over, and thrust his legs theatrically in the air. "It is rough work, but amazingly safe," Caras said. "Okay, that's the humane way, the way professionals do it. And this is the other way, with cables, hobbles and rings known as Running W's and toe tappers. They maim and kill." Holding a set of trip wires in his hands, he went on to say, "It costs thousands of dollars to train a falling horse. This junk's worth $1.98. And who's to blame? Unscrupulous quick-buck artists, legislators that won't enact laws, and a public that just doesn't seem to care."

Caras ended by offering a solution: "Tough laws that are enforced and a public that demands to know what goes on behind the scenes."

Not long after that segment aired, Twinkle Toes's health failed. He was thirty-two, older by far than most horses lived to be. Hayward euthanized him by shooting him to death, a common practice that most horse owners considered humane. "What are you going to do?" Hayward's ex-wife Ellen Powell said years later. "Put your best friend on a truck and send him to the slaughterhouse?"

"It must have really, really, really hurt [Hayward]" to lose Twinkle Toes, Ellen added. But "when you love something . . . that's the kindest thing you can do."

Hayward became a second unit director, orchestrating the kind of action scenes he used to perform in, and he lived another decade before dying of Hodgkin's disease on February 23, 1998.

Coco, the mare Roberson sold to Jack Williams, retired and lived out her final years on Williams's three-hundred-acre ranch, Quail Trail Springs, in Agua Dulce, in northern Los Angeles County. She was thirty-three when she died, and Williams buried her on his property. Williams outlasted Coco by nearly three decades. His own final performance came in 1999, on the movie *Wild, Wild West*, and he won a Golden Boot award from the Motion Picture & Television Fund that year for a lifetime of impressive feats. He was eighty-five when he died of natural causes in 2007.

By 1969 Cocaine had performed in some two hundred movies and television episodes and had executed at least five hundred falls. He had overcome a life-threatening injury and escaped a raging wildfire. He had even survived an earthquake, a 1971 temblor that was strong enough to knock the hinges off the front door of Roberson's house. When the quake erupted, Cocaine pawed the ground and circled the corral, but he was unharmed.

Coke was still working hard. He and Roberson appeared with John Wayne in *The Undefeated*, a 1969 movie shot in Texas, about a Civil War colonel who captures a Confederate company, unaware that the war has ended. From there Roberson trailered Coke to Durango, Colorado, to film *Chisum*, starring Wayne as a New Mexico rancher forced to fend off an unscrupulous land developer. The movie came with a daunting assignment: Roberson was to ride Coke through a wall of flames onto a boardwalk, then dive through a storefront window. Many horses would have refused to go anywhere near an open fire, much less jump head-first through what appeared to be sheer glass. But if Roberson had any doubts about Coke's ability to deliver, he didn't let on.

The day of the shooting, Roberson prepped his horse the usual way: warming him up with a short ride along the perimeter of the set. When the big moment came, Coke showed no hesitation. He trotted confidently through the flames, stepped up onto the boardwalk, and crashed through a window so narrow that Roberson had to duck his head to keep from hitting its frame.

Next came the John Wayne Western *Rio Lobo*, filmed at the Old Tucson stage lot in Arizona. Stuntman Terry Leonard also performed in the movie, and years later he recalled a stunt he was assigned to carry out involving Cocaine. Leonard was no doubt familiar with Coke; he'd gotten to know Roberson on the set of *McLintock!*, and Roberson had invited Leonard to stay at his house for a while. Leonard took the back bedroom and spent the next four months practicing saddle falls in Roberson's backyard.

It had been a long day on the set—it was now 10:00 p.m.—and Leonard was doubling Jorge Rivero, the second lead, who played a Confederate captain who hijacks a Union army payroll train. Wayne often hung around the set after hours to play cards. Still, Leonard was caught off guard when, just before his scene with Coke was about to be filmed, Wayne's custom-made Pontiac—a dark green boat of a station wagon with a raised top designed to accommodate Wayne and his cowboy hat—pulled up.

Wayne's appearance surprised Roberson too. "Hey Duke, what are you doing here?" Roberson said. "I came to see the kid fall the Coke," Wayne replied in his inimitable drawl. After years of working around Cocaine, Wayne had a healthy respect for the horse's athletic prowess. Witnessing Leonard's attempt to handle Coke was worth driving back out to the set.

Leonard was flattered by Wayne's interest, but the arrival of the superstar gripped him with anxiety—he was about to perform the equivalent of kicking a field goal at the Super Bowl. "I'm falling the most famous horse in the movie business, on a John Wayne movie," Leonard thought to himself. "If I miss, I'm never going to get a job again."

More than a hundred cast and crew gathered around to watch Leonard give it a go. His assignment was to lay Coke down at a full-on gallop. Things got quiet on the set, the cameras started to roll, and Leonard spurred Cocaine into a dead run. He needed to catch the horse at exactly the right moment to fall him, but from the instant they set out, the timing was somehow off. To his credit, Leonard aborted the fall rather than try to force Cocaine to the ground.

It was during the filming of *Rio Lobo* that Wayne learned he would be getting an Academy Award for his portrayal of Rooster Cogburn, the grouchy, aging cowboy who wore a patch over one eye in *True Grit*. Wayne was deeply moved by the news. Despite his staggering success at the box office, the Academy of Motion Picture Arts and Sciences had pointedly overlooked him up until now. The filming of *Rio Lobo* was postponed while Wayne flew back to Los Angeles for the Oscar ceremony. "Wow," he told the audience. "If I'd known what I know now, I'd have put a patch on my eye thirty-five years ago."

Back in Tucson the cast, including Jennifer O'Neill, Jack Elam, and Victor French, took that as their cue. The day Wayne was due back on the set, director Howard Hawks handed out eye patches to everyone on the set. Roberson grabbed a couple extra, one for Wayne's horse, Dollor, and one for Cocaine. When Wayne appeared, cast and crew wheeled around to unveil a visual tribute—a sea of eye patches. The Duke was so touched by the gesture that he sniffled back a few tears. With the exception of the horses, so did everyone else.

Wayne rode a handful of different horses over the years. He told author Michael Munn that he'd never cared much for horses, "and I daresay not many of them liked me too much." But he did have a fondness for his last movie horse, Dollor (named for the Spanish word for "sorrow"). Dollor was owned by Dick Webb Movie Productions, which agreed to offer Wayne exclusive use of the horse and not to sell him until Wayne died. The pair performed together in the Duke's last seven movies. In his film *The Shootist*, Wayne altered the script so he could refer to Dollor by name. He tells fellow actor Ron Howard, then a young boy, to take Dollor and "get him a double helpin' of oats."

After Wayne's death, Dollor was sold three times, finally to a Dallas couple who exhibited him in parades but otherwise let him while away his days in spacious quarters, fed imported alfalfa. He died at the age of twenty-seven.

Nearly thirty years of working together had created a close friendship between Wayne and Roberson. The pair were tight enough that when Roberson's young grandson, Charles, saw the two of them dressed alike one day, he marched up to Wayne and demanded, "And what do you do?" Wayne got a kick out of the boy's insouciance. "He laughed real loud, bent down, and put his hands on his knees and his nose right next to Charles's nose," Roberson later recalled. "'You mean you don't know?'" Wayne said. "'I stand in for your Grandpa on the closeups!'"

During a stormy scene in one movie, Coke lay still with a tree placed on top of him—something few horses would have tolerated. Roberson lay next to him and talked him through it. The pair appeared in the Duke's next film, *Big Jake*, about a man estranged from his family who comes back to find a grandson who'd been kidnapped, and in 1972's *The Cowboys*, in which Wayne plays a rancher whose cattle-driving crew abandons him, forcing him to take on a group of schoolboys to do the job.

Roberson loved nothing better than to return from a shoot, open the trailer door, and watch as Cocaine settled back into familiar surroundings. After one such absence, Roberson perched on the top rail of his fence and looked on as Cocaine arched his back and rolled in the sand, extending all four legs in the air. "Feels good to be home, don't it, old-timer?" Roberson told him. Cocaine, he said, "stood up, shook the dirt from his back and neighed loudly."

There were no more horse falls. "Just like an old thoroughbred, you can only run so long, then you got to pull it up and rest awhile," Roberson said.

But Cocaine wasn't done completely.

In 1972 Roberson and Coke began filming yet another Wayne Western, *The Train Robbers*. Shot in Mexico, the movie tells the story of a widow (played by Ann-Margret) who hires a gunman to locate a cache of gold her husband stole from the railroad so she can return the money and start anew. Just as Coke had done in *Chisum*, he needed to dive through a candy-glass window. And this time Roberson was holding the reins of a pack mule that was trailing Cocaine. The mule wasn't expected to go through the window, but the fact that he was right behind Coke could easily have unnerved him. Instead Coke leapt through a twelve-paned window and landed with aplomb on the other side, his red mane flapping from the force of the jump. "There was not another horse alive who would ride through a window without buggering, but Cocaine did it like he was out for a stroll in the park," Roberson later wrote. "'I'll quit when you do,' I told him. 'Damn, you a game old coot!'"

Word quickly spread that twenty-eight-year-old Cocaine had pulled off a major stunt. At the American Humane Association's awards ceremony that year, he was given his second Craven Award, the same prize he had received nineteen years earlier. The AHA's Harold Melniker noted that

13. Cocaine was twenty-eight years old when he and Chuck Roberson blasted through a candy-glass window in the 1973 movie *The Train Robbers*. Courtesy of John Hagner's Hollywood Stuntmen's Hall of Fame.

every animal given an award, including Coke, had been treated properly; the organization wouldn't have honored their performances if they hadn't.

Roberson was getting old for a stuntman. Over the years he'd broken both arms, his back, his leg, several ribs, and more than thirty fingers. He needed to transition to another line of work, one that wouldn't clobber his body quite so much. Roberson became licensed as a thoroughbred trainer in California and Washington state, cashed in some money Jack

Williams had helped him invest, and bought a small ranch a hundred miles north, in Bakersfield. He named his spread White Lane Ranch and moved Cocaine there with him. Roberson's dad, Ollie, came along too. Roberson still took on the occasional assignment, but Coke's performing days were done. Finally the sorrel horse with the white blaze was free to spend the rest of his days nibbling on sweet grass in a meadow and soaking up the California sun.

Five years passed. Cocaine was retired, and it was time for Roberson, now fifty-six, his dark hair softened to gray, to get down out of the saddle too. Spring had blossomed, and the pasture at his ranch had greened up. Two foals had been born in a week's time, and three more would be coming soon. One crisp morning turned cool by a cutting breeze from the southeast, Roberson rested his arms on the fence rail and watched from a distance as Cocaine stuck his nose in the tail of a bay-colored mare and followed her to the water trough. Coke had lost sight in one eye and was starting to lose it in the other. And most of his back teeth were gone; the ones that remained were too worn down to grind food well. For the last three years Roberson had prepared a mix of oats and molasses and fed Coke by hand.

Roberson's father, Ollie, came up behind him and said aloud what was obvious to them both. "He's going blind, son," Ollie said, "and he's limping real bad now on that left hind leg."

"We always fell left, him and me. I favor that leg a little myself now," Roberson replied.

He called out to Coke. The horse did not respond. His hearing was gone too.

"You know what I'm saying, son. Ain't no way around it," Ollie said.

What happened next is uncertain. In his memoir, Roberson wrote that he stood at the fence thinking back on the heyday of Western movies and Cocaine's part in them: his jumps, his drags, and most especially those magnificent falls. Roberson had had lousy luck with romance. He knew fellows who'd stayed married to the same women most of their adult lives. Roberson, on the other hand, had trouble keeping names straight over the breakfast table. His relationship with Cocaine, though, was different. There's a saying that a cowboy has only one good horse in his lifetime. For Roberson, that horse had been Coke.

Roberson later said that his dad watched, silent, as Coke struggled to reach the water trough. That Roberson leapt over the fence, walked over to his horse, and laid a hand on his neck. That Coke startled at the unexpected touch. That Roberson assured him, "Whoa, old son. It's just me."

"He lowered his head and drank deeply," Roberson wrote. "I patted him one more time and left."

He said that he asked his dad to euthanize Cocaine. And that once Coke's life ended, his body be removed. If Coke was buried at the ranch, Roberson said, he couldn't help but think about him every time he walked by that spot. According to this account, Roberson got in his truck and headed north on Interstate 5 toward the racetrack in San Francisco. He didn't want to be anywhere around when Coke breathed his last.

Years later, Charlene Roberson told a different story. She said her dad felt such devotion toward Cocaine that he couldn't begin to imagine seeing him go. Roberson had had many loves in his life, but none compared to his beloved sorrel gelding, the one he'd spared from death years before. The horse who had repaid that favor many times over.

"He said, 'I kept him from the killers before,'" Charlene recalled. "I don't think he could put him down. If [Coke] broke his leg, he couldn't do it."

But Ollie Roberson felt differently, Charlene said. She believes her grandfather was jealous of his son's undying affection for this old, now-crippled horse. On a day when Chuck Roberson was away from the ranch, she said, Ollie took it upon himself to put Cocaine down. When Roberson returned home and discovered his horse's demise, he was enraged. "I never saw my dad mad enough to punch someone, but he was ready to punch Granddad," Charlene said. "He never forgave my granddad for doing that."

However the end came, Roberson was overcome with grief at the loss of his life's partner. He replayed the memory of the first time Coke fell on cue—how his athleticism had stunned everyone lucky enough to have witnessed it. He thought about Coke's race against the Indian ponies at Monument Valley and his remarkably bold countenance, his willingness to do whatever Roberson asked.

"There ain't gonna be another like him, is there?" Roberson thought to himself. It felt as though something great had ended and that nobody completely understood that but him. He hung his head and wept.

But several years after Cocaine's death, a surprise came in the mail. Universal Studios sent Roberson a check for footage of a horse fall he and

Coke had performed two decades earlier. The gag had earned Roberson $250 at the time; Universal was paying him $500 to use it again.

The money was an unexpected bonus. It helped Roberson understand that Cocaine lived on—not in the flesh, of course, but larger than life up on the silver screen. And not just in that one solitary sequence, but in scores of heart-stopping moments that movie lovers could marvel at for years to come.

In his own triumphant way, the horse was immortal.

Epilogue

By the time Chuck Roberson died in 1988 at the age of sixty-nine, his renown as a master stuntman had spread well beyond Western movies' inner circle. He was the inspiration for *The Fall Guy*, a television series starring Lee Majors that appeared for five seasons on ABC in the early 1980s.

He received the Dusty Award for outstanding achievement from the Hollywood Stuntmen's Hall of Fame; Wayne was there to bestow the honor. Wayne also wrote the foreword to Roberson's 1980 memoir; in it, he described Roberson as "the kind of man I could count on to get the job done. But more than that, he has been my *friend*."

Then-president Reagan sent Roberson a telegram when the stuntman fell ill the year before his death. Roberson left behind his third wife, Dollie, whom he met on the set of *The Searchers*, four daughters, and a boatload of lasting images in the movies.

In the years since, protection for movie horses has been iffy. The American Humane Association offers a long list of guidelines for handling horses on the set, and responsible filmmakers have followed them. The introduction of animatronics and computer-generated imagery has also made it possible to film violent scenes without using actual animals. Animatronic horses were substituted for the real thing in at least two movies, *Braveheart* in 1995 and 2000's *The Patriot*.

But the AHA lacks the authority to enforce humane treatment, and the *Hollywood Reporter* and the *Los Angeles Times* have found a disturbing pattern of AHA executives not only overlooking horses' poor treatment but interfering with their own investigators on behalf of the studios. The explosion of cable TV, indie films, and streaming series has made attempts

EPILOGUE

to supervise the welfare of horses and other performing animals that much more difficult.

The fact that so few Westerns are now being made has diminished the need for horses like Cocaine and riders who know how to fall them safely.

ROBERSON MADE THIRTY-TWO FILMS AS A STUNTMAN WITH JOHN Wayne and had minor acting roles in twenty-two of them. Cocaine performed in many of those movies and in others without Roberson.

The Shootist (1976) (stunts) (uncredited)
Rooster Cogburn (1975) (stunt double: John Wayne) (uncredited) (stunts)
McQ (1974) (stunts) (uncredited) . . . Bodyguard
Cahill U.S. Marshal (1973) (stunt coordinator) . . . Leader of Bunch
The Train Robbers (1973) (stunts) (uncredited)
The Cowboys (1972) (stunt double: John Wayne) (uncredited) (stunts) (uncredited)
Big Jake (1971) (stunt double: John Wayne) (uncredited) (stunts) (uncredited) . . . Texas Ranger
Rio Lobo (1970) (stunts) (uncredited) . . . Corporal in baggage car
Chisum (1970) (stunts) (uncredited) . . . Trail herder
The Undefeated (1969) (stunts) (uncredited) . . . Yankee sergeant at river
Hellfighters (1968) (stunts) (uncredited) . . . Firefighter in airplane
The Green Berets (1968) (stunts) (uncredited) . . . Sgt. Griffin
The War Wagon (1967) . . . Brown / outrider
El Dorado (1966) (stunts) (uncredited) . . . Jason's gunman
The Sons of Katie Elder (1965) (stunts) (uncredited) . . . Townsman
Donovan's Reef (1963) (stunts) (uncredited) . . . Festus
McLintock! (1963) . . . Sheriff Jeff Lord
How the West Was Won (1962) (stunts) (uncredited) . . . Officer
Hatari! (1962) (stunt double: John Wayne) (uncredited)
The Man Who Shot Liberty Valance (1962) (stunts) (uncredited) . . . Henchman
The Comancheros (1961) (stunts) (uncredited)
The Alamo (1960) (stunts) (uncredited) . . . Tennessean (segment "It do")
Rio Bravo (1959) (stunt double) (uncredited) (stunts) (uncredited) . . . Gunman

The Barbarian and the Geisha (1958) (stunts) (uncredited)
The Wings of Eagles (1957) (stunt double: John Wayne) (uncredited) (stunts) . . . Officer
The Searchers (1956) (stunts) (uncredited) . . . Ranger at wedding
The Conqueror (1956) (stunts) (uncredited)
Hondo (1953) (stunts) (uncredited) . . . Otawanga / Cavalry sergeant killed in Indian attack
Rio Grande (1950) (stunts) (uncredited) . . . Officer / Indian who fires arrow into Col. York's chest
The Fighting Kentuckian (1949) (stunts) (uncredited) . . . Militiaman
Wake of the Red Witch (1948) (stunts) (uncredited) . . . Seaman
Angel and the Badman (1947) (stunts) (uncredited)

NOTES ON SOURCES

Material needed to tell the story of stunt horses used in Western films, and particularly Cocaine's story, came from scores of documents, published interviews, and biographies. For the sake of brevity, I have condensed the list to sources that were most helpful.

This book would not have been possible had Chuck Roberson not written his memoir, *The Fall Guy: 30 Years as the Duke's Double*, cowritten by author Bodie Thoene using tape recordings Roberson provided her. The book was published by Hancock House in 1980 and reissued in 2022. Chapters 1, 8, 9, 10, 13, 15, 16, 18, and parts of chapters 11 and 14 are based on Roberson's own recollections of his colorful career, and *The Fall Guy* offers the rare insider's look at the life of a stuntman and the making of Western movies from the 1940s through the 1970s.

1. A MORTIFYING GAFFE

An account of Roberson's calamitous horse fall while filming *Rio Grande* is also told in *The Nicest Fella—The Life of Ben Johnson: The World Champion Rodeo Cowboy Who Became an Oscar-Winning Movie Star*, written by Richard D. Jensen and published in 2010.

2. THE LURE OF THE WEST

The most comprehensive source on the development of the Wild West as a larger-than-life American story is Michael Wallis's *The Real Wild West: The 101 Ranch and the Creation of the American West*, published in 1999. Wallis's book traces the Wild West shows that served as a precursor to the silent Westerns and the filmmakers who made them. The biography of

NOTES ON SOURCES

filmmaker Fred J. Balshofer, *One Reel a Week*, provided additional insight into the early days of Westerns, and *The West of the Imagination*, written by William H. Goetzmann and William N. Goetzmann, published in 2009, offered a valuable look at how movies and other art forms worked their way so thoroughly into the American psyche.

3. FIRST CAME FRITZ

The remarkable story of William S. Hart's rise from the New York stage to become the country's first Western superstar and how his pinto pony Fritz helped make that possible is best told in three books: *William S. Hart: Projecting the American West*, written by Ronald L. Davis and published in 2003; Hart's autobiography, *My Life East and West*, originally published in 1929; and Fritz's own "memoir," *Told Under a White Oak Tree*, written by Hart and first published in 1922.

The William S. Hart Park and Museum in Newhall, California, is an excellent place to learn more about Hart and Fritz.

4. THEN CAME TONY

Much has been written about the derring-do of Tom Mix, the Western star who succeeded Hart, and his equally popular horses, all of whom were named Tony. Tucked into several accounts are bits of information about the stunt horses who performed in Tony's stead. *The Amazing Tom Mix: The Most Famous Cowboy of the Movies* by Richard D. Jensen is a thorough and engaging account of Mix's reliance on stunt horses to perform many of "Tony's" tricks. I also turned to *The Fabulous Tom Mix* written by Mix's wife, Olive, and cowritten by Eric Heath and *The Life and Legend of Tom Mix* by Paul E. Mix for insight into Mix's steadfast bond with his steeds. The article "'Tony,' Tom Mix's Horse, Says Goodbye," published by *Movie Classics Magazine* in January 1933, and the 1942 *New York Times* article "Tony, 40 and Ailing, Was Put Down Quietly Today" detail Tony's retirement and the careful steps taken to make certain he rested in peace.

Paula Marantz Cohen's 2001 book *Silent Film and the Triumph of the American Myth* provided additional material on Mix and Tony.

5. TRIP WIRES AND MORE

Movie Horses: Their Treatment and Training by Anthony Amaral, published in 1967, is chock-full of detail about the harsh treatment of horses in early movies and the improvements made in later years to improve their working conditions.

Stunt Man: The Autobiography of Yakima Canutt, published in 1979, is a first-person account of moviedom's wildest tricks as told by the man who invented many of them, most of which involved horses. Child actor Diana Serra Cary, whose father, Jack Montgomery, was called upon to perform some of these perilous stunts, tells the darker side of the story in her equally enthralling book *The Hollywood Posse: The Story of a Gallant Band of Horsemen Who Made Movie History*, published in 1975.

Hollywood Hoofbeats: The Fascinating Story of Horses in Movies and Television, written by Petrine Day Mitchum and Audrey Pavia, published in 2014, is a coffee-table tribute to movie horses that touches on their sometimes-harsh treatment. The article "Before the Production Code: Trips to Hell for a Nickel," written by Susan Doll and published on the *Filmstruck Streamline* blog in 2013, delves into the underbelly of Western movies' earliest days, and I drew material from Harry Carey Jr.'s rollicking memoir *Company of Heroes: My Life as an Actor in the John Ford Stock Company*, published in 2013.

6. RATCHETING UP THE RISKS

I turned to four biographies of Hollywood director Cecil B. DeMille to learn about the iconic epics he filmed, his slavish micromanagement in pursuit of his visions, and the reckless treatment of horses that occurred on his sets. *Empire of Dreams: The Epic Life of Cecil B. DeMille* by Scott Eyman, published in 2010, tells the director's story exceptionally well. *Written in Stone: Making Cecil B. DeMille's Epic The Ten Commandments* by Kathryn Orrison (1999) tracks the enormous undertaking required to make that film. The 1973 biography *Cecil B. DeMille* by Charles Higham recounts the recklessness with which DeMille filmed the silent version of *The Ten Commandments* in 1923. *Cecil B. DeMille: The Art of the Hollywood Epic* by Cecilia DeMille and Mark Alan Vieira (2014) describes the director's contempt for actors who were unwilling to take physical risks.

Diana Serra Cary's *The Hollywood Posse: The Story of a Gallant Band of Horsemen Who Made Movie History* tells how her father and several other stuntmen, incensed over the inhumane treatment of horses, plotted in vain to murder DeMille.

Information on the Hollywood stables that provided horses to studios and the cost of leasing each type of horse came from a June 13, 2012, post, "The Oklahoma Kid and 'Whizzer,'" published on *A Drifting Cowboy* blog, written by Western movie historian Jerry England. Material on Fat Jones and other stable owners also came from *An Illustrated History of Trigger: The Lives and Legend of Roy Rogers' Palomino* by Leo Pando, published in 2010, from Harry Carey Jr.'s memoir, and from *Hollywood Hoofbeats*.

A doctoral dissertation by Harvard student Timothy Stephen McGrath, "Behaving Like Animals: Human Cruelty, Animal Suffering, and American Culture, 1900–Present," written in 2013, probes the brutal conditions many movie horses were forced to endure.

A *New York Times* article published in 1942, "Step Right Up and Call Him 'Breezy'" by Ezra Goodman, helped describe controversial second unit director Breezy Eason's heedless approach to filming Western battle scenes.

7. MAKING HEADWAY AGAINST ABUSE

An article in the December 1936 edition of the *National Humane Review*, "The Charge of the Light Brigade," tells of the astonishment felt by the American Humane Association officials when they realized the studio had disregarded an agreement to remove violent scenes involving horses from the final cut of the film.

The story of Errol Flynn checking out his appearance with a mirror while on horseback and an account of the senseless killing of horses with trip wires while filming *The Charge of the Light Brigade* came from David Niven's memoir *Bring on the Empty Horses*, published in 1975.

The claim that only four horses were killed during the shooting of *Light Brigade* appears in Alan K. Rode's biography of the film's director, *Michael Curtiz: A Life in Film*. Rode also wrote that an investigator for the American Society for the Prevention of Cruelty to Animals tried to borrow $100 from a studio executive.

Timothy Stephen McGrath's dissertation "Behaving Like Animals" explores the challenges horses faced when filming *Light Brigade*.

The most thorough account of the horse dying in *Jesse James* comes from a 2011 article by Michael Gillespie, "The Lake's Deadly Movie Accident," published in the *Lake of the Ozarks News* on October 6, 2011. An account of the incident of the horse's leap into the water was based on "Did Jesse James Jump? Another Look at the Outlaw's Legendary Horse Jump across Devil's Gulch in South Dakota" by Ried Holien, which appeared in *True West* magazine in 2009.

The fallout of the horse's death is recalled in John Baxter's book *Stunt: The Story of the Great Movie Stunt Men*, published in 1974.

The *National Humane Review* chronicled the mounting anger over the incident in a February 1939 article, "Cruelty to Animals in Filming 'Jesse James.'" Turner Classic Movies' website wrote an article about the incident.

8. LEARNING THE ROPES

Additional information about falling-horse trainer Fred Kennedy came from an article by his stepdaughter Pat Mefferd, "Stuntman Fred Kennedy and His Falling Stunt Horses Trixie, Dixie, & Shanghai," published in *Horse Fame* magazine in 2001.

11. LEARNING TO FALL AGAIN

In addition to Chuck Roberson's own description of how he trained Cocaine to fall, I turned to several sources. One of them is "Training a Falling Horse" by veteran trainer Rodd Wolff, which appeared in the Screen Actors Guild and the American Federation of Television and Radio Artists newsletter of December 2011. Audrey Pavia detailed the steps involved in her article "How Stunt Horses are Trained to Fall in the Movies," published by *Horse Illustrated* magazine in June 2014. Pavia also writes about the training involved in *Hollywood Hoofbeats*, the book she cowrote with Petrine Day Mitchum. And John Farkis's book *Not Thinkin' . . . Just Rememberin' . . . The Making of John Wayne's "The Alamo,"* published in 2015, also provided a helpful description of how horses are trained to fall.

Stuntwoman Martha Crawford Cantarini offers a defense of horse-falling in her memoir *Fall Girl: My Life as a Western Stunt Double*, published in 2010. Hal Needham criticizes the practice in his 2011 memoir *Stuntman! My Car-Crashing, Plane-Jumping, Bone-Breaking, Death-Defying Hollywood Life*.

12. TOUGH RIDERS, TOUGH HORSES

Actor Neil Summers's "Western Clipping: Action Actors" column tells the backstories and accomplishments of a number of the Western stuntmen and their horses. John Hagner's "Moab Happenings Archive," part of his Moab, Utah-based Stuntmen's Hall of Fame, was another extremely valuable source.

Les Sellnow's article "Hollywood Horses," which appeared on thehorse.com in 2006, told of some of the stunt horses' exploits. Kevin Conley's book *The Full Burn: On the Set, at the Bar, behind the Wheel, and over the Edge with Hollywood Stuntmen*, published in 2008, describes some of the astounding feats executed in Westerns, and Gene Scott Freese's 2014 book *Hollywood Stunt Performers, 1910s–1970s: A Biographical Dictionary* was a helpful compendium of moviedom's many equine stars.

Actor and stuntman Dean Smith captures the life of a typical stuntman in his memoir *Cowboy Stuntman: From Olympic Gold to the Silver Screen*, published in 2013.

Ellen Powell, the first wife of stuntman and fellow John Wayne double Chuck Hayward, offered several colorful anecdotes about Hayward's falling horse Twinkle Toes and the relationship between the two.

Among the newspaper articles I found useful were the following:

"When John Wayne Refuses to Leap into Raging Torrent, Who Comes to His Aid? A Nebraska Sandhills Boy!" published by the *Lincoln (NE) Journal Star*, January 13, 1957.

Martha Willman's March 7, 1971, article in the *Los Angeles Times*, "Movie Horses Gallop in Shadow of Stars."

"The Accidental Stuntman: A Local Reflects on His Career in Movies," about Terry Leonard, written by Josh Premako and published in the *Santa Clarita Valley Signal*, April 25, 2009.

"Famed Hollywood Stuntman Jack Williams Honored with Plaque on Western Walk" was published in the *Santa Clarita Valley Signal* on April 25, 2008.

The *San Fernando Valley Times* wrote about the lawsuit Williams filed when he felt defamed by critical comments about horse-falling in "$100,000 Suit in Horse Act," published on September 21, 1955.

NOTES ON SOURCES

For information on the steps that were taken to improve working conditions for movie stunt horses, I turned to the following:

"Animals Go Unhurt in Movie 'Fights,'" published by the *Winnipeg Tribune* on April 8, 1949.

"Animals Used in Movies Protected Much Better than Human Stunters," *Clovis (NM) News Journal*, May 5, 1948.

"Movie Animals Virtually Rule" by Harold Heffernan, published by the *Muncie (IN) Star Press*, February 21, 1943.

R. D. Layman's article "Man Who Made Movies Humane," published by the *San Rafael (CA) Daily Independent Journal*, March, 28, 1959.

Author Jane Tompkins West's dim view of the treatment of stunt horses came from her book *West of Everything: The Inner Life of Westerns*, published in 1992.

The 2008 book *Horses at Work: Harnessing Power in Industrial America* by Ann Norton Greene describes the often savage conditions working horses faced in the early days of this country.

14. THE SEARCHERS

Material for this chapter comes in part from Scott Eyman's 1999 book *Print the Legend: The Life and Times of John Ford*. Glenn Frankel's 2013 book *The Searchers: The Making of an American Legend* is an absorbing account of the real-life events that inspired the movie and the making of the film many consider the greatest Western ever made.

Peter Bogdanovich's documentary "Directed by John Ford" offered insight into Ford's personality, and Michael F. Blake's 2003 book *Code of Honor: The Making of Three Great American Westerns* also helped convey the conditions Chuck Roberson and Cocaine would have encountered making the movie.

Harry Carey Jr.'s memoir *Company of Heroes* describes the challenges faced by Cocaine and the other stunt horses that performed in the movie.

15. DOUBLING FOR THE STARS

In addition to Chuck Roberson's memoir, I turned to John Farkis's exhaustive account of the making of John Wayne's pet project *The Alamo* for the ultimate insider's look at what it takes to produce a Western of that magnitude: the sizeable number of horses that had to be purchased and trained, the relationship second unit director Cliff Lyons had with the stuntmen he oversaw, and the effort that went into pulling off one of the most ambitious stunts ever executed by falling horses.

A *Sports Illustrated* article about stunt performers, "Being a Good Sport about It All" by Herman Weiskopf, published January 31, 1972, related Hal Needham's loss of his horse Hondo during filming of the movie *Little Big Man* in Montana.

Material from *Hollywood Hoofbeats*, Anthony Amaral's *Movie Horses*, and Harry Carey Jr.'s *Company of Heroes* all contributed to this chapter, as did the 1962 book *The Western: From Silents to Cinerama* by George N. Fenin and William K. Everson.

Two biographies of John Wayne, Scott Eyman's *John Wayne: The Life and Legend*, published in 2014, and Ronald L. Davis's 1998 book *Duke: The Life and Image of John Wayne* offered keen understanding of Wayne's personality and his fondness for stunt performers like Chuck Roberson.

16. AGING AND STILL FALLING

For details on the death of horse trainer and stuntman Fred Kennedy, I turned to Dan Ford's *Pappy: The Life of John Ford*, published in 1979.

Turner Classic Movies' website also has a story about Kennedy's accident, as does a *Los Angeles Times* article, "Fall in Film Fatal to Actor Fred Kennedy," published December 6, 1958.

Material about the risks of filming *The Conqueror* in St. George, Utah, came from two sources: a June 6, 2015, article in *The Guardian*, "Hollywood and the Downwinders Still Grapple with Nuclear Fallout" by Rory Carroll, and "John Wayne, Susan Hayward, and 90 Other People Developed Cancer after Filming 'The Conqueror' near a Nuclear Testing Site" by Domagoj Valjak, which was published on the vintagenews.com website on February 19, 2018.

Roberson's daughter, Charlene, provided behind-the-scenes happenings during the filming of *The Conqueror*.

17. THE RETURN OF CRUELTY

Newspapers wrote a remarkable amount about the return of trip wires and other cruel practices in the 1970s. Hollywood columnists Gene Handsaker and Gary Deeb wrote several articles noting the problem, among them Handsaker's "Animals Cruelly Treated in Some Foreign Movies," published in the *Lafayette (LA) Daily Advertiser* on September 26, 1970, and "Movie Animals' Welfare Watched by Humane Group," published in the *Joplin (MO) Globe* on May 14, 1971.

Deeb, a syndicated columnist, wrote "AHA Finds Cruelty on Film Often Real," published in the *Syracuse Post-Standard* on June 26, 1982, and "Animal Mistreatment in Films Is Unnecessary," published in the *Santa Fe New Mexican* on February 9, 1984.

Material about the unsuccessful bill brought before the California legislature that would have helped curtail inhumane treatment of movie animals came from Edward Flattau's article "Cruelty to Animals in Movies Bothers Some State Legislature," distributed by Gannett News Service in May 1976.

Jack Valenti's memoir *This Time, This Place: My Life in War, the White House, and Hollywood*, published in 2007, described his desire to abolish the Hollywood Production Code that had forbidden cruelty to animals.

Karen Paterson's article "Movies Are Animal Killers" brought to light some of the problems brought about by the return of trip wires. The *Lincoln (NE) Star* published the story on July 31, 1974. "Shoot-Out at Heaven's Gate" by Les Gapay, published by the *Washington Post* on September 2, 1979, described in gruesome detail animal mistreatment on the set of *Heaven's Gate*.

The anecdote about toe-tappers being used in the movie *The Wind and the Lion* and the tragic accident of Mickey Gilbert's horse Gypsy came from the book *Me and My Saddle-Pal: My Life as a Hollywood Stuntman*, cowritten by Rebecca Rockwell. Terry Leonard's adamant defense of his treatment of horses appears in an interview he gave, "Terry Leonard: Blondes and Hard Ground, Part 2," which appeared on the Prop Store website on September 18, 2012.

18. OUT TO PASTURE

The dwindling popularity of Westerns was discussed in three articles I turned to:

Ken Miyamoto's "Why Did Hollywood Cut Back Significantly on Making Westerns a Few Decades Ago?" published on Quora.com (no date

NOTES ON SOURCES

is listed); "How the West Was Lost (as a Staple of TV)" by Caryn James, published by the *New York Times* on September 15, 1996; and "Cowboy Business" by Thomas Schatz, also published by the *New York Times*, on November 10, 2007.

The anecdote about Terry Leonard's attempt to ride Cocaine in front of John Wayne came from an interview titled "Terry Leonard: Blondes and Hard Ground, Part 2."

An article in the *Bakersfield Californian*, "Chuck Roberson and a Horse Named Cocaine: John Wayne's Daring Stunt Duo" by Bryce Martin included statistics about the number of horse falls Roberson and Cocaine performed, as well as other details. It appeared on April 13, 1975.

Interviews with Charlene Roberson helped explain the circumstances behind Coke's death.

EPILOGUE

The *New York Times* published the article "Flaws Seen in Protection of Animals on the Set" by Michael Cieply on April 14, 2013.

The *New York Times* article "Slipsliding Between Animation and Reality" by John Canemaker appeared on November 24, 1996.

The *Los Angeles Times*' "Questions Raised about Group That Watches Out for Animals in Movies" by Ralph Frammolino and James Bates was published February 9, 2001.

The *Hollywood Reporter* published a scathing piece by Gary Baum, "Animals Were Harmed on Set," on November 25, 2013, which suggested the American Humane Association was ignoring and underreporting incidents of animal abuse on movie and television sets yet continued to bestow the disclaimer saying that "no animals were harmed." Baum followed up with "New Animal Welfare Group Formed to Challenge AHA," which appeared in the *Hollywood Reporter* on January 2, 2014.

The *New York Times* published "HBO Challenged Over Horse Treatment" by Dave Itzkoff on May 4, 2012, after three horses died during the making of the mini-series *Luck*.